GW00731812

BREAKFAST RECIPES

400+ EASY & HEALTHY BREAKFAST RECIPES

By

Nancy Kelsey

NANCY KELSEY

ISBN-13: 978-1537755571
ISBN-10: 1537755579

Table of Contents

BREAKFAST RECIPES

NANCY KELSEY

ALL 3 STEPS OR LESS

Hashbrowns Casserole

Ingredients

- 2 Lbs Frozen Hash Browns
- 1/2 Cup Margarine Or 1/2 Cup Butter, Melted
- 1 (10 1/4 Ounce) Cans Cream Of Chicken Soup
- 1 Pint Sour Cream
- 1/2 Cup Onion, Peeled And Chopped
- 2 Cups Cheddar Cheese, Grated
- 1 Teaspoon Salt
- 1/4 Teaspoon Pepper

Directions

1. Grease with cooking spray, an 11 x 14 baking dish and set the oven to 350° F to preheat.
2. Mix all the Ingredients together, add to the baking dish and bake until brown on top or for 45 minutes.

Variation: -

- You can add cream of mushroom soup as well and it will taste equally good without butter. Fat free sour cream and browned bulk sausage will be nice additions.

3 Meat Breakfast Pizza

Ingredients

- 1 Prebaked Refrigerated 12-Inch Pizza Crust, At Room Temperature
- 1 (2 1/2 Ounce) Packages Country Gravy Mix
- 1 Cup Milk
- 1 Cup Water
- 1 Cup Chopped Sausage Links, Cooked
- 1 Cup Chopped Ham, Cooked
- 1 Cup Bacon Bits, Cooked
- 1/2 Cup Milk
- 2 Tablespoons Margarine
- 8 Eggs
- 1 1/2 Cups Shredded Cheddar Cheese

Directions

1. Add water and milk to a saucepan and set an oven to preheat at 400°F.Whisk the gravy mix to bring to a boil and let it simmer for 2-3 minutes until it becomes thick.
2. Beat eggs with milk. Take a large skillet to melt margarine and add the beaten eggs; scramble it into small chunks.
3. Place the pizza crust on a cookie sheet or stone. Spread the gravy on the pizza, add meat on the gravy layer and top it with the scrambled eggs. Add salt and pepper.

4. Sprinkle a generous amount of cheese on top and bake for 10-15 minutes at 400°F or until the cheese starts to melt and bubble. Take out of the oven and serve hot after cutting into cones.

Variation: -

- You can add green onions to the meat mixture. They taste even better.

Top Breakfast

Ingredients :-

- 2 Tablespoons Butter, Divided (Or To Taste. We Love Lots.)
- 2 Slices Bread, With A Hole Made In The Middle To Fit An Egg Yolk
- 2 Large Eggs
- Salt, To Taste
- Black Pepper, To Taste

Directions:-

1. Melt half of the butter in a large frying pan, over medium heat. Arrange the slices of bread into the frying pan.
2. Crack an egg at the centre of the pan, making a well. Sprinkle salt and pepper. Cook for 2-3 minutes.
3. Add the rest of the butter, and flip over the bread with the egg at the centre in a way that the yolk does not break. Cook for another 2-3 minutes.

Variation: -

- It is a perfect breakfast to be served with berry smoothed and fried turkey bacon.

Healthy Breakfast Bowl

Ingredients

- 1 Apple, Diced
- 150 G Low-Fat Vanilla Yogurt (5 Oz)
- 1/2-1 Teaspoon Ground Flax Seeds

Directions

1. Add all the Ingredients together one after the other in a bowl.
2. Mix and eat.

Variation:

- You can use red apples and lactose free vanilla yogurt.

Microwave Poached Egg on Toast

Ingredients

- 1 Slice Bread, Toasted
- 1 Large Egg
- Butter, To Taste
- Salt, To Taste
- Pepper, To Taste

Directions

1. Butter a toast and flatten it with the back of a fork to make the middle of the toast a little well.
2. Crack an egg into this well of the toast carefully, so that it does not spill.
3. Prick the yolk quickly and bake the toast in the microwave for about 1 minute on 60-70% power or until the egg is cooked.

Homemade Breakfast Sausage

Ingredients

- 1 Lb Ground Pork
- 1 Teaspoon Salt
- 1/2 Teaspoon Ground Black Pepper
- 1 1/2 Teaspoons Sage
- 1 3/4 Teaspoons Thyme Leaves
- 3/4 Teaspoon Savory
- 1 Teaspoon Fennel
- 1/4 Teaspoon Dried Mustard
- 1/8 Teaspoon Clove
- 1/4 Teaspoon Crushed Red Pepper Flakes
- 1/8 Teaspoon Cayenne

Directions

1. Add all the spices in a bowl and mix them well.
2. Spread the spice mix over the meat without mashing the meat too much, to make sure that the sausage is not too tight.

Variation:

- You can omit the savoury and fennel if you like. It will still taste equally good.

Steel Cut Oatmeal for the Crock Pot

Ingredients

- 1 Cup Steel Cut Oats (DO NOT Substitute Old-Fashioned Or Quick-Cooking Oats)
- 4 1/2 Cups Water
- 1/2 Teaspoon Salt
- 2 -3 Tablespoons Butter
- 1/2 Cup Dried Fruit (Raisins, Prunes, Apricots, Dates) (Optional)

Serve with

- Milk, To Taste
- Sugar, To Taste
- Cinnamon, To Taste
- Maple Syrup, To Taste

Directions

1. Add all the Ingredients to a slow cooker of 2 quart. (You can also use a smaller crock pot or crockets, but not a 6 quart cooker).
2. Cover it with a lid and cook for 6-8 hours on LOW heat.
3. If a "crust" is formed, scrape it down and stir.

Variation:

- You can add peanut butter. It really goes well with the oatmeal.

******

Basic Poutine Recipe

Ingredients

- Cooked French Fries
- Cheese Curds (Farmer Cheese Or "Squeaky Cheese")
- Beef Gravy

Directions

1. Add The Cheese Curds And French Fries Together.
2. Pour In Hot Beef Gravy Over The Top And Wait Till The Cheese Melts.
3. Dig In!

Variation:

- You can use a pinch of mozzarella instead of cheese curds and spaghetti sauce instead of beef gravy.

Breakfast Wraps

Ingredients

- 4 Lettuce Leaves (I Prefer Cos, They Recommend Romaine)
- 1 Tablespoon Mayonnaise
- 2 Slices Bacon (Cooked Crisp And Crumbled)
- 4 Tablespoons Cheddar Cheese (Grated Or Shredded, Use Low Fat If You Wish)
- 1/2 Roma Tomato (Small, Diced)

Directions

1. Take 2 of the lettuce leaves and finely slice them.
2. Mix mayonnaise, tomato, cheese and bacon with the lettuce. Add salt and pepper.
3. Use this mixture as the filling for the remaining 2 lettuce leaves. Roll the leaves and enjoy!

Variation:

- You can also add avocadoes to the mixture. They go well.

Breakfast Bars Copycat Recipe

Ingredients

- 1 Cup Spanish Peanut, Peeled And Crushed To A Near Powder
- 1 Cup Rolled Toasted Oats
- 1 Cup Rice Krispies
- 1/2 Cup Miniature Chocolate Chip
- 1/3 Cup Light Karo Syrup
- 36 Ounces Milk Chocolate

Directions

1. Mix all the dry Ingredients and add the Karo syrup to it.
2. Place wax paper in a small pan and pour the mixture into it.
3. Melt the milk chocolate and top it over the pan. Refrigerate for at least one hour or until firm.

Variation:

- You can use dry roasted peanuts and use lined muffin tins instead of pans.

Breakfast Parfait

Ingredients

- 6 Ounces Reduced-Fat Vanilla Yogurt
- 1/2 Cup Canned Crushed Pineapple Or 1/2 Cup Canned Mandarin Oranges
- 1 Tablespoon Toasted Coconut

Directions

1. Put the yogurt in a bowl, top it with pineapple or oranges and coconut.
2. Enjoy!

Variation:-

- You Can Also Add A Little Bit Of Coconut Extract To The Vanilla Yogurt To Support Carry The Tastes.

Devilishly Good Breakfast Sandwich

Ingredients

- 1 whole wheat English muffin
- 1 hard-boiled egg, sliced into 8 pieces
- 2 teaspoons low-fat mayonnaise
- 1 teaspoon mustard
- 1/4 teaspoon vinegar

Directions

1. Make a sauce by mixing the mustard, mayo and vinegar together.
2. Cut the muffins in halves and toast them.
3. Pour the sauce over the toasts and put egg slices on them. Sprinkle salt and pepper.

Variation:-

- You can use Cider vinegar instead of normal vinegar and top it with some paprika and chives. You can also add avocado and tomato.

Honey and Bananas

Ingredients

- 1 Ripe Banana
- 1 Tablespoon Honey

Directions

1. Have the banana slices by dipping them into honey or by making a smoothie out of these two.

Variation:

- You can also add cinnamon to it.

Breakfast Pork Hash

Ingredients

- 1 Cup Leftover Cooked Pork (Shredded Or Diced. I Used A Shredded Crockpot Roast)
- 2 Large Potatoes, Diced Into 1/2-Inch Cubes
- 1/2 Large Onion, Cut Into 1-Inch Squares (Use Any Kind You Like, We Love Red)
- 1 Teaspoon Garlic Powder
- 1/2 Teaspoon Hickory Smoke Salt
- 1 Teaspoon Emeril's Original Essence (Or To Taste)
- 1 Tablespoon Vegetable Oil

Directions

1. Over medium-high heat oil in a skillet. Add the potatoes and onions to it. Season it and stir. Brown them on all sides.
2. Cover it with 1/2 cup water and let it cook for 8 minutes with the lid on. Remove the lid and add the pork.
3. Cook on high heat until the potatoes get a crispy exterior.

Variation:

- You can use paprika, cayenne pepper, dried oregano and dried thyme also.

<u>Breakfast Pitas</u>

Ingredients

- 1 Cup Cooked Ham, Cubed
- 1/3 Cup Onion, Chopped
- 1/3 Cup Green Pepper, Chopped
- 2 Tablespoons Butter
- 3 Eggs, Lightly Beaten
- 1/2 Cup Cheddar Cheese, Shredded
- 1/2 Teaspoon Seasoning Salt
- 1/4 Teaspoon Pepper
- 2 Pita Breads, Halved And Warmed (6 Inches)

Directions

1. Sauté the ham in a large skillet and remove separately.
2. Add the onion and green pepper in butter. Add the eggs and cook. Add the cheese, salt and pepper.
3. When eggs are cooked, spoon it into pita halves.

Breakfast Pie

Ingredients

- 6 Eggs, Beaten
- 1/3 Cup Milk
- 2 Cups Monterey Jack Cheese, Shredded
- 3 Tablespoons Green Onions, Chopped
- 2 Tablespoons Green Peppers, Chopped
- 8 Slices Cooked Bacon, Crumbled
- 2 Cups Hash Brown Potatoes, Refrigerated And Shredded
- 1/2 Teaspoon Salt
- 1/2 Teaspoon Pepper
- 1 Tablespoon Butter, Melted
- Paprika

Directions

1. Mix eggs and milk in a large bowl. Add the onion, cheese, pepper and bacon to it. Grease a 9-in pie plate and pour the entire mixture into it.
2. Place the potatoes over the egg mixture and sprinkle salt and pepper. Add butter and paprika.
3. Bake for 40 minutes at 325 degrees.

Variation:

- You can use different vegetables and serve with sour cream and salsa.

****

Mexi-Potato Breakfast Tostada

Ingredients

- 2 Cups Simply Potatoes® Shredded Hash Browns
- 2 Cups Grated Cheddar Cheese, Loosely Packed
- Olive Oil Flavoured Cooking Spray
- 8 Eggs
- 1/2 Teaspoon Ground Cumin
- 1/2 Teaspoon Kosher Salt
- 2 Slices Bacon, Chopped And Cooked Until Crispy
- 1/4 Cup Diced Red Bell Pepper
- 1/4 Cup Sliced Green Onion
- Cilantro Leaf (To Garnish)

Directions

1. Spread silicone liner and spray it with olive oil in a baking dish. Preheat an oven to 425°F.
2. Put 1/4 cup of Simply Potatoes Shredded Hash Browns at the bottom of the dish evenly and top it with cheese.
3. Bake it in the oven for 15 minutes or until golden brown.

4. Beat eggs with salt, cumin and 2 tablespoons of water. In a medium non stick frying pan cook the eggs to make scrambled eggs.

5. Place the potato disks separately in a dish and top with the scrambled eggs. Garnish with red bell pepper, cooked bacon, cilantro sprigs and green onion.

Variation:

- You can also add a dollop of yogurt and few drops of hot sauce.

Sausage Breakfast Rolls

Ingredients

- 1 Lb Sausage
- 1 (8 Ounce) Packages Cream Cheese
- 1 (8 Ounce) Cans Crescent Rolls

Directions

1. Mix cooked and drained sausage with cream cheese. Put the mix in crescent roll. Roll it and bake for 15 minutes.
2. Store in fridge if left over.

Variation:

- You can use turkey breakfast sausage, scrambled eggs and sliced tomatoes in the roll mix.

Homemade Pancake Syrup

Ingredients

- 3/4 Cup Brown Sugar
- 3/4 Cup White Sugar
- 1 Cup Water
- 1 Cup Corn Syrup
- 3 Drops Maple Flavouring
- 3 Drops Vanilla Flavouring

Directions

1. Mix water and sugar and bring to a boil.
2. Add corn syrup and all the other flavourings.

Apple-Cinnamon Overnight Oatmeal

Ingredients

- 2 Apples, Chopped
- 1 Teaspoon Cinnamon
- 1/3 Cup Brown Sugar
- 2 Cups Old Fashioned Oats (Not Quick-Cooking)
- 4 Cups Water
- 1 Pinch Salt

Directions

1. Mix the apples, brown sugar and cinnamon in a crock pot.
2. Sprinkle the oats over the mix and pour in water and sprinkle some salt. DO NOT STIR!
3. Cook it on Low heat setting for 8-9 hours.

Variation:

- You can also add lime juice, raisins and butter to it.

La Mexicana

Ingredients

- 4 Eggs
- 1 Medium Sized Tomato, Washed And Diced
- 1/4 Onion, Finely Chopped
- 1 -2 Serrano Pepper, Chopped
- 1 Tablespoon Butter
- 1 Tablespoon Oil
- Salt

Directions

1. In a deep skillet melt the butter and add a little oil. Stir in the onion and peppers to sauté them.
2. Add the eggs and the tomato to it.
3. Keep stirring constantly so that it does not stick to the bottom. When eggs are cooked, season it with salt.

Variation:

- You can add bell peppers and cheese to it. Serve with toasts.

Greek Yoghurt and Fruit Salad

Ingredients

- 200 G Greek Yogurt, 8 Oz (FAGE Brand Is Available Overseas, You Can Get A Variety Of Fat Contents, They Are All Delicious)
- Fresh Fruit Salad, Of Your Choice (Try To Use A Variety Of Fresh, Seasonal Fruit, Cut Into Little Pieces)
- 2 Tablespoons Honey (Regular Honey Can Be Used, But Greek Thyme Honey Is Awesome)
- 4 Tablespoons Toasted Walnut Pieces
- Cinnamon

Directions

1. In a sundae glass, layer the fruit salad and yoghurt one after the other.
2. Drizzle some honey and sprinkle cinnamon and walnut pieces.

Variation:

- You can use Greek Gods Plain full fat yogurt and fruits like granny smith apples, strawberries, pineapple, grapefruit and blackberries.

Applesauce-Cranberry Oatmeal

Ingredients

- 3 Tablespoons Oatmeal, Uncooked
- 1 Tablespoon Dried Cranberries
- 1/2 Cup Unsweetened Applesauce
- 1/2 Cup Water
- 1/8 Teaspoon Ground Cinnamon

Directions

1. Add all the Ingredients together and mix well.
2. Microwave it for 1-2 minutes.

Variation:

- You can also use apple-pomegranate flavoured applesauce

Golden Apple Oatmeal

Ingredients

- 1/2 Cup Diced Golden Delicious Apple
- 1/3 Cup Apple Juice
- 1/3 Cup Water
- 1/8 Teaspoon Salt (Optional)
- 1/4 Teaspoon Ground Cinnamon
- 1/4 Teaspoon Nutmeg
- 1/3 Cup Old Fashioned Oats, Uncooked
- Brown Sugar (Optional)
- Milk (Optional)

Directions

1. Mix the apples, spices, juice and water.
2. Bring it to a boil.
3. Add the oats and cook for 7 minutes.
4. Serve with milk and brown sugar.

Variation:

- You can also use dried fruits like cranberries, apricots, dates etc.

Pork Breakfast Sausage

Ingredients

SAGE

- 16 Ounces Ground Pork
- 1 Teaspoon Salt
- 1/2 Teaspoon Dried Parsley
- 1/4 Teaspoon Rubbed Sage (Or More)
- 1/4 Teaspoon Fresh Coarse Ground Black Pepper
- 1/4 Teaspoon Dried Thyme (Or More)
- 1/4 Teaspoon Crushed Red Pepper Flakes (Optional)
- 1/4 Teaspoon Coriander
- 1/4 Teaspoon Msg (Such As Accent Flavour Enhancer)

HOT

- 16 Ounces Ground Pork
- 1 Teaspoon Salt
- 1/2 Teaspoon Cayenne Pepper (Or More)
- 1/4 Teaspoon Rubbed Sage
- 1/4 Teaspoon Fresh Coarse Ground Black Pepper
- 1/4 Teaspoon Crushed Red Pepper Flakes (Or More)
- 1/4 Teaspoon Coriander
- 1/4 Teaspoon Msg (Such As Accent)

MAPLE

- 16 Ounces Ground Pork
- 3 Tablespoons Maple Syrup
- 1 Teaspoon Salt
- 1/2 Teaspoon Msg (Such As Accent)
- 1/4 Teaspoon Coriander

Directions

1. Add all Ingredients to a medium bowl and mix well.
2. Form patties and cook over medium heat in a skillet.

Irish Cream Fruit Dip

Ingredients

- 1 (6 ounce) packages instant vanilla pudding
- 1 cup milk
- 1/2 cup Bailey's Irish Cream
- 1 (8 ounce) containers Cool Whip

Directions

1. Add all Ingredients together.
2. Serve when chilled or immediately.

Variation:

- You can use it with pound cake and strawberries.

Mock Cinnabon (Low Carb)

Ingredients

- 1/2 Cup 1% Fat Cottage Cheese
- 1 (1 G) Packet Sugar Substitute (I Use Equal)
- 7 Pecan Halves, Toasted If You Prefer
- Ground Cinnamon

Directions

1. Mix the sugar substitute and cottage cheese.
2. Top it on the pecan halves and sprinkle cinnamon on it.

Variation:

- You can also use whole milk ricotta with a little more sweetener.

Butter and Honey Sandwiches

Ingredients

- 1 Bagel, Split In Half (You Can Also Use Toast If You Want)
- Smooth Peanut Butter
- Honey

Directions

1. Toast the halves of bagel until golden brown.
2. Spread peanut butter on the toasts.
3. Drizzle some honey on the peanut butter.

Healthful Breakfast Pizzas

Ingredients

- 2 Tablespoons Natural-Style Peanut Butter
- 1 Whole Wheat English Muffin
- 1/2 Tablespoon Apricot Preserves
- 1/4 Cup Banana, Slices

Directions

1. Put the broiler to pre-heat.
2. Broil the muffins until toasted.
3. Spread peanut butter on them and top them with bananas.

Breakfast Quesadillas

Ingredients

- 3 Eggs
- 2 Flour Tortillas (8 Inches)
- 1/2 Cup Shredded Fontina Cheese
- 2 Bacon, Strips Cooked And Crumbled
- 1 Green Onion, Thinly Sliced
- Sour Cream And Salsa (Optional)

Directions

1. Beat the eggs in a bowl and cook in a medium skillet.
2. On a griddle Place the tortillas. Fill half of the tortillas with eggs, bacon, cheese and onion and fold them.
3. Cook the folded tortillas over low heat for 1-2 minutes. Serve with salsa and sour cream.

Variation:

- You can use wholegrain tortillas and sharp cheddar.

Bulgur Breakfast

Ingredients

- 2 Cups Water
- 1 Cup Bulgur
- 1 Cup Unsweetened Applesauce
- 1 -2 Tablespoon Smart Balance Light Butter Spread, I Use Benecol Light Spread
- 2 Tablespoons Honey

Directions

1. Keep water to boil in a skillet. Add the bulgur to it and simmer 20 minutes with cover.
2. Mix Benecol, applesauce and honey.
3. Sprinkle some Cinnamon. Serve.

Variation:

- You can also use sliced almonds and raisins.

Breakfast Smoothie

ingredients

- 1 Cup Frozen Berries (I Used Cherries But Any Dark Frozen Berries Would Be Work Out Wonderfully)
- 1 1/2 Cups Orange Juice
- 1/2 Cup Plain Non-Fat Yogurt
- 1 Tablespoon Honey
- 1 Teaspoon Vanilla
- 1/2 Cup Ice Cube

Directions

1. Blend all the Ingredients together until it is smooth.

Variation:

- You can use strawberries, vanilla yogurt, banana and a teaspoon of canola oil also.

Breakfast Spread

Ingredients

- 1/2 Cup Light Cream Cheese, Softened (Neufchatel Cheese)
- 1/4 Cup Crushed Pineapple, Drained
- 1/4 Cup Finely Chopped Pecans
- 2 Tablespoons Light Brown Sugar

Directions

1. Mix all Ingredients well in a bowl.
2. Serve on top of bagels, English muffins, toast, and waffles or simply with fruits.

Breakfast Banana Split

Ingredients

- 2 Bananas
- 1/2 Cup Vanilla Yogurt
- 1/4 Cup Raspberry Jam (Or Strawberry)
- Nuts
- Chocolate Syrup

Directions

1. Slice ripe, small bananas and arrange them on a salad plate in such a way that they are placed outward from one another.
2. Top the bananas with whipped cream. Drizzle some diluted jam on top. Sprinkle the nuts and chocolate sauce on top.

Variation:

- You can use strawberry jam instead of raspberry jam and vanilla scented granola.

Apple Oatmeal Muffins

Ingredients

- 2 Cups Apples, Peeled And Shredded (= 2 Small Apples)
- 1 1/2 Cups All-Purpose Flour
- 1 Cup Quick Oats
- 2/3 Cup Firmly Packed Brown Sugar
- 1 1/2 Teaspoons Baking Powder
- 1/2 Teaspoon Baking Soda
- 1/2 Teaspoon Salt
- 1/2 Teaspoon Cinnamon
- 1/2 Cup Milk
- 2 Tablespoons Vegetable Oil

Directions

1. Mix all Ingredients together and cook for 15-18 minutes at 375.
2. Check with a toothpick if it comes out clean.

Easy Peasy Breakfast Waffles

Ingredients

- 125 G Butter
- 36 G Sugar
- 15 G Vanilla Sugar
- 3 Eggs
- 200 G Flour
- 2 Teaspoons Baking Powder
- 200 Ml Milk

Directions

1. Mix the butter with vanilla sugar and plain sugar. Add in the eggs. In a separate bowl, mix baking powder with flour.
2. Add the milk and the egg-mixture to it and mix well.
3. Pour the mixture into a lightly greased and well-heated waffle iron. Bake until golden brown.

Variation:

- You can use lavender vanilla sugar instead of vanilla sugar.

Easy Breakfast Casserole

Ingredients

- 10 -12 Eggs
- 12 Ounces Cheddar Cheese, Grated
- 2 (4 Ounce) Cans Chopped Green Chillies
- Salt And Pepper

Directions

1. In a 9 x 13 inch pan spread the grated cheese, after buttering the pan. Beat eggs with salt and pepper.
2. Spread green chillies on the cheese and the eggs on top of the chillies.
3. Bake for 25 to 30 minutes at 350 degrees. Cut into pieces and serve.

Variation:

- Try it with bacon and mushrooms.

Crock Pot Breakfast Apple Cobbler

Ingredients

- 4 Medium Apples, Peeled And Sliced (About 2 Cups)
- 1/4 Cup Honey
- 1 Teaspoon Cinnamon
- 2 Tablespoons Butter, Melted
- 2 Cups Granola Cereal

Directions

1. Place the sliced apples at the bottom of a slow cooker and add the remaining Ingredients one by one.
2. Cover it with a lid and cook it on low heat for 7 to 9 hours (overnight) or on high heat for 2 to 3 hours.
3. Serve hot with milk.

Low Carb Breakfast (Atkins Recipe)

Ingredients

- 2 Ounces Cream Cheese
- 1 (1 G) Packet Splenda Sugar Substitute
- 1 Teaspoon Vanilla Extract
- 1 Egg
- 1 Pinch Cinnamon
- 1/2 Teaspoon Butter

Directions

1. Put cream cheese in coffee cup and soften it in the microwave for 30 seconds.
2. Add eggs and vanilla extract and sweetener to it.
3. Microwave the mix for 45 seconds until it gets a custard consistency. Remove from microwave after it starts to rise and top it with butter and cinnamon.

Winter Toast

Ingredients

- 4 slices bread
- 1 1/2 teaspoons sugar
- 1/4 teaspoon pumpkin pie spice
- 1 tablespoon butter

Directions

1. Toast the bread.
2. At the same time, mix the sugar and the pumpkin pie spruce.
3. Apply butter on toasted bread as well as mix together with the spruce blend.

Breakfast Burros (Burritos)

Ingredients

- 1 Flour Tortilla
- 2 Eggs, Scrambled
- 1/4 Cup Grated Cheddar Cheese Or 1/4 Cup Swiss Cheese Or 1/4 Cup Monterey Jack Cheese

Directions

1. Warm the tortilla in a skillet.
2. Top it with scrambled eggs
3. Sprinkle cheese on it.
4. Fold it and serve hot.

Variation:

- You can add saluted sweet peppers, chopped tomato and onions to the tortilla serve with salsa and sour cream.

Portuguese Healthy Breakfast

Ingredients

- 1 Cup Plain Yogurt
- 4 Tablespoons Corn Flakes Or 4 Tablespoons Muesli
- 1 Piece Of Fruit Kiwi Or 1 Piece Strawberries Or 1 Piece Peaches Or 1/2 Mangoes Or 1/2 Papayas Or 1/2 A Slice Pineapple
- 1 Tablespoon Seeds (Linseed, Sesame, Sunflower ...)
- 1 Teaspoon Honey

Directions

1. Cut fruits into pieces after peeling.
2. Add the fruits, cereals and yogurt together.
3. Sprinkle the seeds on top and drizzle with some honey. Mix everything together and serve.

Irish Breakfast Smoothie

Ingredients

- 1 Cup Cold Strong Irish Breakfast Black Tea
- 1 Cup Frozen Blueberries (Or Raspberries Or Strawberries)
- 1/2 Cup Cranberry Juice (Or Apple Or Other Clear Juice)
- 1/2 Cup Plain Yogurt Or 1/2 Cup Silken Tofu
- 1 Tablespoon Honey

Directions

1. Mix everything together and blend in a blender well until smooth.

Variation:

- You can replace honey with agave nectar and make the same with strawberries. Use thick yoghurt and Melrose's Tea for a different taste.

Orange Oatmeal - 3 Ingredients!

Ingredients

- 1/2 Cup Orange Juice Or 1/2 Cup Peach Juice Or 1/2 Cup Your Favourite Juice
- 1 -2 Teaspoon Dried Cranberries
- 1 (28 G) Packets Instant Oatmeal (Flavour Of Choice Try A Lower Sugar For Your Health)

Directions

1. Mix the juice and the cranberries together and heat them for 30 seconds in a microwavable bowl,
2. Add flavoured oatmeal to it and mix.
3. Cook for another 30 seconds and serve.

Breakfast Bake

Ingredients

- 1 (8 Ounce) Cans Refrigerated Crescent Dinner Rolls
- 1 (8 Ounce) Packages Of Chopped Ham
- 6 Eggs
- 1/2 Cup Milk
- 1/2 Teaspoon Pepper
- 1 Cup Cheddar Cheese, Shredded
- 1 Cup Mozzarella Cheese, Shredded

Directions

1. Preheat an oven to 350 degrees. Unroll the crescent dinner rolls in a 13x9 baking dish.
2. Press it firmly to seal the dish properly.
3. Arrange the ham on it. Beat the eggs with milk and pepper and it pour over the ham. Cover it with cheese and for 25 minutes.

Variation:

- You can also use bacon or spicy sausage.

Wagon Wheel Breakfast Pie

Ingredients

- 1 1/2 Cups Frozen Hash Brown Potatoes, Thawed
- 3 Tablespoons Cream Cheese, Softened
- 2 Tablespoons Milk, Plus
- 2 Tablespoons Milk
- 1 Green Onion
- 1/8 Teaspoon Salt
- 1 Dash Pepper
- 4 Uncooked Breakfast Sausage Links
- 1/4 Cup Baking Mix (Like Bisquick)
- 1 Egg
- 1 Dash Ground Nutmeg
- 1 Dash Paprika

Directions

1. In a 7-inch pie plate spray non-stick cooking spray and add the hash browns coated. Mix cream cheese, milk, salt and pepper and onion separately in a bowl and pour it over the potatoes.

2. Cut the sausage lengthwise and arrange on the potatoes. In another small bowl mix the egg, biscuit mix, remaining milk and nutmeg to make it smooth.

3. Pour it over the sausages and sprinkle paprika on top. Bake it for 25-30 minutes at 400 or until golden brown.

Turkey Breakfast Sausage Patties

Ingredients

- 1 Lb Ground Turkey
- 1 Teaspoon Salt
- 2 Teaspoons Sage
- 1 Teaspoon Fennel Seed
- 1 Teaspoon Thyme
- 1 Teaspoon Black Pepper
- 1/2 Teaspoon White Pepper
- 1/2 Teaspoon Cayenne
- 1/4 Teaspoon Garlic Powder
- 1/8 Teaspoon Ground Cloves
- 1/8 Teaspoon Nutmeg
- 1/8 Teaspoon Allspice

Directions

1. Mix all Ingredients and blend well and add it to the meat.
2. Refrigerate the meat overnight. Make patties out of the meat and cook.
3. Cook only until they start to turn the colour from pink, but are still juicy.

Variation:

- You can use star anise instead of fennel and omit the thyme if you do not have. Surprisingly, adding maple syrup to it enhances the taste!

*****

Bacon and Tater Tots Crock Pot Breakfast

Ingredients

- 1 Lb Frozen Tater Tots
- 1/2 Lb Diced Canadian Bacon
- 1 Onion, Chopped
- 1 Green Bell Pepper, Chopped
- 1 1/2 Cups Shredded Cheddar Cheese
- 1/4 Cup Grated Parmesan Cheese
- 6 Eggs
- 1/2 Cup Whole Milk
- 2 Tablespoons Flour
- Salt And Pepper

Directions

- Add 1/3 of the tater tots, onions, bacon, green peppers and the cheeses to a 4-5 quart crock pot.
- Make layers with same repetition so that the cheeses are always on top.

- Whisk the eggs, flour and milk with salt and pepper to taste. Add this mixture to the pot and cover it. Cook on low heat, overnight.

****

Omani Breakfast Tea

Ingredients

- 3 Cups Water
- 3 Tablespoons Sugar
- 2 Tea Bags Or 2 Teaspoons Loose Tea
- 1 Tablespoon Fresh Ginger Or 1 Tablespoon Ground Ginger Or 1 Teaspoon Ground Cardamom
- 1 Cup Evaporated Milk

Directions

1. Add water, sugar and tea to a teapot and boil for 2–3 minutes over high heat.
2. Pour in the canned milk and the ground cardamom and boil further.
3. Remove from heat before it spills out of the teapot and add ginger at this time. Strain and serve piping hot.

Variation:

- You can use sugar instead of honey and raw milk instead of evaporated milk.

******

Breakfast Burritos

Ingredients

- 1/2 Lb Bulk Italian Sausage, Crumbled
- 2 Tablespoons Olive Oil
- 1/2 Cup Chopped Onion
- 1 Garlic Clove, Minced
- 1 Jalapeno, Seeded And Minced
- 1 Large Tomato, Diced
- 2 Cups Trimmed Cooked And Diced Artichoke Hearts (Not Marinated)
- Salt And Pepper, To Taste
- 3 Large Eggs
- 8 Medium Flour Tortillas
- 2 Cups Grated Monterey Jack Cheese Or 2 Cups Cheddar Cheese

Directions

1. Cook sausage over medium heat in a skillet. Add olive oil to sausage. Add the garlic, onion and jalapeno and cook for a few

minutes. Add the tomatoes and artichokes and cook for 3-4 minutes.

2. Add salt and pepper according to taste. Then add the eggs and cook further.

3. Heat the tortillas on a griddle. Fill the tortillas with this mixture and sprinkle with cheese. Fold the ends of the tortillas and serve.

Variation:

- You can also use avocado, potato and green salsa.

LOW CARB BRACKFAST RECIPES

Apple Buckwheat Muffins

Ingredients

- 1/4 Cup Buckwheat Flour
- 1 Tablespoon Baking Powder
- 1/2 Tablespoon Cinnamon Powder
- 1/8 Tsp Salt (Course)
- 2 Eggs (Large And Farm Fresh)
- ½ Piece Banana, Mashed
- 1/4 Cup Honey
- 1/2 Finely Diced Sweet Apple
- 1/4 Cup Walnuts, Chopped

Instructions:-

1. Pre-heat oven to 350 degrees. In a muffin tin, prepare four baking cups.
2. Whisk together flour, baking powder, salt, and cinnamon in a large bowl until the mixture is even. In another container, mix the wet ingredients – egg, honey, and banana – until smooth.
3. Combine wet and dry ingredients before folding in walnuts and apples.

4. Fill the tops of the lined cups with batter. Fill the remaining cups halfway with water.

5. Bake your muffins for around 30 minutes. Keep baking until a poking toothpick comes out clean. When done, let the muffins cool. Serve and enjoy a hearty breakfast muffin!

****

Low Carb Pumpkin Spice Pancakes

Ingredients:-

- 1 Scoop Protein Powder (For Reduced Carb Content)
- ½ Cup Shredded Pumpkin (Cooked)
- 1 Tablespoon Cinnamon Powder
- ½ Tablespoon Baking Powder
- 2 Egg Whites
- ½ Cup Uncooked Oatmeal
- ½ Cup + 3 Tablespoons Water
- Honey

Instructions:-

1. Mix dry ingredients in a bowl and sift.

2. When done, prepare a large blender. Mix the wet and dry ingredients. In a low setting, turn on the blender to mix the ingredients smoothly. Do not mix the ingredients for an extended period of time.

3. You may manually mix the ingredients, but using a blender will be handy if your shredded pumpkin is not so soft in texture.

4. Set the batter aside.

5. Spray a heated pan with cooking oil. Over medium heat, pour about a quarter cup of batter onto the pan.

6. Cook until bubbles emerge to the top and the edges look solid. Flip the pancake. You should have a golden brown color, but with a more golden accent.

7. When done, serve with a teaspoon of honey. This recipe makes three servings for you and your family to enjoy.

<u>Cheese and Ham Scrambled Eggs</u>

Ingredients:-

- Butter
- 8 Ounces Of Smoked Ham, Diced
- 6 Fresh Eggs
- 2 Tablespoons Of Heavy Cream
- Salt And Pepper
- 1 Tablespoon Minced Chives
- 2 Ounces Shredded Cheese

Instructions:-

1. In a large bowl, whisk the eggs with heavy cream until frothy. Season with salt and pepper to your liking.
2. In a large, non-stick skillet, heat a tablespoon of butter. Be careful not to burn the butter and keep your flames low.
3. Sauté the ham in melted butter until it starts to brown.
4. Pour in the egg and cream mixture. Whisk with the ham and scramble over medium-low heat. Avoid overcooking to preserve soft texture.
5. Lastly, toss in the chives and cheese. Keep scrambling until the cheese starts to melt.
6. Transfer to a plate and serve hot! This delightful breakfast makes 4 servings.

Microwave Poached Eggs

Ingredients

- 1 Large Egg
- 1/8 Teaspoon White Vinegar
- 1/3 Cup Water
- Salt And Pepper

Instructions:-

1. In a 6-ounce custard cup mix white vinegar and water together.
2. In the same cup, break an egg and its yolk by pricking with a toothpick.
3. Cover it with a plastic wrap.
4. Cook for 1 minute in microwave or until it is done.
5. Experiment with the cooking time, depending on taste preference and microwave wattage system.
6. Remove egg from hot water immediately to stop cooking process.
7. Serve with salt and pepper.

Baked Ham and Cheese Omelette Roll

Ingredients

- 6 Eggs
- 1 Cup Milk
- 1/2 Cup All-Purpose Flour
- 1/2 Teaspoon Salt
- 1/4 Teaspoon Black Pepper
- 1 Cup Cooked Ham, Chopped Or 9 Slices Of Any Deli Ham
- 1 Cup Shredded Sharp Cheddar Cheese

Instructions:-

1. Preheat an oven to 450 degrees.
2. Grease a 9 x 13 baking dish or pan or lay butter paper on the dish.
3. Make a fluffy mixture of milk and eggs by beating them together.
4. Into this mix, add salt, pepper and flour.
5. Make a smooth batter by whisking properly.
6. Pour batter on the greased dish and bake for 10 - 15 minutes.
7. After 6 minutes interval, sprinkle cheese on top.
8. Bake for about 5 minutes, until cheese melts.
9. Roll the omelet and slice it to serve hot.

Sausage Gravy

Ingredients

- 1 Lb Pork Sausage
- 1/3 Cup Flour
- 1 Quart Milk
- 1 Dash Pepper
- Pillsbury Grands Refrigerated Buttermilk Biscuits

Instructions:-

1. After cooking the sausages in a skillet, drain all the remaining fat.
2. On the cooked sausages, sprinkle some flour to coat them well.
3. Cook these flour coated sausages for about 5 - 7 minutes.
4. Add the milk to it and cook it further to make it thick.
5. Sprinkle pepper and serve hot spreading over biscuits.

<u>Scrambled Eggs</u>

Ingredients

- 8 Eggs
- 2 Tablespoons Sour Cream
- 1 Tablespoon Water
- Salt & Freshly Ground Black Pepper
- 2 Tablespoons Butter
- 1/2-3/4 Cup Grated Cheddar Cheese (I Use Sharp)

Instructions:-

1. Beat sour cream, eggs and water in a medium size bowl.
2. Add salt and pepper to it to.
3. Whisk properly to make it fluffy.
4. Melt butter in a nonstick frying pan.
5. Add the egg mix to it and stir occasionally.
6. As egg cooks, add cheese.
7. When it reaches the desired consistency, serve with biscuits.

Breakfast Burritos

Ingredients:-

- 12 Eggs, Beaten
- 1 Lb Bulk Sausage, Cooked (Or Crumbled Links)
- 1/2 Cup Chunky Salsa (Your Choice Of Heat)
- 2 Cups Cheddar Cheese, Shredded
- 24 Flour Tortillas (You Can Also Use Whole Wheat)
- Optional Ingredients
- 1 Green Pepper, Finely Diced (Optional)
- 6 Potatoes, Shredded And Fried Until Cooked Through (Optional) Or 6 Hash Browns (Optional)
- Jalapeno, Slices (Optional)
- 1 (4 Ounce) Cans Chopped Green Chilies (Optional)
- 1 -2 Garlic Clove, Finely Minced (Optional)
- 1 Onion, Finely Diced (Optional)
- 1 Tomatoes, Peeled And Chopped (Optional)
- 2 Green Onions, Sliced With Tops (Optional)

Instructions: -

1. In a large skillet, scramble eggs, sausages and salsa.
2. Warm the tortillas for 20-30 seconds in the microwave.
3. Put 1/2 cup of the scrambled eggs and roll them burrito-style.

4. On a lightly greased cookie sheet, wrap the burrito and freeze it.

5. Freeze them even for a month.

6. When serving, unwrap them and microwave for 2 minutes until heated through.

7. Or you can also thaw burritos and wrap in a foil to bake for ten minutes at 350 degrees in the oven.

QUICK AND HEALTHY RECIPES

<u>Bacon Waffles</u>

- **Prep Time:** 15 mins
- **Total Time:** 35 mins
- **Servings:** 8

Ingredients

- 1/2 Lb Sliced Bacon
- 2 Cups All-Purpose Flour
- 2 Tablespoons Sugar
- 2 Teaspoons Baking Powder
- 1 Teaspoon Salt
- 1 1/2 Cups Milk
- 2 Tablespoons Unsalted Butter, Melted
- 2 Large Eggs, At Room Temp
- Maple Syrup

Directions

1. To make this recipe at first you need to cook crumble, crispy bacon
2. Preheat it and then put flour, baking powder, sugar as well as salt in a bowl and mix them properly.
3. Put a cup full with milk into microwave and keep it for 1 minute. Then, take a bowl and mix warm milk with melted

butter and eggs. Put some other liquid ingredients into the flour mixture in order to blend it properly.

4. Turn on your waffle iron with the help of cooking spray. Keep the bacon properly in the waffle iron and spread the batter over every iron. Spread 1/8 of bacon on its top. Close the iron and wait until it's done.

5. Taste it with tepid syrup.

Pancakes

- **Prep Time:** 5 mins
- **Total Time:** 10 mins
- **Yield:** 9 small pancakes

Ingredients

- 1 Egg
- 3/4 Cup Milk
- 2 Tablespoons Butter Or 2 Tablespoons Margarine, Melted
- 1 Cup Flour
- 1 Tablespoon Sugar
- 1 Teaspoon Baking Powder
- 1/2 Teaspoon Salt

Directions

1. Beat eggs into a bowl and make them fluffy
2. Put melted butter and milk into it also put some dry ingredients like salt, pepper and mix properly.
3. Heat a fry pan and add a coating of little butter on it.
4. Put a drop of water into the pan when it is hot enough then add some of the batter (approx ¼ cups) into the fry pan and spread it with a spoon.
5. When it starts to break then try to cook the other side.

Breakfast Shepherd's Pie

- **Prep Time:** 15 mins
- **Total Time:** 45 mins
- **Serves:** 6, **Yield:** 1 pan

Ingredients

- 6 Cups Simply Potatoes Diced Potatoes With Onion
- 6 Slices Bacon
- 6 Eggs
- 1 Cup Red Bell Pepper
- 1/4 Cup Green Onion, Diced
- 1/4 Cup Feta
- 1 Cup Shredded Cheddar Cheese
- 1 Tablespoon Salt
- 1 Tablespoon Pepper
- 1 Tablespoon Paprika
- 1/4 Cup Canned Chopped Jalapeno
- 1 Tablespoon Onion Powder
- 2 (12 Ounce) Cans Corn Beef Hash
- 2 Tablespoons Olive Oil
- 1 Garlic Clove

Directions

1. Take 6 slices of bacon and make them crispy. Put olive oil into the pan and fry small dices of onions and chopped garlic.

2. Make a mixture of 6 eggs in a bowl. Add proper amount of salt, pepper and feta cheese in it. And then put 6 slices bacon into it.

3. Mix it with the cooked onion and garlic and then pre heat it.

4. Put olive oil in pan and heat it, add diced potatoes, chopped red pepper, jalapenos, salt and pepper, onion powder and paprika. Blend them all properly.

5. Make at least 2 cans of beef hash in other pan. And when the egg mixture is ready then spread the beef has on top of it.

6. Add the potato mixture on top of the hash. Spread cheddar cheese on it.

7. Put it into the oven for at least 10 minutes. And the food is ready.

Creme Brulee French Toast

- **Prep Time:** 15 mins
- **Total Time:** 1 hr
- **Serves:** 4, **Yield:** 9 slices

Ingredients

- 1/2 Cup Butter
- 2 Cups Brown Sugar
- 1/4 Cup Light Karo Syrup
- 9 Slices Italian Bread (Sliced 1-Inch Thick) Or 9 Slices Challah (Sliced 1-Inch Thick)
- 1 Dozen Egg
- 1 Pint Heavy Cream
- 1 Teaspoon Vanilla
- Cinnamon

Directions

1. Mix brown sugar and butter with Karo syrup in a saucepan and boil it properly.
2. Add sliced bread into the mixture. And also add eggs, vanilla and cream over the bread. Spread some cinnamon over it.
3. Keep it in the refrigerator for a night. Then bake it at 350 degrees.

Ham and Eggs Benedict

- **Prep Time:** 7 mins
- **Total Time:** 17 mins
- **Servings:** 4

Ingredients

- 4 Frozen Biscuits
- 2 Tablespoons Butter, Melted
- 3 Tablespoons Fresh Chives, Chop And Divide
- 1 (1 Ounce) Package Hollandaise Sauce Mix (Or Make Your Own)
- 1 Cup Milk
- 1 Tablespoon Lemon Juice
- 3/4 Cup Cooked Ham, Chopped
- 1/4-1/2 Teaspoon Ground Red Pepper (Optional)
- 1/2 Teaspoon White Vinegar
- 4 Large Eggs
- 2 Cups Loosely Pack Arugula (Optional)
- 1 Small Avocado, Sliced (Optional)
- Black Pepper, To Taste

Directions

1. Bake biscuits properly then mix it with melted butter, chives and blend them.
2. Bake them at 375 degrees in order to toast it.

3. Use milk and lemon juice to make Hollandaise and don't use butter in it. Heat the Saute ham for 3 minutes in skillet to make it brown.

4. Keep the hollandaise sauce warm and mix it with ham and red pepper. Add water to it and boil it.

5. Put white vinegar and then add eggs one at a time into it.

6. Then keep it for 3 to 5 minutes and then trim it with sharp knife.

Twisted Bacon

- **Prep Time:** 5 mins
- **Total Time:** 15 mins
- **Servings:** 6-8

Ingredients

- 1 lb lean bacon
- 1/2-2 teaspoon black pepper (optional)
- 2 teaspoons brown sugar (optional)

Directions

1. Preheat the oven at first at 400 degrees Fahrenheit. Put some bacon on pan, spread black pepper as well as brown sugar.
2. You need to bake it at least for 10 minutes and then remove the fat from your pan. You need to make the bacon crispy so bake it for 5 more minutes.
3. Put it on a paper towel as it is ready.

Cinnamon Roll Waffles

- **Prep Time:** 30 mins
- **Total Time:** 50 mins
- **Yield:** 12 4

Ingredients

WAFFLES

- 1 3/4 Cups All-Purpose Flour
- 2 Tablespoons Granulated Sugar
- 1 Teaspoon Baking Powder
- 1/2 Teaspoon Baking Soda
- 1/4 Teaspoon Salt
- 2 Large Eggs
- 2 Cups Buttermilk
- 1/4 Cup Vegetable Oil
- 1 Teaspoon Vanilla Extract

CINNAMON TOPPING

- 1/2 Cup Butter, Melted
- 3/4 Cup Brown Sugar, Packed
- 1 Tablespoon Ground Cinnamon

CREAM CHEESE TOPPING

- 4 Tablespoons Butter
- 2 Ounces Cream Cheese
- 3/4 Cup Powdered Sugar
- 1/2 Teaspoon Vanilla Extract

Directions

1. Take a medium bowl, put some flour, baking powder, sugar, baking soda and salt into it and mix it properly.
2. In another bowl blend eggs, oil, buttermilk and vanilla and put some dry ingredients. And make the batter properly.
3. Put a non-stick spray on a heated waffle iron and pour the batter into it. Follow the instruction of waffle iron and bake it properly. You can use a form to set aside finished waffles and keep the waffles warm.
4. For cinnamon topping: mix butter, cinnamon and sugar in a bowl and keep it in a small zip packet.
5. For cream cheese topping: put butter and cream in microwave and heat them for 30 to 60 seconds. Stir properly.
6. Put the drizzle cinnamon topping on the waffles and drizzle cream cheese on the top and then serve it.

Lavender Pancakes With Honey

- **Prep Time:** 5 mins
- **Total Time:** 20 mins
- **Serves:** 4-6, **Yield:** 12.0 Pancakes

Ingredients

- 8 Ounces Plain Flour
- 1 Tablespoon Brown Sugar
- 1/2 Teaspoon Powdered Dried Lavender Flowers
- 1/4 Teaspoon Salt
- 4 Teaspoons Baking Powder
- 2 Eggs
- 1 Cup Milk
- 1 Teaspoon Vanilla Extract
- 5 Tablespoons Butter, Melted And Allowed To Cool Slightly
- Cooking Spray Or Butter
- Lavender Honey, To Serve
- Cream, To Serve
- Butter, To Serve

Directions

1. Mix all the needed dry ingredients in a bowl. Add eggs, vanilla extract and milk into it and whisk them properly. You need to make the batter thick so blend them with melted butter.

2. Put fry pan and spread cooking oil into it. Put the pancake batter in proper amount and cook them until the bubbles come up.

3. Use a spatula to flip the pancakes and cook them for few more seconds. Keep the heat proof plate in the oven and make the batter warm. Put lavender honey and cream or butter and lavender honey on it.

4. Eat it with fruits.

Parmesan and Green Onion

- **Prep Time:** 2 mins
- **Total Time:** 20 mins
- **Servings:** 1

Ingredients

- 1 Slice Ham, Thin
- 1 Egg
- 2 Teaspoons Parmesan Cheese, Grated
- 1 Tablespoon Green Onion, Chopped
- Smidge Oil
- Salt
- Pepper

Directions

1. Preheat your oven to 375F. Put oil in it and put the ham inside it.
2. Break your egg in the centre.
3. Put green onion as well as cheese on the top of it.
4. Add salt and pepper. Bake it for 20 minutes then enjoy it.

Great Easy Crepes

- **Prep Time:** 5 mins
- **Total Time:** 20 mins
- **Servings:** 6

Ingredients

CREPES

- 1 1/2 Cups Milk
- 1 Cup Flour
- 2 Eggs
- 1 Tablespoon Sugar
- 1 Pinch Salt

FILLING

- Jam
- Whipped Cream
- Fresh Fruit

TOPPING

- Maple Syrup
- Nutella
- Powdered Sugar

Directions

1. Preheat your non stick pan then mix all the ingredients in the blender.
2. Put little butter on the pan. Then pour the whole batter in the pan in order to cover the bottom of it.
3. When it becomes golden then flip it.
4. Spread some topping like jam, fresh fruit, whipped cream, maple syrup etc.

Apple Stuffed French Toast

- **Prep Time:** 10 mins
- **Total Time:** 30 mins
- **Servings:** 2

Ingredients

- 1 Large Apple
- 1 Teaspoon Butter, Melted
- 1/2 Teaspoon Sugar
- 1 Dash Cinnamon
- 1/2 Cup Half-And-Half
- 1 Large Egg
- 1 Teaspoon Vanilla
- 1/2 Teaspoon Sugar
- 1/4 Teaspoon Cinnamon
- 1/4 Teaspoon Nutmeg, Grated
- 2 Slices Day Old Bread, Like Brioche (Very Thick Slices)
- 2 Tablespoons Unsalted Butter
- Confectioners' Sugar (Optional)

Directions

1. Preheat your non stick pan then mix all the ingredients in the blender.
2. Put little butter on the pan. Then pour the whole batter in the pan in order to cover the bottom of it.

3. When it becomes golden then flip it.

4. Spread some topping like jam, fresh fruit, whipped cream, maple syrup etc.

Baked Ham and Cheese Omelet Roll

- **Prep Time:** 10 mins
- **Total Time:** 30 mins
- **Servings:** 4-6

Ingredients

- 6 Eggs
- 1 Cup Milk
- 1/2 Cup All-Purpose Flour
- 1/2 Teaspoon Salt
- 1/4 Teaspoon Black Pepper
- 1 Cup Cooked Ham, Chopped Or 9 Slices Of Any Deli Ham
- 1 Cup Shredded Sharp Cheddar Cheese

Directions

1. Preheat your over. Crack eggs and add milk to make it fluffy.
2. Put salt, pepper and flour to it and blend it to make it smooth. Then pour it into a pan and bake for 10 to 15 minutes until the eggs are cooked.
3. Spread chopped ham or you can also put some slices of ham on the top of it. Then spread some cheese.
4. Then bake it for more than 5 minutes to melt the cheese. Then roll up the omelette in the pan. You can serve with seam side.

Low Carb Breakfast Balls

- **Prep Time:** 20 mins
- **Total Time:** 50 mins
- **Serves:** 12, **Yield:** 48 meatballs

Ingredients

- 2 Lbs Bulk Pork Sausage
- 1 Lb Ground Beef
- 3 Eggs
- 2 Tablespoons Dried Onion Flakes
- 1/2 Teaspoon Black Pepper
- 1/2 Lb Sharp Cheddar Cheese, Shredded

Directions

1. Mix the ingredients properly and blend them. Form them into a shape of small balls and put them in the boiler pan.
2. Bake them for 25 minutes. When they become cool then you can put them into different zip bags and keep them in refrigerator.
3. Then eat it for your breakfast.

Waffle

- **Prep Time:** 20 mins
- **Total Time:** 25 mins
- **Servings:** 6

Ingredients

- 1 1/2 Cups All-Purpose Flour
- 1 Teaspoon Salt
- 1/2 Teaspoon Baking Soda
- 1 Egg
- 1/2 Cup Granulated Sugar
- 1 Tablespoon Granulated Sugar
- 2 Tablespoons Butter, Softened
- 2 Tablespoons Shortening
- 1/2 Cup Half-And-Half
- 1/2 Cup Milk
- 1/4 Cup Buttermilk
- 1/4 Teaspoon Vanilla

Directions

1. Mix flour, baking soda and salt in a bowl and blend them properly.
2. Beat the egg in another medium bowl and mix it with butter and sugar to make it smooth.

3. Then add butter milk, milk as well as vanilla and mix it properly.

4. Put the dry ingredients mixture into the egg mixture. You can keep it chill for overnight to make the batter perfect.

5. Put light coating of vegetable oil on your waffle iron and heat it.

6. Then slowly put the batter in the waffle iron and cook for 3 to 4 minutes until the waffles are brown.

<u>Pancakes With Orange Honey Sauce</u>

- **Prep Time:** 15 mins
- **Total Time:** 45 mins
- **Servings:** 4

Ingredients

BLOOD ORANGE HONEY SAUCE

- 1/2 Cup Honey
- 1/2 Cup Blood Orange Juice, Strained
- 1 1/2 Teaspoons Cornstarch Or 1 1/2 Teaspoons Cornflour
- 1 Tablespoon Butter
- 8 Ounces Fresh Strawberries, Quarter

PANCAKE

- 1 1/2 cups all-purpose flour, sifted
- 3 1/2 teaspoons baking powder, sifted
- 1/2 teaspoon salt, sifted
- 1 tablespoon white sugar, sifted
- 1 egg
- 3 tablespoons butter, melted and slightly cooled
- 1 1/2 cups milk
- cooking spray, for pan

Directions

1. Blood Orange Honey Sauce: In a small sauce pan add blood orange juice, honey and corn flour and whisk them properly to blend the ingredients.

2. Keep your saucepan on a medium heat and boil the mixture. You need to cook this mixture properly until the sauce begins to boil. Then you can remove it from the heat.

3. Add some butter into it and whisk it properly and then keep it aside and try to keep it cool. You need to do it until the pancakes are ready.

4. Pancakes: take a large bowl and put sifted flour, salt, sugar and baking powder and mix them properly. You can make a small circle at the middle of the bowl with the needed dried ingredients.

5. Put egg at the middle of the bowl and add melted butter. You also need to add milk into it and mix it properly to make it smooth. Use proper amount of milk into it.

6. Use the cooking spray and put oil on your pancake pan or non stick pan and keep it over medium heat.

7. When the pan is hot then put ¼ cup of the mixture in the pan. When the one side of the pancake becomes brown then flip it and cook the other side. Repeat this step until you have the batter in the bowl.

8. You need to divide these pancakes equally on the plates and then add blood orange honey sauce on the top of it and you can also add some strawberries on top of the sauce.

9. Enjoy your dish.

Crumpets With Cheese & Bacon

- **Prep Time:** 10 mins
- **Total Time:** 20 mins
- **Servings:** 4

Ingredients

- 4 Crumpets
- 1/4 Cup Cheddar Cheese, Grated
- 50 G Bacon (One Large Slice Or Rasher)
- 1/4 Teaspoon Ground Pepper (Optional)
- 1/4 Teaspoon Ground Paprika (Optional)

Directions

1. Cook bacon lightly in a non stick fry pan and keep it aside.
2. Spread cheese properly over every crumpet and also add pepper and paprika on the bacon.
3. Then discard fat and the rind from bacon and then place it over the top.
4. Grill it at least for 5 to 10 minutes and when the cheese melted into the crumpet then you can serve it.

Crunch French Toast

- **Prep Time:** 10 mins
- **Total Time:** 20 mins
- **Serves:** 4-5, **Yield:** 12.0 slices

Ingredients

- 3 Cups Cap'n Crunch Cereal
- 5 Eggs
- 1 Teaspoon Sugar
- 3 Tablespoons Milk
- 1/2 Cup Cooking Oil

Directions

1. Take a blender mix 3 cups of Cap'n Crunch Cereal. Pour it on a large bowl and keep it aside.
2. Take eggs and crack them in a bowl, then add sugar and milk. Blend it properly with a fork and make it smooth.
3. You can put the bread in refrigerator overnight because it will not fall apart easily in the mixture.
4. Put the frying pan on the oven and preheat oil into it.
5. Now you have to dip bread into the egg mixture and also add the Cap'n crunch mixture into it to make it proper.
6. Then cook it for at least a minute until it becomes golden brown. And place it on a place. Serve this item with syrup.

Peppered Sausage Gravy and Biscuits

- **Prep Time:** 15 mins
- **Total Time:** 30 mins
- **Servings:** 5

Ingredients

- 1 Lb Jimmy Dean Mild Sausage (Any Pork Sausage)
- 2 Teaspoons Minced Garlic
- 1/4 Cup Butter
- 1/3 Cup All-Purpose Flour
- 1/4 Teaspoon Ground Pepper
- 1/4 Teaspoon Seasoning Salt
- 1/4 Teaspoon Basil
- 1 (14 Ounce) Cans Ready-To-Serve Chicken Broth
- 1/4 Cup Half-And-Half
- 1 (12 Ounce) Cans Pillsbury Refrigerated Buttermilk Biscuits

Directions

1. Bake biscuits properly, fry the sausage in a large skillet.
2. Put the sausage in the pan and two table spoon of garlic. Put it on the low heat in order to make the gravy.
3. Put melted butter, flour, salt, pepper and basil into it. Then you can add chicken broth.
4. Try to thicken the gravy and then add sausage to the mixture. Then keep it for 5 minutes and serve.

Blueberry Almond Crepes

- **Prep Time:** 20 mins
- **Total Time:** 40 mins
- **Servings:** 18

Ingredients

- 4 Eggs
- 1 Cup Flour
- 1 Cup Milk
- 1 Tablespoon Light Brown Sugar
- 1/4 Teaspoon Almond Extract
- 1 (16 Ounce) Containers Cottage Cheese
- 2 Egg Yolks
- 3 Tablespoons Sugar
- 1/2 Cup Sugar
- 1 Tablespoon Orange Zest
- 1/2 Cup Chopped Blanched Almond
- 2 Tablespoons Cornstarch
- 2/3 Cup Orange Juice
- 4 Cups Blueberries (Fresh Or Frozen)
- 1/2 Cup Toasted Sliced Natural Almonds

Directions

1. For crepes: mix all the needed ingredients and make it smooth.
2. Use non stick cooking spray and heat it properly.

3. Put the pan on the oven and add 3 tablespoons of butter and make even layers.

4. Cook one side of it until it becomes brown. You need to pit it for 1 minute and your crepes will be ready.

5. To prepare filling:

6. Take a blender and put cottage cheese, 3 tablespoons sugar, egg yolks, sugar and peeled orange. Combine it properly.

7. Add some chopped almonds; mix it properly to make it smooth.

8. Blueberry sauce: Take saucepan and mix sugar and cornstarch in it. Stir it in blueberries and orange juice.

9. To assemble: Put two tablespoons of filling on each crepe and roll on the baking sheet.

10. Cover it and place it in the refrigerator until it becomes ready for serving. At that time preheat your oven at 300 degrees. And bake it for 15 minutes.

11. Spread blueberry sauce and almond on it.

Egg Lasagna

- **Prep Time:** 45 mins
- **Total Time:** 1 hr 20 mins
- **Servings:** 12-15

Ingredients

- 1 Lb Diced Bacon
- 1 Large Onion, Chopped
- 1/3 Cup Flour
- 1/2-1 Teaspoon Salt
- 1/4 Teaspoon Pepper
- 4 Cups Milk
- 12 Lasagna Noodles, Cooked And Drained
- 12 Hard-Boiled Eggs, Sliced
- 2 (8 Ounce) Cups Shredded Swiss Cheese
- 1/3 Cup Grated Parmesan Cheese
- 2 Tablespoons Minced Fresh Parsley

Directions

1. Cook the bacon properly, drain it and fill it with drippings.
2. Put sauté onion in the dripping.
3. Mix it with flour and pepper and blend it properly. Then stir it with milk.
4. You need to boil and cook it for 2 minutes.

5. Then make layers of four noodles, egg and bacon. Spread cheese and sauce.

6. Spread parmesan cheese and parsley. And keep it for 15 minutes.

7. Bake them and serve.

Cornmeal Molasses Pancakes

- **Prep Time:** 10 mins
- **Total Time:** 15 mins
- **Yield:** 16 pancakes

Ingredients

- 1 Large Egg, Beaten
- 1 1/4 Cups Buttermilk
- 1 Tablespoon Dark Molasses
- 1 Teaspoon Dark Molasses
- 1/4 Cup Butter, Melted
- 1 Cup Unbleached All-Purpose Flour
- 1/2 Teaspoon Salt
- 1/2 Teaspoon Baking Soda
- 2 Teaspoons Baking Powder
- 1/2 Cup Yellow Cornmeal

Directions

1. Take a bowl and combine egg, buttermilk, molasses and melted butter with it.
2. Add salt, flour, baking soda and baking powder. Put cornmeal and stir it properly and make the batter lumpy.
3. Cook it properly until it gets brown and then serve it with syrup.

Cornmeal Sourdough Waffles

- **Prep Time:** 20 mins
- **Total Time:** 40 mins
- **Yield:** 14 waffles

Ingredients

- 1/2 Cup Sourdough Starter
- 2 -2 1/2 Cups Buttermilk, Divided
- 2 Tablespoons Sugar
- 1 Cup White Flour
- 1 Cup Whole Wheat Pastry Flour
- 3 Eggs, Egg And White Separated
- 1 Cup Yellow Cornmeal
- 2 -3 Tablespoons Butter, Melted
- 1 Teaspoon Baking Soda
- 1 Teaspoon Salt
- 1 Teaspoon Vanilla
- 1 Teaspoon Cinnamon (Optional)

Directions

1. Take a large mixing bowl and mix it with 2 cups buttermilk, wheat flour, and sugar and combine it properly.
2. Next morning preheat your waffle iron and pt eggs in it to make it stiff.

3. Put egg yolks then add cornmeal, salt, cinnamon, butter and soda and add extra buttermilk in it.

4. Bake it according to the proper direction. Cool it in refrigerator. Then before serving reheat it.

<u>Creole Breakfast Stack</u>

- **Prep Time:** 15 mins
- **Total Time:** 35 mins
- **Servings:** 4

Ingredients

- 3 Tablespoons Olive Oil, Divided
- 1/2 Medium Yellow Onion, Chopped
- 1/4 Cup Celery, Diced
- 1 Small Red Bell Pepper, Chopped
- 2 Large Garlic Cloves, Minced
- 2 Plum Tomatoes, Seeded, Diced
- 1 Cup Chicken Broth
- 2 Bay Leaves
- 1 1/2 Teaspoons Cajun Seasoning
- 2 Teaspoons Worcestershire Sauce
- Hot Sauce, To Taste
- 3 Green Onions, Thinly Sliced
- Salt, To Taste
- Black Pepper, To Taste
- 12 Medium Shrimp, Deveined
- 2 Cups Simply Potatoes® Shredded Hash Browns
- 4 Eggs

Directions

1. Put 2 teaspoons oil in a saucepan. Then add chopped onion, bell pepper, garlic, celery and cook it properly. Then add chopped tomato and cook for 2 minutes.

2. Add seasonings, hot sauce, and chicken broth and Worcestershire sauce in it. Stir it properly. While you simmer the sauce then put some amount of olive oil and keeps it warm. Put a hot skillet and make patties with spatula. Then add some salt. And cook it.

3. Chopped the shrimp add sauce and shrimp and cook it. Mix it with green onions. Remove bay leaves. Put the cooked potatoes on the plate and serve it with sauce and egg.

<u>Berry-Stuffed French Toast</u>

- **Prep Time:** 15 mins
- **Total Time:** 15 mins
- **Servings:** 4

Ingredients

- 2 Cups Fresh Mixed Berries, About 1/2 Lb (Blueberries, Sliced Strawberries, Raspberries Or Blackberries)
- 2 Tablespoons Powdered Sugar
- 1/3 Cup Fat-Free Sweetened Condensed Milk
- 1 (6 Ounce) Containers Low-Fat Vanilla Yogurt
- 10 Ounces French Bread (1 Small Loaf)
- 1 Egg
- 1 Egg White
- 1/3 Cup Low-Fat Milk
- 1 Teaspoon Granulated Sugar
- 1 Teaspoon Vanilla Extract
- 1/4 Teaspoon Cinnamon
- Nonstick Cooking Spray

Directions

1. Put berries into a small bowl and spread with sugar. To make the sauce take some berries and sweet condensed milk and yogurt and blend them properly.

2. Cut the breads and make small pockets into it. Put the remaining berries and other stuff into it.

3. Mix it with egg and milk, sugar, cinnamon and vanilla. Heat it on a large non stick skillet. Cook the bread it gets brown.

4. Spread sauce and arrange the French toast and serve it properly.

Sausage Crescent Breakfast

- **Prep Time:** 5 mins
- **Total Time:** 30 mins
- **Servings:** 8

Ingredients

- 1 1/2 Lbs Pork Sausage, Mild Or 1 1/2 Lbs Hot Pork Sausage, Your Preference
- 1 (8 Ounce) Cans Refrigerated Crescent Dinner Rolls
- 2 2/3 Cups Mozzarella Cheese Or 2 2/3 Cups Monterey Jack Cheese, Shredded
- 1 Garlic Clove, Minced
- 4 Large Eggs, Beaten
- 3/4 Cup Milk
- 1/4 Teaspoon Salt
- 1/8 Teaspoon Pepper
- Cayenne Pepper (Optional)

Directions

1. Mix brown sausage and garlic in a skillet and makes it crumble.
2. Put crescent roll in a big dish and spread garlic, sauce and cheese over it.
3. Mix eggs with other ingredients.
4. Baked it for 15 minutes and then enjoy it.

Blueberry Pancakes, Milk-free, Egg-free

- **Prep Time:** 5 mins
- **Total Time:** 15 mins
- **Yield:** 6 pancakes

Ingredients

- 1 Cup White Flour
- 3 Tablespoons White Sugar
- 2 1/4 Teaspoons Baking Powder
- 1/4 Teaspoon Salt
- 2 1/2 Tablespoons Margarine
- 3/4 Cup Water
- 1 Eggs Or 2 Tablespoons Water
- 1/2 Cup Fresh Blueberries Or 1/2 Cup Frozen Blueberries

Directions

1. Put sift flour, baking powder, sugar and salt together in a medium bowl
2. Put 2 ½ Tbsp, margarine into the frying pan and keep it until it gets melted.
3. Put the melted margarine in a small bowl adds egg and water and mixes it properly.
4. Put blueberries and dry blueberries and then add liquids. And make it lumpy

5. Now cook the pancakes. You can cook it over the medium high heat until its bottoms get browned.

6. Enjoy it with honey, maple syrup and brown sugar.

****

Eggs in a Nest

- **Prep Time:** 15 mins
- **Total Time:** 55 mins
- **Serves:** 4-6, **Yield:** 12.0 hash brown/egg cups

Ingredients

- 3 Cups Simply Potatoes® Shredded Hash Browns
- 1/3 Cup Green Onion (Chopped)
- 1/4 Teaspoon Pepper
- 1/4 Teaspoon Salt
- 1 1/2 Cooking Oil
- 1/3 Cup Red Bell Pepper (Chopped)
- 1/3 Cup Bacon (Diced)
- 5 Eggs (Beaten)
- 1/4 Cup Milk
- Salt And Pepper
- 1/4 Cup Cheddar Cheese (Grated)

Directions

1. Preheat your oven to 400 degrees and grease the muffin pan properly

2. Mix it with potatoes, hash browns which are shredded, pepper, green onion, oil and salt.

3. Put the potatoes in 12 muffin cups and bake for 25 minutes.

4. Fry the bacon and also the red bell peppers for at least 7 minutes.

5. Add eggs and milk with the bacon. Put some salt.

6. Put the bacon mixture with hash onion cups.

7. Spread cheese and cook for 15 minutes.

Sugar and Spice Bacon

- **Prep Time:** 5 mins
- **Total Time:** 25 mins
- **Servings:** 3

Ingredients

- 6 Slices Bacon Or 6 Slices Turkey Bacon
- 1 Tablespoon Brown Sugar
- 1 Tablespoon Sugar Or 1 Tablespoon Splenda Sugar Substitute
- 1/2 Teaspoon Cinnamon
- 1/4 Teaspoon Nutmeg (Fresh Grated Is Best)
- 1/8 Teaspoon Allspice
- 1/8 Teaspoon Clove
- 1/8 Teaspoon Garlic Salt
- 1 Pinch Cayenne

Directions

1. Preheat your oven to 350°.
2. Put bacon slices and bake at least for 10 minutes.
3. Mix other ingredients. Add some garlic powder.
4. After baking, spread sugar on each side of the bacon. And then put it on the oven again. And make it crispy.
5. Enjoy your dish.

Everyday Breakfast Banana Split

- **Prep Time:** 5 mins
- **Total Time:** 5 mins
- **Servings:** 1

Ingredients

- 1 Banana, Split Lengthwise
- 1/2 Cup Yogurt, Any Flavor You Like
- 1/4 Cup Granola Cereal Or 1/4 Cup Cereal
- 1/4 Cup Blueberries Or 1/4 Cup Other Berries
- Chocolate (Optional) Or Fruit Syrup (Optional)
- Whipped Cream (Optional)
- 1 Maraschino Cherry

Directions

1. Put banana in a medium bowl and put some yogurt on it.
2. Spread granola or cereal on yogurt and also some berries.
3. Add some chocolate and fruit on the top
4. Then you can garnish it with cherry and whipped cream.

Hash Browns Omelet

- **Prep Time:** 10 mins
- **Total Time:** 40 mins
- **Servings:** 4-6

Ingredients

- 6 Slices Bacon
- 2 Cups Hash Browns
- 1/4 Cup Chopped Onion
- 5 Eggs
- 1/4 Cup Milk Or 1/4 Cup Cream
- 1/2 Cup Shredded Cheese, Your Favorite

Directions

1. Fry bacon on a fry pan and keep it aside.
2. Put some grease on the pan and add hash browns, salt and onion and also pepper.
3. When potatoes starts to get browned the remove it from the oven.
4. Add eggs, milk, pepper and salt. And pour it over hash brown mixture.
5. Make the bacon crispy and spread on top and add cheese. And cook it for 15 to 20 minutes.

Brunch Pigs in a Blanket

- **Prep Time:** 8 mins
- **Total Time:** 28 mins
- **Yield:** 15 pancakes

Ingredients

- 1 1/2 Cups Original Bisquick Baking Mix
- 1 Cup Milk
- 1 Egg
- 1/4 Cup Fresh Blueberries (Optional)
- 15 Breakfast Sausage Links (Brown N' Serve Pre-Cooked, Original)
- Nonstick Cooking Spray
- 6 Ounces Pure Maple Syrup

Directions

1. Preheat your oven to 250*F. and also the pre cooked sausage. You need to put the maple syrup in the microwave.
2. Mix milk, bisquick, eggs and blueberries. Put a large non stick skillet on the oven. Use 2 full Tbsps of batter to make the pancakes. It is better to make the pancakes slowly. Cook both the sides properly.

3. When it is ready then put 1 cooked and warmed breakfast sausage in the middle of the pan cakes. Serve it with maple syrup.

****

Breakfast Sausage Cups

- **Prep Time:** 10 mins
- **Total Time:** 27 mins
- **Servings:** 5

Ingredients

- 1 (10 1/4 Ounce) Pillsbury Grands Refrigerated Buttermilk Biscuits (5 To A Can)
- 1/2 Lb Sausage
- 1 Egg
- 1 Teaspoon Milk
- 1/3 Cup Salsa (Mild Or Hot)
- 1/2 Cup Cheddar Cheese, Shredded

Directions

1. Fry sausage and make it crispy. Spread vegetable oil make holes on the biscuits.
2. Divide the crumbles sausage to make each biscuit. Put beaten eggs and milk.

3. Then make a mixture on the sausage. Add 1 tablespoon of salsa on the sausage and put some shredded cheese on the top of it.

4. You can also put muffin tip on the top of it while baking.

5. Bake it for 17 minutes.

<u>Waffle-Style French Toast</u>

- **Prep Time:** 15 mins
- **Total Time:** 55 mins
- **Servings:** 8

Ingredients

- 4 Large Eggs
- 1 Cup Milk
- 1 Teaspoon Vanilla
- 1 Tablespoon Sugar
- 1/2 Teaspoon Salt
- 8 Slices Day Old Challah (1-Inch Thick Slices) Or 8 French Bread (1-Inch Thick Slices)

Directions

1. Preheat waffle iron with the help of cooking spray.
2. Whisk eggs in a pie plate and mix it with milk, sugar, salt and vanilla.
3. Slice bread in the egg mixture
4. Then you need to fry the slices on the waffle iron and make it light brown
5. Serve it with powdered sugar or warm syrup.

Ham Breakfast Casserole

- **Prep Time:** 1 hr
- **Total Time:** 2 hrs
- **Servings:** 4

Ingredients

- 8 Slices White Bread (Or Any Bread You Like)
- 1 Cup Ham, Diced
- 1/2 Cup Sliced Mushroom
- 3/4 Cup Cheddar Cheese, Shredded
- 4 Eggs, Beaten
- 1 1/3 Cups Milk
- 1 Teaspoon Dried Onion Flakes
- 1 Teaspoon Dried Parsley Flakes
- 1/2 Teaspoon Lemon Pepper

Directions

1. Put 4 pieces of bread in a baking dish.
2. Spread mushrooms, cheese, ham over the top of it.
3. Use 4 pieces of bread to cover it.
4. Mix eggs and skim milk in a bowl. Then add onion flakes, lemon pepper and parsley flakes. And mix it properly.
5. Pout the egg mixture on the bread
6. Put it in the refrigerator for 1 hour.
7. Then take it out and bake it for 1 hour.

8. Then serve it.

*****

Baked Oatmeal

- **Prep Time:** 10 mins
- **Total Time:** 55 mins
- **Servings:** 6

Ingredients

- 1/3 Cup Butter
- 2 Large Eggs
- 3/4 Cup Brown Sugar
- 1 1/2 Teaspoons Baking Powder
- 1 1/2 Teaspoons Vanilla
- 1 Teaspoon Nutmeg Or 1 Teaspoon Cinnamon
- 1/4 Teaspoon Salt
- 1 Cup Milk
- 2 Tablespoons Milk
- 3 Cups Oatmeal (Regular Or Quick)

Directions

1. Put melt butter

2. Put eggs in baking dish and beat them properly. Add brown sugar, vanilla, cinnamon, baking powder and nutmeg and salt. And mix it well.
3. Mix it in butter and also in milk and add oats. Stir properly and put it in refrigerator overnight.
4. Bake it and uncover after 35 to 45 minutes.
5. Serve with hot milk.

******

Southern Eggs Benedict

- **Prep Time:** 24 hrs
- **Total Time:** 24 hrs 30 mins
- **Servings:** 4

Ingredients

- 2 Cups Cooked Grits
- 4 Eggs
- 1/2 Lb Country Ham
- 1 Tablespoon Parsley (Chopped)
- 1 Garlic Clove, Minced
- 1/2 Cup Mayonnaise
- 1 Teaspoon Tabasco Sauce
- 1 Tablespoon Lemon Juice
- 1 Tablespoon Creole Mustard

- 36 Small Shrimp
- 1/2 Cup Heavy Cream
- 1/2 Tablespoon Paprika

Directions

1. One day before you need to cook the grits as per the directions written on the package. Keep it in freeze to cool it and spread the cookies so that they become thick. It is important to make them stiff and dry.
2. Then in the morning combine all the ingredients in the bowl and remove the shrimp.
3. You need to cut the grits into 4 parts and make it like a bread or English muffin. Add flour on the grits and make them brown.
4. Fry the grits on your pan with butter and oil. Cut the ham in right proportion so that you can put it on the grit cakes.
5. Make egg poach and also put the ham on it. Then spread some paprika and serve.

Hamburgers W/ Eggs

- **Prep Time:** 8 mins
- **Total Time:** 23 mins
- **Servings:** 4

Ingredients

- 1 1/2 Lbs Ground Sirloin, Shaped Into 4 Patties
- 4 Teaspoons Butter
- 4 Tablespoons Butter
- 4 Eggs
- 6 -12 Anchovy Fillets (Optional)
- 2 Tablespoons Capers, Drained
- 1 Tablespoon Parsley, Finely Chopped
- Salt & Freshly Ground Black Pepper

Directions

1. Spread salt and pepper and bake the hamburgers. Put the patties on a warmed platter and start to cook the eggs.
2. Put 4 Tbsps of butter in a skillet and heat it and minutely break the eggs and cook them properly and make it firm. Place eggs on the patties.
3. Spread eggs and pepper and salt. Designed it with anchovies on the top of eggs.
4. Add parsley and capers in it. When the butter become brown then pour sauce on it and serve it with hot sauce.

Pepperoni Omelet

- **Prep Time:** 10 mins
- **Total Time:** 30 mins
- **Servings:** 1-2

Ingredients

- 3 Medium Eggs
- 1/2 Teaspoon Tabasco Sauce
- 1 Medium Potato
- 1 Medium Onion
- 1 Medium Tomatoes, Coarsely Diced
- 50 G Pepperoni, Thinly Sliced
- 50 G Tasty Cheese, Grated
- 1/4 Teaspoon Ground Black Pepper

Directions

1. Break eggs in a bowl with tobacco sauce; mix it with grated onion and potato.
2. Put diced tomato in it and mix properly.
3. Place the mixture into a small skillet with oil and fry it with medium temperature.
4. Then put the pepperoni slices over its top and spread grated cheese
5. Put grinned pepper on its top.
6. Cook it for 15 to 20 minutes

Breakfast Brownies

- **Prep Time:** 17 mins
- **Total Time:** 32 mins
- **Serves:** 9, **Yield:** 9 Pieces

Ingredients

- 3/4 Cup Bisquick
- 1/4 Cup Cocoa
- 1/4 Cup Sugar
- 3/4 Cup Skim Milk
- 1/4 Cup Applesauce
- 1 Egg
- 1 3/4 Cups Raisin Bran Cereal

Directions

1. Heat the oven into 425 degrees. Take a 9 inch square pan and mix it with all ingredients apart from cereal and then stir it properly.
2. Put it into the pan and bake it for 15 minutes and cut into pieces.

Toad

- **Prep Time:** 35 mins
- **Total Time:** 1 hr 35 mins
- **Servings:** 4

Ingredients

- 125 G Plain Flour
- 4 Eggs
- 480 Ml 2% Low-Fat Milk (Or 240ml Milk And 240ml Water)
- 1 Pinch Salt
- 1 Tablespoon Malt Vinegar
- 4 Tablespoons Drippings Or 4 Tablespoons Lard
- 12 Links Pork Sausages
- 2 Large Onions, Sliced
- 1 Tablespoon Dried Herbs

Directions

1. Preheat your oven. Then put the flour into large bowl. Then break eggs into it. add some milk and water and mix it properly to combine.
2. Add little amount of salt and vinegar and put it there for 30 minutes.
3. Add sausage in it and make it brown. Then place it on the oven and cook for 10 minutes.

4. Place a frying pan on the oven and fry the onions till it become golden. Add some mixed herbs and salt and pepper.
5. Turn on the oven.
6. Take the sausages out from the oven and spread it over the onions. Put the batter on it and bake for 25 minutes.
7. Then cook for more 10 minutes and make it golden
8. Serve it with gravy.

<u>Belgian Waffles</u>

- **Prep Time:** 10 mins
- **Total Time:** 30 mins
- **Yield:** 16 waffles

Ingredients

- 2 cups flour
- 4 teaspoons baking powder
- 1/2 teaspoon salt
- 1/4 cup sugar
- 2 eggs, separated
- 1/2 cup oil
- 2 cups milk

Directions

1. Put the dry ingredients in a big bowl.
2. Put the eggs in a separate bowl.
3. Beat the eggs in a small bowl. Online the white part of the eggs and make it stiff.
4. Put egg yolks, oil and milk and stir properly.
5. Then add other dry ingredients and mix properly.
6. Then put it in the white eggs.

Eggs Benedict Wrap

- **Prep Time:** 15 mins
- **Total Time:** 25 mins
- **Servings:** 4

Ingredients

- 3 Tablespoons Butter
- 2 1/2 Cups Mushrooms, Sliced
- 1 (1 Ounce) Envelope Hollandaise Sauce Mix, Such As Knorr
- 3/4 Cup Milk
- 3 Tablespoons Sun-Dried Tomatoes, Chopped
- 1 3/4 Cups Smoked Ham, Cut Into Strips
- 6 Eggs
- 1/3 Cup Milk
- Salt
- Pepper
- 3 Tablespoons Butter
- 4 Flour Tortillas, Burrito Size

Directions

1. Put a small skillet and melt butter then add mushrooms into it and cook it for 10 minutes.
2. You need to make the hollandaise sauce. Use 3 to 4 cup of milk and add dried tomatoes into it. Then keep it aside.

3. Cook the ham and make it brown. Add beaten eggs, salt, pepper and milk. Then melt the butter and cook eggs and make scrambled eggs.

4. For the wrap you need to warm the tortilla and put it on the top of the eggs mushroom, ham and hollandaise sauce.

5. Fold the tortilla and cut it into halves.

6. Then enjoy your breakfast and serve it to others as well.

Banana Bread Muffins

- **Prep Time:** 15 mins
- **Total Time:** 35 mins
- **Yield:** 15-16 Muffins

Ingredients

- 2 Cups Flour
- 1 Teaspoon Baking Soda
- 1/4 Teaspoon Salt
- 1/2 Cup One Stick Butter
- 3/4 Cup Brown Sugar
- 2 Large Eggs, Beaten
- 3 -4 Over Ripe Bananas

Directions

1. You need to preheat your oven to 350°F and then put cup cake in with the spray and vanilla pam.
1. Take a big bowl and mix flour soda and salt into it.
2. Then in another bowl put butter, cream and sugar together.
3. Stir the eggs and smashed bananas in order to blend properly.
4. Put the proper amount of banana into the muffin in order to fill it.
5. Then bake it for 20 minutes.
6. Your breakfast will be ready then you can enjoy it at your table.

Egg and Bacon Tarts

- **Prep Time:** 10 mins
- **Total Time:** 30 mins
- **Servings:** 6

Ingredients

- 6 Slices Sandwich Bread, Crusts Removed
- 30 G Butter, Melted
- 6 Eggs
- 3 Slices Bacon, Chopped
- 1 Tablespoon Chopped Fresh Parsley

Directions

1. Put butter in each side of a bread.
2. Then put it into patty tins with grease.
3. Crack an egg into the bread. Put proper amount of bacon on it. Always put chopped bacon on it.
4. Then spread little parsley on it.
5. Then bake it in a moderate oven for at least 20 minutes and let the eggs get firmed.
6. You can serve it warm or cold as you like.
7. You should put it in air tight container and put it in the fridge for 3 days.

Shredded Potato Baskets

- **Prep Time:** 10 mins
- **Total Time:** 40 mins
- **Serves:** 4, **Yield:** 12 baskets

Ingredients

- 1 (20 Ounce) Packages Simply Potatoes® Shredded Hash Browns
- 1 Large Egg
- 2 -3 Tablespoons Flour
- 1 (12 Ounce) Packages Shredded Cheddar Cheese
- 8 Ounces Bacon, Cooked And Crumbled

Directions

1. Preheat your oven at 375 degrees F. Then you need to put non stick muffin tins and use cooking spray. Then keep it aside.
2. Take a big bowl put potatoes, flour and add eggs into it. And mix it together. Divide it properly for the each muffin. Use the back of a spoon then press the potato mixture. And make well into that.
3. Put it on the oven and bake for 25 minutes and make it brown.
4. Set it aside from the oven and divide the shredded cheese properly in the cups and put crumbled bacon on it. Put it in the oven for 5 to 10 minutes. When the baskets are golden brown and the bacon and cheese is hot melted then put it aside.

5. After 5 minutes you can serve it. Gently place it on the serving platter and serve to your guest.

Note: It is an amazing dish for breakfast. But you should always remember to keep it aside at least for 5 minutes before serving it.

Bacon, Egg & Cheese Tacos

- **Prep Time:** 5 mins
- **Total Time:** 25 mins
- **Servings:** 4

Ingredients

- 2 Tablespoons Butter
- 1 Onion, Chopped
- 8 Eggs, Beaten
- 1/2 Cup Milk
- 1/2 Teaspoon Salt
- 1 Lb Bacon
- 2 Cups Cheese, Shredded
- 2 Cups Salsa
- Sour Cream
- Taco Shell, Hard & Soft

Directions

1. Take a large baking sheet and cover it with foil and place sliced bacon strips in it. You need to place it in a cold oven and turn on the heat to 400 degree F.
2. Then cook it for 20 minutes. But do not overcook it.
3. Preheat your skillet and put melted butter in it.
4. Add sauté onion and make it brown as well as caramelized. You should not skip this step.

5. You need to beat the eggs and a make a mixture with milk and salt. You need to add onions and cook properly.
6. Heat the required taco shells.
7. Then add scrambled eggs, put cheese on the top of it, then bacon, sour cream and salsa.
8. Then serve it in a big plate.

Grilled Cheese French Toast

- **Prep Time:** 2 mins
- **Total Time:** 7 mins
- **Yield:** 3 sandwiches

Ingredients

- 2 Large Eggs
- 1/3 Cup Buttermilk Or 1/3 Cup Low-Fat Milk
- 6 Slices White Bread
- 3 Slices American Cheese
- 3 Slices Crispy Cooked Bacon, Sliced In Half (Optional)
- 2 Tablespoons Butter
- Syrup (Optional) Or Raspberry Jam, Garnish (Optional)

Directions

1. Put 1 tablespoon of butter and heat a griddle.
2. Put eggs and buttermilk
3. Dip bread and cover it with egg mixture and put it on the hot griddle and make it brown both of its sides. Then put cheese on its sides.
4. Places 2 slices of bacon on it then put 3 slices of bread.
5. Then you need to put the other 3 slices of bread and cooked it with bacon.
6. Flip it and use butter on its other side. Then garnish it with syrup and raspberry jam.

7. You will love it at your breakfast.

******

Mexican Breakfast

- **Prep Time:** 20 mins
- **Total Time:** 35 mins
- **Servings:** 4

Ingredients

- 1 Teaspoon Olive Oil
- 1 Medium Onion, Chopped
- 2 Garlic Cloves, Chopped
- 1 Large Anaheim Or New Mexican Green Chili Pepper (Or 2 Small Hot Chile Peppers, Cut Into 1/4-Inch Dice)
- 1 Medium Sweet Potato, Peeled And Cut Into 1/4-Inch Dice
- 2 Medium Tomatoes, Cut Into 1/4-Inch Dice
- 2 Cups Bpa-Free Canned Black Beans, Drained And Rinsed Well (Or Cooked Black Beans)
- 1 Teaspoon Ground Cumin
- 1 Teaspoon Chili Powder
- 1 Teaspoon Smoked Paprika
- Olive Oil Flavored Cooking Spray
- 4 Large Eggs
- 4 Tablespoons Finely Chopped Cilantro Leaves
- 1 Ounce Queso Fresco, Separated Into 4 Pieces

- 2 Ounces Avocados, Thinly Sliced

Directions

1. Preheat you oven to at least 450 degree F. Heat oil in a big saucepot with medium high temperature. Put onions, pepper, potato and garlic into it. Then cook it for 5 minutes.
2. Again add beans, chilli powder, tomatoes and paprika. Cover it and cook at least for 20 minutes. When the potatoes gets soften then you can remove it.
3. Put ramekins with cooking spray and put 1 cup vegetable mixture in the ramekins. Place it in a way so that each ramekin gets the mixture. Spread the outside edges of it.
4. Make a well in the middle of it and break one egg into it.
5. You need to bake it for 5 minutes.
6. When the eggs are ready the put the ramekins again on the oven and boil for 5 minutes. When the eggs gets soften then put it aside from the oven.
7. Spread cheese, cilantro and slices of avocado on it.
8. Serve it immediately.

Spicy Hash Browns

- **Prep Time:** 15 mins
- **Total Time:** 45 mins
- **Servings:** 5

Ingredients

- 2 Tablespoons Olive Oil
- 1 Teaspoon Paprika
- 3/4 Teaspoon Chili Powder
- 1/2 Teaspoon Salt
- 1/4 Teaspoon Red Pepper, Ground
- 1/8 Teaspoon Black Pepper
- 6 1/2 Cups Baking Potatoes, Diced (About 2-1/2 Lbs)
- Cooking Spray

Directions

1. Preheat the oven at 400 degrees Fahrenheit.
2. Mix olive oil, red powder, paprika, salt, chilli powder, and black pepper in a big bowl; stir it well.
3. Put diced potatoes and mix it well for coating. .
4. Put the potatoes as a single layer on the cookie sheet which should be coated with the cooking spray.
5. Bake it at 400 degrees F at least for 30 minutes or until it gets browned.
6. Serve it.

Basic Pancake Syrup

- **Prep Time:** 2 mins
- **Total Time:** 7 mins
- **Yield:** 2 cups

Ingredients

- 1 cup sugar
- 1 cup brown sugar
- 1 cup corn syrup
- 1 cup water
- 1 teaspoon vanilla

Directions

1. Boil it properly with all the ingredients together and cook at least for 3 minutes.
2. Put it in a bottle and store in fridge.
3. Serve it with any type of pancakes. It helps to increase the taste of pancakes.

CROCK POT BREAKFAST RECIPE

SLOW-COOKED SCRAMBLED EGGS WITH GREEN HERBS

- Total Time: 30 min
- Prep: 20 min
- Cook: 10 min
- Yield: 4 servings

INGREDIENTS:-

- 10 Extra-Large Eggs
- 6 Tablespoons Whole Milk Or Half-And-Half
- 1 Teaspoon Kosher Salt
- 1/2 Teaspoon Freshly Ground Black Pepper
- 2 Tablespoons Minced Fresh Parsley Leaves
- 2 Tablespoons Minced Scallions, White And Green Parts
- 2 Tablespoons Minced Fresh Dill
- 2 Tablespoons Unsalted Butter

DIRECTIONS:-

1. The egg, milk, salt, pepper, parsley, scallions and dill are being mixed in a large bowl.
2. They are being whisked together.
3. The butter is being melted in a large omelet pan, and then egg mixture is being added.
4. This is being cooked over a low flame. Fold the food item over with a rubber spatula.

5. Seasoning is being done and is served hot.

*****

SLOW-COOKER WHOLE-GRAIN BREAKFAST PORRIDGE

- Total Time: 14 hr 5 min
- Prep: 5 min
- Inactive: 12 hr
- Cook: 2 hr
- Yield: 6 to 8 servings

INGREDIENTS

- 3/4 Cup Dehulled Whole Barley
- 3/4 Cup Steel-Cut Oats
- 1/2 Cup Cornmeal (Not Coarsely Ground)
- 3 Tablespoons Light Brown Sugar, Plus More For Sprinkling
- 1 Teaspoon Pure Vanilla Extract
- 1 Cinnamon Stick
- Kosher Salt
- Topping Suggestions: Milk, Chopped Dried Fruit, Fresh Fruit Or Nuts

DIRECTIONS

1. All the INGREDIENTS are combined with 4 ½ cups of eater and half teaspoon salt is added in a slow cooker. Let it sit for a night for a minimum of 8 hours.

2. In the next day, the slow cooker is set to high and cooks it until the grains are soft.

3. It is being done in 2 hours and continues stirring halfway through.

4. Settle the porridge in the serving bowl and add toppings for example milk, dried fruits, fresh nuts.

SLOW COOKER OVERNIGHT BREAKFAST CASSEROLE

- Total Time: 8 hr 30 min
- Prep: 30 min
- Cook: 8 hr
- Yield: 12 Servings

INGREDIENTS

- 2 Packages (12 Ounces, Each) Johnsonville Hot &Spicy Breakfast Sausage
- 1 Cup Chopped Green Onions
- 1 Sweet Red Bell Pepper, Chopped
- 1 Can (4 Ounces) Diced Mild Green Chilies
- 1/4 Cup Chopped Fresh Cilantro
- 1 Package (30 Ounces) Frozen Shredded Hash Brown Potatoes
- 1 -1/2 Cups Shredded Cheddar Cheese
- 12 Eggs
- 1 Cup Milk
- 1/2 Teaspoon Salt
- 1/8 Teaspoon Pepper

DIRECTIONS

1. The sausages are being cooked in the direction mentioned in the packets ad cut these in 1/4th slices and set it aside.
2. Green onions red pepper, chilies and cilantro and now set this aside.

3. With the vegetable cooking spray the interior of a 5 to 6 quart slow cooker.

4. Now 1/3 rd of the hash browns, sausages green onions mixture and cheese into the crock and layer it.

5. Repeat the same process. In the bowl beat the egg milk salt pepper and pour over the layers ingredient.

6. Then cook for 7 to 8 hours until the temperature rises to 160F and then serve.

SLOW-COOKED SCRAMBLED EGGS WITH CAVIAR

- Total Time: 15 min
- Prep: 5 min
- Cook: 10 min
- Yield: 2 servings

INGREDIENTS

- 4 extra-large eggs
- Splash half-and-half
- Pinch kosher salt
- Pinch freshly ground black pepper
- 2 tablespoons (1/4 stick) unsalted butter, divided
- 2 slices toasted brioche
- 2 teaspoons malossol caviar, osetra or sevruga

DIRECTIONS

1. Half of the egg with salt and pepper and whisk it. Then heated butter is being added in a large sauté.

2. Add the eggs and stir constantly over low heat. After cutting the heat, add one more tablespoon of butter and stir until melted.

3. Season it before serving hot on a slice of toasted brioche.

SLOW-COOKED SCRAMBLED EGGS WITH GOAT CHEESE

- Total Time: 15 min
- Prep: 10 min
- Cook: 5 min
- Yield: 6 servings

INGREDIENTS

- 16 Extra-Large Eggs
- 1/2 Cup Milk Or Half-And-Half
- 1 1/2 Teaspoons Kosher Salt
- 3/4 Teaspoon Freshly Ground Black Pepper
- 4 Tablespoons (1/2 Stick) Unsalted Butter, Divided
- 6 Ounces Fresh Goat Cheese, Such As Montrachet, Crumbled
- 2 Tablespoons Minced Fresh Chives

DIRECTIONS

1. Charcoal grill is being heated and is spreader them in one dense layer.
2. Eggs are being whisked with milk, salt, and pepper. 2 tablespoons of butter is added in omelet pan over the grill.
3. Then off the grill and add the goat cheese, chives, and the rest of butter.
4. Stir and let the egg for 30 seconds till the butter melt.
5. Serve hot with seasoning.

CROCK POT EGGS BENEDICT

- Prep Time: 30 mins
- Total Time: 3 hrs 30 mins
- Servings: 12

INGREDIENTS

- 1 Dozen Hard-Boiled Egg, Cut Up
- 1 (16 Ounce) Packages Little Smokies Sausages, Smokie Cheese Links (Cut Into Small Pieces Or Use The "Little Smokies")
- 1/2 Cup Butter Or 1/2 Cup Margarine
- 1/4 Cup Flour
- 1/2 Cup Milk
- 1/2 Lb Velveeta Cheese
- 1 (10 3/4 Ounce) Cans Cream Of Mushroom Soup (99.9% Fat-Free Works Fine)
- 6 English Muffins (Or Use Crimp Bread)

DIRECTIONS

1. On a low heat mix the butter with the flour and whisk on milk.
2. Add Soup and Velveeta cheese until the cheese melts. Hard boiled eggs and smokie cheese links are added.
3. Refrigerate it in a crock pot. Or you can bake it at 325 degrees for 20 minutes before serving.
4. English muffin is being halved, and it serves with it.

OVERNIGHT CROCK POT OATMEAL

- Prep Time: 15 mins
- Total Time: 8 hrs 15 mins
- Servings: 2-4

INGREDIENTS

- 2 Cups Oats
- 4 Cups Water
- 1/2 Cup Brown Sugar
- 1/2 Teaspoon Cinnamon
- 1/4 Teaspoon Nutmeg
- 1 Apple, Diced
- 1 Cup Raisins (I Used Dates Because I Don't Like Raisins)
- 1/2 Cup Chopped Nuts

DIRECTIONS

1. The crock pot is being sprayed with the cooking spray.
2. All the INGREDIENTS are mix and covered and cooked for over 8 hours and set it for overnight.

CROCKPOT BREAKFAST OMELETTE

- Prep Time: 25 mins
- Total Time: 7 hrs 25 mins
- Servings: 15

INGREDIENTS

- 12 Eggs
- 1 (32 Ounce) Bags Frozen Hash Brown Potatoes (Partially Thawed)
- 1 Lb Bacon, Cut Into Small Pieces (Fried And Drained)
- 1/2 Cup Diced Onion
- 1/2 Cup Diced Green Pepper
- 3/4 Lb Shredded Cheddar Cheese
- 1 Cup Milk
- 1/2 Teaspoon Salt

DIRECTIONS

1. The crock pot is being greased with butter, and the INGREDIENTS are being layered from the bottom to the top taking half of the INGREDIENTS each time which includes potatoes, bacon, onions and peppers, cheese. Whisk egg, milk, and salt and pour the mixture over the layer.
2. Cook for nearly 7 to 8 hours.

CROCK POT BREAKFAST CASSEROLE

- Prep Time: 20 mins
- Total Time: 8 hrs 20 mins
- Servings: 8

INGREDIENTS

LAYERS

- 1/2 Lb Sausage Or 1/2 Lb Ham
- 1/2 Lb Bacon
- 1 (32 Ounce) Bags Frozen Hash Brown Potatoes
- 1 -2 Bell Pepper, Chopped
- 1/2 Onion, Chopped
- 3 -4 Cups Cheese, Shredded
- Olive

MIX

- 12 Eggs
- 1 Cup Milk
- Salt, To Taste
- Pepper, To Taste

DIRECTIONS

1. The sausage and bacon are being browned. In the crock pot, the INGREDIENTS are being layered.
2. Te first layer has to be meat and then mix the egg and milk and salt and pepper and pour over the top.
3. Cook it for 8 hours.

<u>SLOW-COOKER BREAKFAST CASSEROLE</u>

- Prep Time: 0 mins
- Total Time: 10 hrs
- Servings: 4

INGREDIENTS

- 16 Ounces Hash Browns, Frozen
- 1/2 Lb Bacon, Cooked And Crumbled
- 1/2 Medium Onion, Diced
- 1/2 Medium Bell Pepper, Diced
- 3/4 Cup Cheddar Cheese, Shredded
- 6 Eggs
- 1/2 Cup Milk
- 1/2 Teaspoon Salt
- 1/2 Teaspoon Pepper

DIRECTIONS

1. The frozen hash brown is being placed at the bottom of the crock pot and then the bacon onions, bell pepper, and cheese is being layers.
2. Repeat the same things and end with cheese.
3. Whisk egg, milk, salt, pepper together and pour over the crock pot.
4. Cover and cook for 8 to 10 hours.

BACON AND TATER TOTS CROCK POT BREAKFAST

- Prep Time: 15 mins
- Total Time: 12 hrs 15 mins
- Servings: 6-8

INGREDIENTS

- 1 Lb Frozen Tater Tots
- 1/2 Lb Diced Canadian Bacon
- 1 Onion, Chopped
- 1 Green Bell Pepper, Chopped
- 1 1/2 Cups Shredded Cheddar Cheese
- 1/4 Cup Grated Parmesan Cheese
- 6 Eggs
- 1/2 Cup Whole Milk
- 2 Tablespoons Flour
- Salt And Pepper

DIRECTIONS

1. Layer The INGREDIENTS With One Third Of Tater Tots, Bacon, Onions, Green Peppers And Cheeses.
2. Repeat The Layers With The Cheese On The Top. Mix Egg, Milk, Flour And Whisk It. Season It With Salt And Pepper To Taste.
3. Pour This Mixture Over The Crock Pot.
4. Cook It Low Which May Take Nearly 4 Hours.

CROCK POT SAUSAGE AND MUSHROOM BAKE

- Prep Time: 15 mins
- Total Time: 6 hrs 15 mins
- Servings: 6

INGREDIENTS

- 2 Tablespoons Oil
- 1 Onion, Sliced
- 450 G Potatoes, Thinly Sliced
- 450 G Sausages, Skinned And Halved
- 1 (450 G) Cans Baked Beans
- 200 G Button Mushrooms, Halved
- 1 -2 Teaspoon Chili Powder (Or To Personal Taste)
- 1 Tablespoon Tomato Paste
- 2/3 Cup Water
- Salt And Pepper, To Personal Taste

DIRECTIONS

1. Oil is being heated, and onion and potatoes are being sautéed gently for 5 minutes.
2. The remaining INGREDIENTS are being mixed and are being seasoned with salt and pepper and bring to boil.
3. Transfer to crock pot for 6 to 10 hours it is being cooked

FRUIT & NUT OATMEAL CROCK POT

- Prep Time: 10 mins
- Total Time: 8 hrs 10 mins
- Servings: 4

INGREDIENTS

- 4 1/2 Cups Water
- 1 Cup Steel Cut Oats
- 1 Pinch Salt
- 1 Tablespoon Butter
- 1/4 Teaspoon Cinnamon
- 1/4 Cup Dried Apples Or 1/4 Cup Dried Blueberries Or 1/4 Cup Dried Cranberries Or 1/4 Cup Dried Cherries
- 1/4 Cup Toasted Chopped Pecans

DIRECTIONS

1. In a small crock pot place all the INGREDIENTS (except pecans) and cook for nearly 7 hours.
2. The oats in the INGREDIENTS will thicken up. Serve with milk, cream, sweetener, fresh fruits and serve with the toppings of pecans.

SLOW COOKER BAKED BEANS WITH MAPLE SYRUP

- Prep Time: 10 mins
- Total Time: 9 hrs 10 mins
- Servings: 8-10

INGREDIENTS

- 4 Cups Dry White Beans (1 Bag 907 G Or 2 Lbs) Or 4 Cups Navy Beans (1 Bag 907 G Or 2 Lbs)
- Water, For Soaking
- 6 Cups Cold Water (For Cooking)
- 1 Cup Maple Syrup
- 1/2 Cup Ketchup
- 1/2 Lb Streaky Salt Pork, Rind Removed And Diced (I Used Bacon)
- 2 Onions, Coarsely Chopped
- 1 Tablespoon Dijon Mustard
- 1 Teaspoon Salt
- 1/2 Teaspoon Ground Pepper

DIRECTIONS

1. The beans are placed in large bowls and are being soaked in water overnight.
2. Rinse and drain before preparation. In a slow cooker, all the INGREDIENTS are mixed and are cooked for 8 to 9 hours on low and another 6 hours on high flame. Seasoning has to be done before the serving.

EARLY RISER CROCK POT BREAKFAST

- Prep Time: 10 mins
- Total Time: 7 hrs 10 mins
- Servings: 6

INGREDIENTS

- 16 Ounces Tator Tot Potatoes, Divided In Half
- 2 Tablespoons Onions, Chopped, Divided In Half
- 8 Ounces Ham, Chopped, Divided In Half
- 1 1/2 Cups Sharp Cheddar Cheese, Divided In Half
- 32 Ounces Egg Substitute
- 1/2 Teaspoon Salt
- 1/2 Teaspoon Pepper
- 1/4 Teaspoon Dried Mustard (Optional) Or 1/4 Teaspoon Thyme (Optional)

DIRECTIONS

1. Cook the crock pots in a slow cooker for 6 hours or less. Layer the potatoes, onion, ham and cheese.
2. Remember not to touch the cheese on the side of the crock pot as it will burn the cheese. Repeat the layers with the ingredients.
3. The egg beater is being dumped in salt, pepper and dried mustard. You may also try thyme or Italian.
4. Put the cap of the seal and shake it well. Pour this mixture on the layers and cover the crock. Heat a bit and cook for 6 hours.

QUINOA AND BARLEY BREAKFAST PORRIDGE

- Prep Time: 5 mins
- Total Time: 45 mins
- Servings: 4

INGREDIENTS

- 1/2 Cup Barley (I Prefer Hulled To Pearled)
- 1/2 Cup Quinoa
- 1 Pinch Salt
- 4 Cups Water
- Dried Fruits (Optional, Such As Raisins, Cranberries Or Cherry)
- Honey (Optional) Or Maple Syrup (Optional) Or Sugar (Optional)
- Spices, Such As Cinnamon, Nutmeg, Cardamom (Optional)
- Milk (Optional) Or Yogurt (Optional)

DIRECTIONS

1. Barley, quinoa, salt and water and mix this and cook at low heat. This is for crock pot method.
2. For stove top method you have to boil the INGREDIENTS and continue till all water is absorbed.
3. Then fluff the INGREDIENTS and put in serving the dish.

4. Add sweetener dried fruits and spices. You can also serve it with milk or yogurt. In the case of vegan cancel the milk and yogurt or soy milk.

****

APPLE DUMPLINGS!

- Prep Time: 15 mins
- Total Time: 6 hrs 15 mins
- Servings: 6

INGREDIENTS

- 4 Granny Smith Apples, Peeled And Sliced Thin
- 1/4 Cup Golden Raisin
- 1 1/2 Tablespoons Flour
- 1/2 Cup Apple Juice
- 1/3 Cup Sugar
- 2 Tablespoons Butter, Melted
- 1 Teaspoon Vanilla Extract
- 3/4 Teaspoon Cinnamon
- 1/4 Teaspoon Nutmeg

Drop Dumplings

- 4 Ounces Cream Cheese
- 1/3 Cup Plain Yogurt (I Used A Thick, Greek-Style)
- 1 Egg, Beaten

- 1 Cup Flour
- 1/3 Cup Quick-Cooking Oatmeal
- 1/3 Cup Sugar
- 1 Teaspoon Baking Powder
- 1/2 Teaspoon Vanilla Extract
- 1/2 Teaspoon Cinnamon
- 1 Dash Salt

To Garnish

- Chopped Toasted Walnuts Or Pecans

DIRECTIONS

1. The crock pot liner has to be greased. Mix the apple slices and raisins with flour.
2. Place it in the crock pot. Add apple juice with melted butter sugar vanilla extract and other spice. Pour this over the apple.
3. Cook for nearly 5 hours.
4. For the dumpling pat mix all the INGREDIENTS and then pour the dumpling batter over the mixture in crock pot.
5. Put the temperature at high and cook for more than 1 hour.
6. Serve 2 dumplings with lots of apple sauce and topped with toasted crunchy walnuts and a little cream.

GOLDILOCK'S PORRIDGE

- Prep Time: 5 mins
- Total Time: 8 hrs 5 mins
- Servings: 2-4

INGREDIENTS

- 1/4 Cup Pearl Barley
- 3/4 Cup Oatmeal
- 2 Cups Milk
- 1/2 Cup Heavy Whipping Cream
- 2 Tablespoons Melted Butter
- 1 1/2 Tablespoons Brown Sugar
- 1 Tablespoon Real Maple Syrup
- 1/4 Cup Golden Raisin
- 1/8 Cup Chopped Pecans
- 3/8 Teaspoon Salt
- 1 Dash Cinnamon

DIRECTIONS

1. With cooking spray, spray the inside of the crock pot. All the INGREDIENTS are stirred and are cooked overnight for 8 to 9 hours.
2. Cook at a low temperature.

BREAKFAST APPLE COBBLER

- Prep Time: 15 mins
- Total Time: 8 hrs 15 mins
- Servings: 2-3

INGREDIENTS

- 2 Medium Tart Apples
- 2 Tablespoons Splenda Brown Sugar Blend Or 1/4 Cup Brown Sugar
- 1/4 Teaspoon Cinnamon
- 2 Teaspoons Lemon Juice
- 1 Tablespoon Butter, Melted
- 1/2 Cup Granola Cereal (With Fruit And Nuts)
- Milk (Optional)
- Cream (Optional)

DIRECTIONS

1. Apples are being sliced and are placed in Crockett. All the INGREDIENTS are mixed and are stirred thoroughly.
2. Cook it for 8 to 10 hours and serve with the toppings o your choice.

CHINESE BREAKFAST RICE SOUP

- Prep Time: 20 mins
- Total Time: 10 hrs 50 mins
- Servings: 4-6

INGREDIENTS

- 1 cup calrose rice (or a premium Japanese-style rice such as Nishiki)
- 2 tablespoons vegetable oil
- 10 cups chicken broth or 10 cups turkey broth
- 2 teaspoons salt
- 1 tablespoon finely minced cilantro (stems)
- 1 cup plain soymilk (optional)
- For serving
- Chopped Fresh Cilantro Leaves
- Minced Green Onion
- Oyster Sauce
- Soy Sauce
- Hot Pepper Sauce, Such As Sriracha (Or Tabasco)

DIRECTIONS

1. Wash and soak rice for 30 minutes. Then heat the oil in a slow cooker setting at HIGH.
2. Finally, drain the water. The rice is being added to the oil and is cooked until it smells toasty.

3. All the stocks, salt, cilantro stems are added. These are being stirred well and mix the liquid and the rice well.

4. Cover and cook on HIGH for 1 and half hours stirring it occasionally.

5. Minced green onions and chopped cilantro leaves are being given with soy sauce or oyster sauce.

HEALTHIEST OVERNIGHT MAPLE OATMEAL

- Prep Time: 10 mins
- Total Time: 7 hrs 10 mins
- Servings: 6

INGREDIENTS

- 2 Cups Steel Cut Oats (Do Not Substitute)
- 6 Cups Water
- 1/2 Cup Dried Cherries Or 1/2 Cup Raisins Or 1/2 Cup Cranberries
- 1 Teaspoon Cinnamon
- 1/4 Cup Ground Flax Seeds
- 1/2 Cup Blueberries Or 1/2 Cup Bananas Or 1/2 Cup Walnuts

DIRECTIONS

1. 4-5 quart of slow cooker is being sprayed with non stick cooking spray.
2. Add oats water, maple syrup, and dried fruits cinnamon and ground flaxseed and set the cooker to Low.
3. Cook for 7 to 8 hours.
4. When it is served, add blueberries, banana slices, and walnuts.

BACON AND GRUYERE PAIN PERDU

- Prep Time: 45 mins
- Total Time: 2 hrs 45 mins
- Servings: 6

INGREDIENTS

- Unsalted Butter
- 8 Ounces Bacon
- 2 Large Shallots, Finely Chopped (About Ã 1/2 Cup)
- 5 Large Eggs
- 2 Cups Whole Milk
- 1/4 Teaspoon Freshly Grated Nutmeg
- Salt
- Fresh Ground Black Pepper
- 1 Cup Freshly Grated Parmigiano-Reggiano Cheese
- 6 Cups Day-Old French Bread Cubes, 1-Inch
- 1/2 Cup Grated Gruyere Cheese Or 1/2 Cup Emmenthaler Cheese

DIRECTIONS

1. The slow cooker is being layered with the butter. Cook the bacon in a large skillet over medium heat until it turns crispy.
2. Crumble the bacon after draining the water. Except 1T fat all are being poured from the skillet. The shallots are being added and cooked until they get soft.

3. Beta the eggs in a separate bowl stir the bacon shallot and parmesan. Place bread cubes in another bowl.
4. Now pour the egg mixture over the cubes and stir well. Scrape it in slow cooker. The bread cubes have to be pressed into the liquid. Sprinkle it with gruyere.
5. Cover and cook for nearly 2 hours. Insert a knife in the center and it should come out clean. Serve hot.

SPICY TOMATO JUICE

- Prep Time: 15 mins
- Total Time: 11 hrs 15 mins
- Serves: 8, Yield: 1 quart (approximately)

INGREDIENTS

- 4 Lbs Fresh Tomatoes
- 1/2 Cup Celery
- 1/4 Cup Onion
- 6 Slices Beets
- 2 Tablespoons Lemon Juice
- 1 1/2 Teaspoons Sugar
- 1/2 Teaspoon Salt Substitute
- 1/2 Teaspoon Mixed Spice
- 4 Teaspoons Reduced-Sodium Worcestershire Sauce
- 1/2 Teaspoon Tabasco Sauce (Optional)

DIRECTIONS

1. Tomatoes, celery, onions, and beets are being chopped. Cook them at low temperature in a crock pot.
2. Cook for 8 to 10 hours. The mixture is being pressed through the sieve.
3. Again cook the juice for half an hour in the crock pot. Add the remaining INGREDIENTS and cook for 15 minutes and then chill.

GREEK YOGURT

- Prep Time: 24 hrs
- Total Time: 24 hrs
- Serves: 8, Yield: 4 cups

INGREDIENTS

- 1/2 Gallon Skim Milk
- 1/2 Cup Plain Fat Free Greek Yogurt (Fat Free& With Active Cultures)

DIRECTIONS

1. For nearly 2 and half hours cook the milk. Then cool it for 100 to 110 degrees.
2. Take 2c of cooked milk and mix it with the yoghurt and then place it again in crock pot. Wrap the whole crock pot in thick towels and let it sit overnight. Then drain with a fine sieve or cheesecloth.
3. Place yoghurt in the container and put it in the fridge. The more time it will rest it will be tastier. And more you drain, it becomes thicker. Sweetened it with honey and frozen berries can be added.

BAKED OATMEAL

- Prep Time: 5 mins
- Total Time: 8 hrs 5 mins
- Serves: 8-10, Yield: 8.0 bowls

INGREDIENTS

- 2 Cups Old Fashioned Oats
- 1 Cup Cream
- 1/2 Cup Light Brown Sugar
- 1 Cup Melted Butter
- 1/2 Cup Hot Water
- 2 Cups Dried Fruit
- 2 Cups Chopped Walnuts

DIRECTIONS

1. All the INGREDIENTS are being mixed and is cook overnight till morning in a slow cooker

FRUITY BREAKFAST CEREAL

- Prep Time: 10 mins
- Total Time: 6 hrs 10 mins
- Yield: 10 cups

INGREDIENTS

- 5 Cups Water
- 2 Cups Seven-Grain Cereal
- 1 Medium Apple, Peeled And Chopped
- 1 Cup Unsweetened Apple Juice
- 1/4 Cup Dried Apricot, Chopped
- 1/4 Cup Dried Cranberries
- 1/4 Cup Raisins
- 1/4 Cup Chopped Dates
- 1/4 Cup Maple Syrup
- 1 Teaspoon Ground Cinnamon
- 1/2 Teaspoon Salt
- Chopped Walnuts (Optional)

DIRECTIONS

1. Combine the INGREDIENTS and cook then at LOW in a slow cooker.
2. Cook it for 7 hours or until the fruits are softened. Sprinkle walnuts over the servings.

MORNING CASSEROLE

- Prep Time: 30 mins
- Total Time: 10 hrs 30 mins
- Servings: 6

INGREDIENTS

- 1 (32 Ounce) Bags Frozen Hash Brown Potatoes
- 1 Lb Bacon, Diced Cooked And Drained Or 1 Lb Cooked Ham, Cubed
- 1 Medium Diced Onion
- 1 Green Bell Pepper, Diced
- 1 1/2 Cups Shredded Cheddar Cheese Or 1 1/2 Cups Monterey Jack Cheese
- 1 Dozen Egg
- 1 Cup Milk
- 1 Teaspoon Salt
- 1 Teaspoon Pepper (More Or Less To Taste)

DIRECTIONS

1. Layer the slow cooker with frozen potatoes in the bottom and then by bacon, then by onions, green pepper, and cheese.
2. Repeat it for two or three layers and on the uppermost have the layer of cheese. Beat the egg, milk, salt and pepper together and pour over the slow cooker mixture. Cook for 10 to 12 hours.

TAPIOCA PUDDING

- Prep Time: 20 mins
- Total Time: 3 hrs 20 mins
- Servings: 4

INGREDIENTS

- 3 1/2 Ounces Large Pearl Tapioca, Approximately 1/2 Cup
- 2 Cups Cold Water
- 2 1/2 Cups Whole Milk
- 1/2 Cup Heavy Cream
- 1 Egg Yolk
- 1/3 Cup Sugar
- 1 Lemon, Zest Of
- 1 Pinch Salt

DIRECTIONS

1. Mix tapioca with water and let it stand for 8 hours covered. Then rinse the water and put it in slow cooker.
2. Mix milk cream and salt as per taste. For 2 hours it needs to be cooked in HIGH. In another bowl whisk egg and sugar.
3. A small amount of tapioca is being mixed with the egg and then put this in the slow cooker.
4. Repeat with the rest of eh tapioca. Cook for 15 minutes and stir it one time. Put the ready pudding in a bowl wrapped with plastic wrap.
5. Allow to cool and pour it in the fridge. Serve it chilled.

HOT OATMEAL AND RICE

- Prep Time: 10 mins
- Total Time: 9 hrs 10 mins
- Servings: 4

INGREDIENTS

- 1 Cup Steel Cut Oats
- 1 Cup Short-Grain Brown Rice
- 2 Tablespoons Oat Bran Or 2 Tablespoons Toasted Wheat Germ
- 1 Pinch Sea Salt
- 5 Cups Water

DIRECTIONS

1. All the INGREDIENTS are added in a slow cooker and is stirred. Cover and cook for 7 to 9 hours. Stir the cereals and scoop in the bowl.
2. Serve with milk, soy milk light cream and honey.

GOOD-FOR-YOU GRANOLA

- Prep Time: 5 mins
- Total Time: 6 hrs 5 mins
- Serves: 6, Yield: 6 cups

INGREDIENTS

- 2 1/2 cups old fashioned oats
- 1 cup chopped pecans
- 3/4 cup coconut flakes
- 1/3 cup wheat germ
- 2 tablespoons sesame seeds (optional)
- 1/2 cup honey
- 1/4 cup frozen apple juice concentrate, thawed
- 2 tablespoons brown sugar
- 1 teaspoon vanilla
- 1/2 teaspoon cinnamon
- 1 (6 ounce) bags dried cranberries

DIRECTIONS

1. In a slow cooker stir, the oats, nuts, coconuts wheat germ and sesame seeds are stirred together.
2. In a microwave safe bowl, mix honey, apple juice sugar, vanilla, and cinnamon. Microwave for 1 minute. Pour this mixture over the slow cooker and stir it well.

3. Cook for 1 hour without any lid. Reduce to low. Over and again cook for 4 to 5 hours until the granola are golden and dry. Stir cranberries and store in airtight container

NEW BREAKFAST CASSEROLE

- Prep Time: 0 mins
- Total Time: 10 hrs
- Servings: 6

INGREDIENTS

- 1 (32 Ounce) Bags Frozen Southern Style Hash Brown Potatoes
- 1 Lb Bacon, Cut, Fried And Drained
- 1 Lb Sausage, Crumbled, Browned And Drained
- 1/2 Cup Diced Onion
- 1 Green Pepper, Diced
- 3/4 Lb Cheddar Cheese, Diced
- 1 Dozen Egg
- 1 Cup Milk
- 1/2 Teaspoon Dry Mustard
- Salt And Pepper

DIRECTIONS

1. Frozen potatoes, bacons onions, green pepper, cheese are layered in the crock pot in two or three layers.
2. Complete the layer with cheese. Whisk eggs, milk, and mustard salt and pepper together. Pour it over the whole mixture.
3. Cook this for nearly 10 to 12 hours.

SCRAMBLED EGGS

- Prep Time: 40 mins
- Total Time: 4 hrs 40 mins
- Servings: 12

INGREDIENTS

- 8 Slices Bacon
- 3 Cups Sliced Mushrooms
- 3 Tablespoons Butter
- 16 Eggs
- 1 Cup Half-And-Half Or 1 Cup Milk
- 1 (10 Ounce) Cans Condensed Cream Of Mushroom Soup
- 2 Tablespoons Chopped Fresh Chives
- 4 Italian Plum Tomatoes, Quartered,Sliced
- 2 Cups Shredded Cheddar Cheese
- Salt & Pepper

DIRECTIONS

1. Fry the bacon until it is crisp. Drain them on paper towels. Crumble the bacon and put them aside.
2. In the drippings add the mushroom and cook for 4 minutes stirring occasionally. Remove them from the skillets.

3. Then melt the Marge in skillet over medium heat and whisk half egg salt pepper and pour it over the skillet. Stir the soup frequently.

4. Place the other half of the egg in the slow cooker. Top it with half of the cooked mushroom tomatoes cheese crumbled bacon.

5. Repeat these layers and cover and cook for 4 hours.

CHERRY OATMEAL

- Prep Time: 5 mins
- Total Time: 4 hrs 5 mins
- Servings: 6-8

INGREDIENTS

- 3 Cups Steel Cut Oats Or 4 Cups Old Fashioned Oats
- 8 1/2 Cups Water
- 1 Cup Splenda Granular, Sugar Substitute
- 2 (16 Ounce) Bags Frozen Cherries (Trader Joes)
- Cinnamon
- 1 Teaspoon Almond Extract

DIRECTIONS

1. Mix all the INGREDIENTS in a crock pot and cook on HIGH for nearly 4 hours.
2. But if you are cooking on the stove then cook on top of the stove and follow the usual cooking timing for cooking oat.

VEGETARIAN BREAKFAST CASSEROLE

- Prep Time: 20 mins
- Total Time: 7 hrs 20 mins
- Serves: 6, Yield: 1 Casserole

INGREDIENTS

- 1 (14 Ounce) Packages Soy Sausage (I Use Gimme Lean)
- 4 Ounces Diced Green Chilies, Undrained
- 1 Medium Bell Pepper, Chopped (Red Or Green)
- 1 Medium White Onion, Chopped
- 1 Summer Squash, Sliced
- 2 Carrots, Sliced
- 2 Cups Fat Free Mozzarella Cheese
- 2 Cups Egg Substitute
- 1/2 Cup Water

DIRECTIONS

1. After greasing the crock pot layer all the INGREDIENTS that is meat, onion, squash, carrots, pepper, chilies and cheese. Repeat these layers for several times and pour water over the layer.

2. Whisk egg and pour it over the layers. Cover the entire food item and cook for 7 to 8 hours. To spice it up add sauce or sour cream.

EASY OVERNIGHT OATMEAL

- Prep Time: 10 mins
- Total Time: 7 hrs 10 mins
- Servings: 8

INGREDIENTS

- 4 Cups Milk
- 1/2 Cup Brown Sugar
- 2 Tablespoons Butter
- 1/2 Teaspoon Salt
- 1 Teaspoon Cinnamon
- 2 Cups Old Fashioned Oats (Not Quick Cooking Oats) Or 2 Cups Steel Cut Oats (Not Quick Cooking Oats)
- 2 Cups Chopped Apples
- 1 Cup Raisins
- 1 Cup Chopped Walnuts

DIRECTIONS

1. With non-stick cooking spray coat the interior of the crock pot. Mix all the INGREDIENTS and place in the crock pot.
2. Cover the lid and set to Low for a night (7 to 8 hours). Stir well and scoop into individual bowls and serve.
3. Be careful that you don't overcook the food.

CREAMY RICE PORRIDGE WITH RAISINS

- Prep Time: 10 mins
- Total Time: 8 hrs 10 mins
- Servings: 3

INGREDIENTS

- 1 cup medium grain rice, such as Calrose (or short-grain rice such as Arborio)
- 2 cups water
- 1 1/2 cups evaporated skim milk
- 1/2 teaspoon salt
- 1/2 cup raisins

DIRECTIONS

1. Mix the INGREDIENTS mentioned in a slow cooker and set the cooking temperature at LOW.
2. Cook the items for 6 to 8 hours. Keep eye on the INGREDIENTS becoming tender and creamy.
3. Then stir the mixture and serve hot from the pot.

OVERNIGHT OATMEAL

- Prep Time: 0 mins
- Total Time: 8 hrs
- Servings: 1-10

INGREDIENTS

- 1 Cup Steel Cut Oats
- 4 Cups Water
- 1 Pinch Salt

DIRECTIONS

1. Water is mixed with the oats and put it in the crock pot and set the temperature at the LOW cover the pot and let it stay for an overnight cook.
2. Then stir it in salt before serving

CHOCOLATE BLINTZES

- Prep Time: 5 mins
- Total Time: 1 hr 20 mins
- Serves: 1, Yield: 1 blintzes

INGREDIENTS

- 3 Ounces Chocolate Syrup (Can Be Sugar-Free)
- 3 Ounces Frozen Blintz (One Blintz- Can Be More Of Course, Though Cooking Times May Vary)

DIRECTIONS

1. In the chocolate syrup put the blintzes and put the bag in the crock pot.
2. Set the temperature as HIGH and cook for 75 minutes and then few hours at LOW.

POACHED EGGS IN SPICY TOMATO SAUCE

- Prep Time: 30 mins
- Total Time: 2 hrs 30 mins
- Servings: 8

INGREDIENTS

- 2 Tablespoons Olive Oil
- 1 Medium Onion, Sliced
- 2 Medium Red Bell Peppers Or 2 Medium Green Bell Peppers, Chopped
- 2 Garlic Cloves, Finely Chopped
- 1 Small Jalapeno, Seeded And Finely Chopped
- 28 Ounces Crushed Tomatoes
- 28 Ounces Diced Tomatoes, Drained
- 2 Teaspoons Smoked Paprika
- 1 Teaspoon Ground Turmeric
- 1 Teaspoon Sugar
- Salt And Pepper
- 8 Large Eggs
- Za'atar Spice Mix

DIRECTIONS

1. Heat oil at medium heat.

2. Add the onion and sauté till soft. Stir in pepper garlic and Jalapeno. Cook for 10 minutes.

3. Put this in the slow cooker and add tomatoes, paprika, turmeric, sugar salt and pepper to taste. Stir it to mix well.

4. Cover and set the temperature at HIGH. Now break one egg and gentle slip in the sauce.

5. Do the same thing with the remaining eggs. Sprinkle the eggs and cook for 10 minutes. Serve the sauce with the eggs and serve with hot fresh pita bread for dipping.

STRAWBERRY BANANA & PEAR BUTTER

- Prep Time: 30 mins
- Total Time: 14 hrs 30 mins
- Yield: 2 cups

INGREDIENTS

- 6 Cups Peeled Cored Chopped Ripe Pears
- 1 (11 1/2 Ounce) Cans Kern's Strawberry-Banana Nectar
- 1 Cup Sugar
- 1/4 Teaspoon Ground Cardamom
- 1 Teaspoon Vanilla Extract

DIRECTIONS

1. In the crock pot cook the pears and nectar for 1 hour. Mix all INGREDIENTS reduce the temperature to LOW and cook for 8 hours.
2. Stir the mixture occasionally. Smash the fruits which are softened with the help of potato smasher.
3. Keep notice and stir it occasionally such that it is not stick to the bottom and get thickened.
4. After it gets thickened, cool it down and spoon in the container with ½ inch top sauce.
5. Cool to in fridge and cover while refrigerating.

FOSTER OATMEAL

- Prep Time: 5 mins
- Total Time: 8 hrs 5 mins
- Serves: 2, Yield: 2

INGREDIENTS

- 2 Cups Oats
- 2 Chopped Bananas
- 4 Tablespoons Toasted Pecans
- 4 Tablespoons Caramels
- 2 Tablespoons Rum Extract
- 2 Cups Cream

DIRECTIONS

1. Combine the INGREDIENTS and cook in a slow cooker overnight.
2. Put in it excess of caramel and cream over it

HOMEMADE LOW FAT YOGHURT

- Prep Time: 5 mins
- Total Time: 12 hrs 5 mins
- Serves: 8, Yield: 0.5 cup

INGREDIENTS

- 6 Cups Water
- 1 Cup Low-Fat Powdered Milk
- 1/2 Cup Yogurt

DIRECTIONS

1. In a crock pot add 6 cups of water and milk powder whisking it thoroughly.
2. On low temperature leave it for 4 hours to cook. Then take the lid off and allow the mixture to cool down.
3. Then stir the yoghurt. Then again put the lid and leave the crock pot for 8 hours.
4. Then whisk these and transfer it to the water tight container and put in the fridge.

<u>CREAMY OATMEAL WITH DRIED FRUIT</u>

- Prep Time: 10 mins
- Total Time: 9 hrs 10 mins
- Servings: 3

INGREDIENTS

- 1 Cup Steel Cut Oats
- 2/3 Cup Dried Tart Cherries Or 2/3 Cup Dried Sweetened Cranberries
- 1/3 Cup Chopped Dried Fig
- 1/3 Cup Chopped Dried Apricot
- 4 1/2 Cups Water
- 1/2 Cup Half-And-Half

DIRECTIONS

1. In a slow cooker mix all the ingredients.
2. Cook in LOW temperature and keep it overnight before it is fully done.

MILLET PORRIDGE WITH DATES

- Prep Time: 5 mins
- Total Time: 9 hrs 5 mins
- Servings: 4

INGREDIENTS

- 1 Cup Cracked Millet Or 1 Cup Millet
- 3 1/2 Cups Water
- Salt (A Pinch)
- 1/2 Cup Evaporated Milk (Or Whole Milk Or Light Cream)
- 1/4-1/2 Cup Chopped Pitted Dates

DIRECTIONS

1. Mix millet, water, salt in a slow cooker and combine.
2. Cover and cook for nearly 8 hours or overnight. Stir it occasionally during cooking.
3. Before it is done, stir it with the milk and dates turning the temperature to high.
4. Stir the porridge and serve with milk and honey.

BREAKFAST CASSEROLE

- Prep Time: 10 mins
- Total Time: 8 hrs 10 mins
- Servings: 8

INGREDIENTS

- 1 Lb Frozen Hash Browns, Partially Thawed
- 2 Cups Low-Fat Cheddar Cheese, Shredded
- 6 Large Eggs
- 1 1/2 Cups Egg Substitute
- 1 Cup Skim Milk
- 1/2 Teaspoon Salt
- 1/4 Teaspoon Pepper

DIRECTIONS

1. With cooking spray, spray the inside of the slow cooker.
2. The hash brown is being topped with cheese and put it in slow cooker.
3. Repeat the remaining hash brown in the same way. In another bowl mix the eggs and its substitute.
4. Pour this mixture over the layer and allow it to cook for 8 hours

MULTIGRAIN PORRIDGE

- Prep Time: 15 mins
- Total Time: 6 hrs 15 mins
- Servings: 10

INGREDIENTS

- 2 Tablespoons Butter
- 3/4 Cup Brown Rice
- 1/4 Cup Quinoa
- 1 Cup Rolled Oats
- 1 Cup Steel Cut Oats
- 2 Granny Smith Apples, Cored And Diced
- 2 Teaspoons Vanilla Extract
- 2 Teaspoons Ground Cinnamon
- 1/4-1/3 Cup Brown Sugar
- 10 Cups Water

DIRECTIONS

1. The slow cooker should be of 6 quarts and put butter on the inside of the cooker.
2. Wash brown rice and quinoa by water and dump in the slow cooker.
3. Add the apples, oats, vanilla, cinnamon and brown sugar.
4. Pour 10 cups of water and slow cook for 6 hours. When the brown rice gets tender opens the lid and stir well.
5. Then allow the porridge to cool down and serve

MOZZARELLA, SAUSAGE, AND SUN-DRIED TOMATO BREAD PUDDING

- Prep Time: 20 mins
- Total Time: 2 hrs 20 mins
- Servings: 6

INGREDIENTS

- 3/4 Cup Sun-Dried Tomato
- 2 Tablespoons Olive Oil
- 1 Large Onion, Chopped
- 3 Sweet Italian Sausages
- 6 Cups Day Old Italian Bread, Lightly Toasted (Cut Into 1-Inch Cubes)
- 5 Large Eggs
- 2 Cups Milk
- Salt And Pepper
- 8 Ounces Mozzarella Cheese Or 8 Ounces Provolone Cheese, Chopped

DIRECTIONS

1. With non-stick cooking spray, spray the inside of the slow cooker.

2. Put the sun-dried tomatoes with warm water and the drain the water. Heat oils in skillet and sauté the onions until brown and soft. Crumble the sausages in the pan. Place the bread cubes in the slow cooker and pour the sauce over it and toss it well. In another bowl blend the egg and put in milk salt pepper. Pour this mixture over the bread cubes and sprinkle cheese.

3. Cover and cook for one and a half hours on high. Cut the bread pudding and serve.

WARM APPLE BREAKFAST CEREAL

- Prep Time: 30 mins
- Total Time: 8 hrs 30 mins
- Servings: 6

INGREDIENTS

- 8 Granny Smith Apples, Cored, Peeled, And Quartered (Braeburn, Golden Delicious)
- 2 Tablespoons Lemon Juice
- 3 Tablespoons Honey Or 3 Tablespoons Sorghum
- 1 1/2 Teaspoons Ground Cinnamon
- 2 1/2 Cups Granola Cereal
- 3 Tablespoons Unsalted Butter, Melted
- 1/3 Cup Toasted Chopped Pecans
- Nonfat Yogurt (Plain Or Vanilla)

DIRECTIONS

1. Grease the slow cooker and put the apples in it. Sprinkle honey and cinnamon.
2. Top this with cereal and sprinkle butter.
3. Cover and cook for 8 hours.
4. Serve after topped it with pecans and dollops of yoghurts.

MUSHROOM PAIN PERDU

- Prep Time: 45 mins
- Total Time: 2 hrs 45 mins
- Servings: 6

INGREDIENTS

- 3 Tablespoons Unsalted Butter, Plus More For The Cooker
- 1 (10 Ounce) Packages Sliced Mushrooms
- 1 Small Onion, Finely Chopped
- Salt
- Fresh Ground Pepper
- 5 Large Eggs
- 2 Cups Whole Milk
- 1/2 Cup Freshly Grated Parmigiano-Reggiano Cheese
- 1/4 Teaspoon Freshly Grated Nutmeg
- 6 Cups Day-Old French Bread Cubes, Lightly Toasted, 1-Inch Cubes
- 1/2 Cup Grated Gruyere Cheese Or 1/2 Cup Emmenthaler Cheese

DIRECTIONS

1. Grease the inside of the slow cooker with butter. Melt the 3 T butter in a skillet over medium heat.
2. Add mushrooms, onions and cook till mushrooms get golden.

3. Add salt and pepper as per the taste. In another bowl, whisk eggs, milk, parmesan, nutmeg salt and pepper to taste. Stir with the mushrooms.

4. Place the bread cubes in a bowl and pour this mixture over the bread cubes. Pres the bread cubes into the liquid and set the slow cooker at HIGH temperature for one and a half hours.

5. Serve hot.

APPLE-PECAN BREAD PUDDING

- Prep Time: 30 mins
- Total Time: 5 hrs 30 mins
- Servings: 6

INGREDIENTS

- Cooking Spray
- 4 Cups Toasted Bread Cubes (Approximately 8 Slices)
- 2 Granny Smith Apples, Peeled, Cored, And Diced
- 1/4 Cup Butter, Melted
- 1/2 Cup Coarsely Chopped Pecans
- 1 Cup Raisins
- 1 Cup Brown Sugar
- 2 Teaspoons Pumpkin Pie Spice
- 3 Eggs
- 2 Cups Half-And-Half

DIRECTIONS

1. Spray stoneware inside the slow cooker. Put toasted bread into the cooker and add dice apples.
2. Mix the bread and apple with butter. Dumped in pecans raisins, brown sugar and sprinkle pumpkin pie spice.
3. Stir gently to mix the INGREDIENTS gently. Beat a half egg and pour from the top. Cook for 4 to 5 hours on HIGH .pudding is done when it is browned on the top. Serve warm with vanilla ice cream as a dessert.

PEACHES (OR OTHER FRUIT) AND CREAM CASSEROLE

- Prep Time: 5 mins
- Total Time: 3 hrs 5 mins
- Servings: 4-6

INGREDIENTS

- 3 Cups Almond Milk
- 2 Egg Whites
- 2 Teaspoons Vanilla Extract
- 1/4 Teaspoon Almond Extract
- 1/2 Teaspoon Ground Cinnamon
- 1 1/2 Cups Peach Slices (Or Blueberries Or Cherries)
- 1/4 Cup Brown Sugar
- 1 1/2 Cups Oatmeal

DIRECTIONS

1. Grease crock pot. In a bowl combine milk, egg whites cinnamon and pour it in pot. In the same bowl combine peaches with brown sugar.
2. Add milk to the mixture.
3. Cover and cook for 4 hours at LOW temperature.

FARINA PORRIDGE

- Prep Time: 5 mins
- Total Time: 9 hrs 5 mins
- Servings: 4

INGREDIENTS

- 1/2 Cup Cream Of Wheat Or 1/2 Cup Farina
- 1/3 Cup Wheaten A Toasted Wheat Cereal
- 4 1/2 Cups Water
- 1 Pinch Salt

DIRECTIONS

1. Mix the INGREDIENTS in the slow cooker and cook over 7 to 9 hours. Stir it and whisk it.
2. Scoop into bowl and serve with milk and brown sugar

BAGEL BREAKFAST CASSEROLE

- Prep Time: 5 mins
- Total Time: 3 hrs 5 mins
- Servings: 4

INGREDIENTS

- 3 Plain Bagels, Ripped Into Small Pieces
- 2 Cups Egg Whites
- 1 Cup Crumbled Turkey Sausage
- 1/2 Cup Diced Turkey Bacon
- 1/4 Cup White Onion, Chopped
- 3/4 Cup Low-Fat Cheddar Cheese Or 3/4 Cup Fat-Free Cheddar Cheese

DIRECTIONS

1. The slow cooker is greased with non-stick cooking spray. Put bagel pieces in it.
2. Mix egg whites, turkey sausages and bacon and onion. Pour it over the bagels. On the top add cedar cheese.
3. Cover and cook on high for 3 hours and low for 6 to 7 hours.
4. Cook it until egg is set and bacon is cooked

CREAM AND CHIVE WAFFLES WITH SAUSAGE AND LINGONBERRY

- Prep Time: 20 mins
- Total Time: 45 mins
- Servings: 4

INGREDIENTS

- 1 Tablespoon Extra Virgin Olive Oil
- 1 Lb Ground Pork Or 1 Lb Ground Chicken Or 1 Lb Ground Turkey Breast
- 2 Teaspoons Fennel Seeds
- 2 Teaspoons Paprika Or 2 Teaspoons Smoked Sweet Paprika
- 1 Tablespoon Fresh Flat-Leaf Parsley, Finely Chopped
- 1 Tablespoon Grill Seasoning, Preferred Brand Montreal Steak Seasoning
- 1 Cup Lingo Berry Preserves
- 2 Cloves
- 1 Cinnamon Stick
- 1 Tablespoon Lemon Juice
- 1 Dash Water
- 1 1/2 Cups All-Purpose Flour
- 1 1/2 Teaspoons Baking Powder
- 1 1/2 Teaspoons Baking Soda
- 1 -2 Pinch Salt
- 2 Teaspoons Sugar
- 1 Pinch Freshly Grated Nutmeg

- 3 -4 Tablespoons Chopped Chives
- 1 Cup Milk
- 1 Cup Sour Cream
- 2 Large Free-Range Eggs
- 4 Tablespoons Melted Butter, Divided

DIRECTIONS

1. Heat olive oil in skillet and mix the meat with fennel paprika parsley and grill seasoning.

2. Make 2 to 3 inch patties and add hot skillet on it. Preheat waffle iron. Warm preserves with cloves cinnamon lemon and water over low heat. Remove the cinnamon and cloves stick.

3. Mix all the dry INGREDIENTS in a mixing bowl. Mix milk, sour cream, and half melted butter and mix the batter. Brush the waffle iron with the remaining butter and cook the waffles.

4. The batter should fill 4 section iron 3 times, making 12 waffles 3 per portion. Serve 3 waffles and 2 patties with lingo berry syrup.

SWEET & SPEEDY BREAKFAST OAT

- Prep Time: 10 mins
- Total Time: 11 mins
- Serves: 1, Yield: 1 muffin

INGREDIENTS

- 3 Tablespoons Oat Bran
- 1 Egg
- 1 G Stevia (1 Packet)
- 1/2 Teaspoon Baking Soda
- 1 Teaspoon Vanilla Extract (I Like A Lot Of Vanilla, But This Depends On Your Taste)
- 2 Teaspoons Ground Cinnamon (Depends On Your Taste, Other Spices Can Be Used)

DIRECTIONS

1. Mix egg and Stevia thoroughly.
2. Add cinnamon baking soda, vanilla extract, and oat bran and again mix it well.
3. Let it rest for few times so that oats absorb the liquid.
4. Microwave on little heat until the batter becomes solid

CROCK POT WESTERN OMELET CASSEROLE

- Prep Time: 10 mins
- Total Time: 12 hrs 10 mins
- Servings: 10-12

INGREDIENTS

- 1 (32 Ounce) Packages Frozen Hash Browns
- 1 Lb Ham, Extra Lean, Cooked And Cubed
- 1 Medium Onion, Diced
- 1 Medium Green Bell Pepper, Diced
- 1 1/2 Cups Shredded Monterey Jack Cheese Or 1 1/2 Cups Cheddar Cheese
- 12 Eggs
- 1 Cup Skim Milk
- 1 Teaspoon Salt
- 1 Teaspoon Black Pepper, To Taste

DIRECTIONS

1. Spray with nonstick cooking oil and place the frozen potatoes on the bottom of the crock pot.
2. Add layers of ham, onion, green pepper, cheese. Repeat it again for two or three times and have a top layer of cheese. In another bowl mix egg milk, salt, and pepper.
3. Pour it over the layers and turn on low.
4. Allow it to cook for 10 to 12 hours.

SLOW COOKER FRENCH TOAST CASSEROLE

- Prep Time: 10 Mins
- Total Time: 6 hrs 10 mins
- Serves: 6, Yield: 1 Casserole

INGREDIENTS

- 12 Slices Whole Wheat Bread
- 6 Eggs
- 1 Teaspoon Vanilla
- 2 Cups Fat-Free Evaporated Milk
- 2 Tablespoons Dark Brown Sugar
- 1 Teaspoon Cinnamon
- 1/4 Teaspoon Nutmeg

DIRECTIONS

1. Spray the slow cooker with nonstick spray. Put the bread layer in the slow cooker.
2. Whisk egg vanilla, evaporated milk brown sugar and cinnamon with nutmeg in another bowl. Pour it over the bread.
3. Cover and cook it for 6 to 8 hours and then remove the lid and cook uncovered for 30 minutes.

CROCK POT CHEESY HASH BROWNS

- Prep Time: 5 mins
- Total Time: 8 hrs 5 mins
- Servings: 6-8

INGREDIENTS

- 6 Cups Frozen Hash Browns
- 2 Cups Cheddar Cheese
- 1 Cup Milk
- 1/2 Cup Half-And-Half
- 1/3 Cup Green Onion, Sliced Thin
- 1 Cup Frozen Peas
- 1 Teaspoon Salt
- 1 Teaspoon Pepper
- 1 Teaspoon Paprika

DIRECTIONS

1. Mix hash brown, onion, peas in croc. Seasoning is added to cheese and milk. Cover and cook for 6 to 8 hours or high for 3 to 4 hours

BREAKFAST IN A CROCK POT

- Prep Time: 10 mins
- Total Time: 10 hrs 10 mins
- Servings: 12

INGREDIENTS

- 32 Ounces Frozen Hash Browns
- 1 Lb Cooked Lean Ham, Cubed Or 1 Lb Cooked Bacon
- 1 Diced Onion
- 1 Diced Green Pepper
- 1 1/2 Cups Shredded Cheese
- 12 Eggs
- 1 Cup Skim Milk
- 1 Teaspoon Salt
- 1 Teaspoon Black Pepper

DIRECTIONS

1. Separate the potatoes ham, vegetable, and cheese and make several layers with the ingredients. Start with hash brown and end with cheese.
2. Beat egg, salt, and pepper and pour the mixture over the layers.
3. Cover and cook for 10 to 12 hours on LOW heat overnight.

Christmas Morning Crock Pot Breakfast

- Prep Time: 15 mins
- Total Time: 15 mins
- Servings: 12

INGREDIENTS

- 32 Ounces Frozen Hash Brown Potatoes (Diced)
- 1 Lb Bacon, Diced Cooked And Drained Or 1 Lb Cooked Ham, Cubed
- 1 Onion, Diced
- 1 Green Bell Pepper, Diced
- 1 1/2 Cups Cheddar Cheese, Shredded
- 12 Eggs
- 1 Cup Milk
- 1 Teaspoon Salt
- 1 Teaspoon Pepper (More Or Less To Taste)

DIRECTIONS

1. Layer up potatoes, bacon, onion, green pepper and cheese in the slow cooker.
2. Repeat this layers for two or three times and ends with cheese. Whisk eggs milk, salt and pepper and pour the mixture over the layer. Cover it and turn low.
3. Cook for 10 to 12 hours. Tortillas and salsa can be added with extra cheese

CROCK POT HUEVOS RANCHEROS

- Prep Time: 5 mins
- Total Time: 4 hrs 5 mins
- Servings: 8

INGREDIENTS

- 1 Tablespoon Butter
- 10 Eggs, Beaten
- 1 Cup Light Cream
- 8 Ounces Mexican Blend Cheese, Shredded
- 1/2 Teaspoon Pepper
- 1/4 Teaspoon Chili Powder
- 1 Garlic Clove, Crushed
- 1 (4 Ounce) Cans Chopped Green Chilies, Drained
- 1 (10 Ounce) Cans Red Enchilada Sauce
- 4 Ounces Sharp Cheddar Cheese, Shredded
- 8 Tortillas

DIRECTIONS

1. Crock pot is being greased with butter and set aside. Whisk egg, cream, Mexican cheese, and pepper and chili powder in other bowl.
2. Also, add garlic and chilies and stir it well. Pour this mixture into the crock pot and cook on LOW for 3 hours and 45

minutes. Unlit it and ass enchilada sauce and cheddar cheese. Again put the lid till the sauce is warm.

3. Then add tortillas and egg before serving.

*****

POTATO, SAUSAGE AND EGG BREAKFAST

- Prep Time: 5 mins
- Total Time: 8 hrs 5 mins
- Servings: 6

INGREDIENTS

- 1 (16 Ounce) Boxes Sausage Links, Cooked
- 1 (16 Ounce) Packages Frozen Hash Browns
- 1 Small Onion, Diced
- 8 Eggs
- 2 (10 3/4 Ounce) Cans Cream Of Mushroom Soup
- 3 Tablespoons Water
- Salt
- Pepper

DIRECTIONS

1. Put the hash browns and onions in the crock pot. Lay links on the top of the onions. Eggs water, soup salt, and pepper are being mixed and pour evenly on the hash brown and onion layers.

2. Cook on LOW temperature for nearly 8 hours.

***

GRAIN BREAKFAST IN THE CROCK POT

- Prep Time: 5 mins
- Total Time: 6 hrs 5 mins
- Servings: 3-6

INGREDIENTS

- 2 1/2 Tablespoons Bulgur Wheat
- 2 1/2 Tablespoons Brown Rice
- 2 Tablespoons Barley
- 2 Tablespoons Quinoa
- 1/4 Cup Rolled Oats
- 1 Cup Apple, Diced
- 1 1/2 Teaspoons Ground Cinnamon
- 3 Cups Water
- 1 Tablespoon Vanilla Extract

DIRECTIONS

1. All the INGREDIENTS are being mixed well in the crock pot. Cover and cook at temperature LOW for 6 to 8 hours. Before serving the dish, stir it well and add more water if required.

CROCK POT LITTLE RED ROOSTER BREAKFAST

- Prep Time: 10 mins
- Total Time: 10 hrs 10 mins
- Servings: 4

INGREDIENTS

- 4 Large Potatoes
- 1 Onion, Peeled And Chopped
- 1 Tablespoon Unsalted Butter
- 4 Slices Bacon
- 1/4 Lb Cheddar Cheese

DIRECTIONS

1. First, you have to fry the bacon and slice potatoes and chop the onions and grate the cheese.
2. Then layer with the potatoes, butter, onion, bacon, and cheese.
3. Make 2 layers and cook for high at least for 8 to 10 hours.

CROCK POT SAUSAGE AND EGG CASSEROLE

- Prep Time: 15 mins
- Total Time: 10 hrs 15 mins
- Servings: 6-8

INGREDIENTS

- 1 Dozen Beaten Egg
- 14 Slices Bread
- 2 1/4 Cups Milk (Lowfat Or Skim Is Ok)
- 2 1/2 Cups Grated Cheddar Cheese Or 2 1/2 Cups Monterey Jack Cheese
- 1 Lb Sausage, Cooked And Drained
- 1/2 Teaspoon Salt
- 1 Teaspoon Pepper (More Or Less To Taste)
- 2 Teaspoons Mustard (Optional)
- 1 Small Diced Onion (Optional)
- 2 Cloves Crushed Garlic (Optional)
- 3 -5 Dashes Of Your Favorite Hot Pepper Sauce (Not Opt. In My House) (Optional)

DIRECTIONS

1. Grease the crock with butter. Spread mustard on one side of bread and cut it into a large square.
2. Make layers in the pot of bread followed by sausage, cheese, ending with cheese layer. Whisk eggs milk salt and pepper together. Pour the mixture over the layer and cook by covering.

3. Cook it for 12 hours.

*****

SLOW COOKER EGG CASSEROLE WITH SAUSAGE AND RED PEPPER

- Prep Time: 20 mins
- Total Time: 4 hrs 20 mins
- Servings: 8

INGREDIENTS

- 1 Lb Italian Sausage
- 4 Slices Bread, Torn Into Pieces
- 1 Red Pepper, Seeded And Diced
- 1/2 Cup Red Onion, Chopped
- 12 Eggs
- 1/4 Cup Milk
- Salt And Pepper, To Taste

DIRECTIONS

1. Brown the sausages in a medium skillet. Spray the bottom with non-stick cooking spray. Add bread pieces, diced red pepper, chopped red onion and browned sausages to the base of the slow cooker.

2. Now in another bowl, mix the egg with milk and salt and pepper. Pour this mixture over the bread and sausage in slow cooker. Cook on HIGH for 4 hours.

3. Enjoy the preparation with sausages and red pepper and some fresh fruits along with it.

****

SLOW COOKER BREAKFAST CASSEROLE

- Prep Time: 30 mins
- Total Time: 8 hrs 30 mins
- Servings: 12

INGREDIENTS

- 2 (12 Ounce) Packages Johnsonville Hot & Spicy Breakfast Sausage
- 1 Cup Chopped Green Onion
- 1 Red Sweet Bell Pepper, Chopped
- 1 (4 Ounce) Cans Diced Mild Green Chilies
- 1/4 Cup Chopped Fresh Cilantro
- 1 (30 Ounce) Packages Frozen Hash Brown Potatoes
- 1 1/2 Cups Shredded Cheddar Cheese
- 12 Eggs

- 1 Cup Milk
- 1/2 Teaspoon Salt
- 1/8 Teaspoon Pepper

DIRECTIONS

1. Combine green onions, red pepper, chilies. Cilantro and set aside.
2. Cook sausages as per the direction in packages. Spray the interior of the slow cooker with vegetable cooking spray.
3. Layer with hash brown sausages green onion and cheese into the crock. Repeat this again for two or three layers. Beat eggs milk, salt, and pepper. Pour this mixture over the layer.
4. Cover and cook for 7 to 8 hours.
5. Note that the temperature should be 160 F. Then serve your food.

HAM AND TATER TOTS CROCK POT BREAKFAST

- Prep Time: 5 mins
- Total Time: 10 hrs 5 mins
- Servings: 5-8

INGREDIENTS

- 1 Lb Frozen Tater Tots
- 1/2 Lb Diced Ham
- 1 Chopped Onion
- 1 Green Bell Pepper, Diced
- 1 Cup Shredded Cheddar Cheese
- 6 Eggs
- 1/2 Cup Milk

DIRECTIONS

1. Tater tots, hams, green pepper, and cheese, are being layered in the crock pot.
2. Repeat this layer for two or three times and end with cheese. In another mixing bowl mix the eggs and milk and whisk it. Add salt and pepper to taste.
3. Then pour this mixture over the layers and cover it.
4. Then cook it in Low temperature for 12 hours.

BREAKFAST IN CROCK POT

- Prep Time: 5 Mins
- Total Time: 10 Hrs 5 Mins
- Servings: 10-12

INGREDIENTS

- 1 Lb Country Sausage
- 1 (2 Lb) Packages Frozen Hash Browns
- 1 (10 1/2 Ounce) Cans Cream Of Mushroom Soup
- 1 Cup Sour Cream
- 1 (8 Ounce) Containers Cream Cheese
- 12 Eggs
- 1 1/2-2 Cups Cheese

DIRECTIONS

1. Crumble sausages in a skillet. Whisk eggs in another bowl. Stir everything until hash brown is thoroughly coated. Spray crock pot with Pam and then put the hash brown into it.
2. Cook this for 8 to 10 hours in low and high for 4 to 6 hours.

APPLE PEAR BREAKFAST COBBLER FOR THE CROCK POT

- Prep Time: 20 mins
- Total Time: 8 hrs 20 mins
- Servings: 6

INGREDIENTS

- 3 Apples
- 3 Pears
- 1/3 Cup Brown Sugar
- 1 Tablespoon Flour
- 1 Tablespoon Lemon Juice
- 1/3 Cup Apple Cider
- 1 Teaspoon Ground Cinnamon
- 1 Teaspoon Apple Pie Spice
- 2 Tablespoons Butter
- 3 Cups Granola Cereal (With Or Without Raisins)

DIRECTIONS

1. Spray the crock pot with non-stick cooking oil. Apples and pears are being peeled off. And put them in the crock pot.
2. In a jar mix the brown sugar, lemon juice apple cider and spices in a tight fitting jar.
3. Close the jar tightly and shake well so that all get mixed so that there are no lumps in the jar. Put 2 T butter n the apples and pears and spread the granola over the fruits.

4. Cover and cook on low for 8 hours.

5. Remove lid and allow cooling for 10 minutes. And serve with milk and a bit ice cream.

******

MAPLE, PECAN AND BROWN SUGAR CROCK POT STEEL CUT OATS

- Prep Time: 5 mins
- Total Time: 8 hrs 5 mins
- Servings: 4

INGREDIENTS

- 1 Cup Steel Cut Oats, Uncooked
- 1/2 Teaspoon Salt
- 4 1/2 Cups Water
- 1/2 Cup Chopped Pecans
- 1/4 Cup Brown Sugar
- 2 Tablespoons Maple Syrup

DIRECTIONS

1. Combine all INGREDIENTS in crock pot. Cover and cook them in low for 8 hours. Stir all nuts and brown sugar.

2. Spread the syrup with each serving you serve.

CROCK POT BAKED APPLES

- Prep Time: 10 mins
- Total Time: 5 hrs 10 mins
- Servings: 3

INGREDIENTS

- 3 Medium Baking Apples, Washed &, Cored
- 1 Tablespoon Raisins
- 2 Tablespoons Sugar
- 1/2 Teaspoon Cinnamon
- 1 Tablespoon Butter
- 1/2 Cup Water

DIRECTIONS

1. Apples are being put in the Crockpot along with the raisins and sugars. Fill the centers of the apple. Sprinkle with cinnamon and butter.
2. Cover and cook for 7 to 9 hours.

PUMPKIN PIE STEEL CUT OATS/OATMEAL FOR SLOW COOKER

- Prep Time: 5 mins
- Total Time: 8 hrs 5 mins
- Serves: 4, Yield: 3-4 cups

INGREDIENTS

- 1 Cup Steel Cut Oats
- 1 Cup Low-Fat Milk
- 3 Cups Water
- 1/8 Teaspoon Salt
- 3/8 Teaspoon Cinnamon, Divided (1/4 In With Oats, 1/8 In With Pumpkin)
- 1/8 Teaspoon Ginger
- 1/16 Teaspoon Nutmeg
- 1 Pinch Clove
- 1/4 Cup Canned Pumpkin Puree
- 2 Tablespoons Brown Sugar

DIRECTIONS

1. Oats milk, water, salt and 1/4th cinnamon are mixed in crock pot. Cool it overnight and it will get thickened.
2. As you cool more it will get thicker. Stir the left over cinnamon ginger nutmeg and cloves into pumpkin puree.
3. Then add the oatmeal with brown sugar. Give toppings with blueberries and additional brown sugar.

BREAKFAST CASSEROLE (CROCK POT)

- Prep Time: 15 mins
- Total Time: 10 hrs 15 mins
- Servings: 12

INGREDIENTS

- 30 ounces frozen hash brown O'Brien potatoes (cubes, with onion and pepper)
- 1/4 lb bacon, cooked
- 3/4 lb sausage, cooked
- 1 1/2 cups cheddar cheese, shredded
- 12 eggs
- 1 cup milk
- 1 teaspoon pepper

DIRECTIONS

1. Spray the crock pot with cooking spray. Layer with frozen potatoes ad followed by meat and then cheese.
2. Repeat these for two layers and end with a cheese layer. In another bowl whisk eggs milk and pepper together. Pour this mixture over the layer.
3. Cover it and cook for nearly 8 to 10 hours.

CROCK POT EGG CASSEROLE

INGREDIENTS

- 16 Ounces Frozen Hash Brown Potatoes
- 1/2 Lb Cooked Ham, Cubed
- 1/2 Onion, Chopped
- 1/2 Green Bell Pepper, Chopped
- 1/2 Tablespoon Olive Oil
- 3/4 Cup Cheddar Cheese, Shredded
- 6 Eggs
- 1/2 Cup Milk
- 1/4 Teaspoon Salt
- 1/4 Teaspoon Pepper

DIRECTIONS

1. With non stick spray, spray the interior of the slow cooker. In a small skillet onions green pepper are being cooked in olive oil. Cool for 10 minutes.
2. Place frozen hams in slow cooker. Ham onion green pepper and cheese are being layered.
3. This layer is being repeated for two or three times. In another bowl mix egg milk and other seasoning.
4. Mix it well and pour the mixture over the layer. Cover and cook for 5 to 6 hours.

CROCK POT METHOD FOR POLENTA GRITS OR MUSH

- Prep Time: 10 mins
- Total Time: 8 hrs 10 mins
- Servings: 8

INGREDIENTS

- 7 -8 Cups Boiling Water Or 7 -8 Cups Milk Or 7 -8 Cups Soymilk Or 7 -8 Cups Vegetable Broth
- 1 1/2-2 1/2 Teaspoons Salt, To Taste
- 2 Cups Cornmeal
- 1 Teaspoon Butter (Optional) Or 1 Teaspoon Olive Oil (Optional)
- Cooking Spray

DIRECTIONS

1. The slow cooker is being spread with the cooking spray and turns the heat on HIGH.
2. Add the liquid of 8 cups of coarse cornmeal, 7 finer grinds, salts and cornmeal.
3. And stir it very well. Cover it and cook for 1 hour on high temperature. Stir it well again at low temperature. Cover and stir it occasionally.
4. Again cook for 9 hours till it is tender.

CROCKPOT IRISH OATMEAL

- Prep Time: 5 hrs
- Total Time: 13 hrs
- Servings: 4-6

INGREDIENTS

- 1 Cup Steel Cut Oats
- 4 Cups Water
- 1 Apple, Peeled, Cored, Chopped
- 1/2 Cup Raisins
- 1 Teaspoon Cinnamon
- 1/4 Cup Brown Sugar
- 2 Tablespoons Honey
- 1/2 Teaspoon Salt
- 1 Tablespoon Cream (I Use 2% Milk)
- 2 Tablespoons Irish Whiskey (Don't Have It So I Leave It Out)

DIRECTIONS

1. Mix all INGREDIENTS well and cook the INGREDIENTS in crock pot. You have to cook it for 8 hours.

CROCK POT STEEL CUT OATS

- Prep Time: 10 mins
- Total Time: 8 hrs 10 mins
- Servings: 4

INGREDIENTS

- 1 Cup Steel Cut Oats
- 1 Apple, Coarsely Chopped
- 1 Teaspoon Cinnamon
- 1 Teaspoon Allspice
- 1 Teaspoon Nutmeg
- 4 1/2 Cups Skim Milk

DIRECTIONS

1. Mix the entire ingredient. Put the mixture in the slow cooker and set the heat as LOW.
2. Cover and cook for 8 to 9 hours.

CREAMY CROCKPOT OATMEAL

- Prep Time: 5 mins
- Total Time: 10 hrs 5 mins
- Servings: 6

INGREDIENTS

- 2 Cups Regular Oats (Not Quick Cooking) Or 2 Cups Steel Cut Oats
- 5 Cups Water
- 1/2 Cup Packed Brown Sugar
- 1/2 Teaspoon Ground Cinnamon
- 1/4 Teaspoon Ground Nutmeg
- 1/4 Teaspoon Salt
- 1 1/2 Tablespoons Melted Butter
- 1 Teaspoon Vanilla
- 1 Apple, Peeled, Cored And Diced
- 1 Cup Golden Raisin

DIRECTIONS :

1. Mix all the INGREDIENTS in crock pot before night. Cover them and cook o low heat.
2. Then you can serve it in the morning with milk and brown sugar. You can also add sliced banana coconut or raspberries

GLUTEN FREE CROCK POT BREAKFAST GRAINS

- Prep Time: 5 mins
- Total Time: 6 hrs 5 mins
- Servings: 3-6

INGREDIENTS

- 2 1/2 Tablespoons Buckwheat Groats
- 2 1/2 Tablespoons Brown Rice
- 4 Tablespoons Quinoa
- 1/4 Cup Rolled Oats
- 1 Cup Apple, Diced
- 1 1/2 Teaspoons Ground Cinnamon
- 3 Cups Water
- 1 Tablespoon Vanilla Extract

DIRECTIONS

1. Mix all the INGREDIENTS in crock pot and ix very well. Cover it and cook for 6 to 8 hours. before serving it stir very well and add water if it is required

CROCKPOT CHEESY POTATOES

- Prep Time: 10 mins
- Total Time: 4 hrs 10 mins
- Servings: 12

INGREDIENTS

- 1 (32 Ounce) Packages Southern Style Hash Brown Potatoes
- 1/8-1/4 Cup Melted Butter
- 1 (10 Ounce) Cans Cream Of Chicken Soup
- 1/2 Cup Chopped Onion
- 1 Cup Sour Cream
- 1 -2 Cup Cheddar Cheese, Grated

OPTIONAL TOPPINGS

- French-fried onions or potato chips or corn flakes

DIRECTIONS

1. Grease the crock pot and mix all the ingredients. But keep aside the sour cream and cheese and cook on low for 4 to 6 hours.
2. When it is all done, mix all INGREDIENTS and then you can add toppings. For oven mix all INGREDIENTS and pour into pan.

CROCKPOT BREAKFAST CASSEROLE (PALEO)

- Prep Time: 10 mins
- Total Time: 8 hrs 10 mins
- Serves: 4-6, Yield: 4.0

INGREDIENTS

- 8 Eggs, Whisked
- 1 Sweet Potatoes Or 1 Yam, Shredded
- 1 Lb Pork Sausage, Broken Up
- 1 Yellow Onion, Diced
- 1 Tablespoon Garlic Powder
- 2 Teaspoons Dried Basil
- Salt And Pepper, To Taste
- Other Chopped Vegetables, To Taste (Peppers, Zucchini, Etc.)

DIRECTIONS

1. With coconut oil grease the crock pot and shred the sweet potatoes. All the INGREDIENTS are being mixed well ad cooked for 6 to 8 hours.
2. Spoon it in serving plates and serve to eat.

STEEL CUT OATMEAL CROCK POT

- Prep Time: 5 mins
- Total Time: 8 hrs 5 mins
- Servings: 5

INGREDIENTS

- 1 Cup Steel Cut Oats
- 1 Cup Milk
- 4 Cups Water

DIRECTIONS

1. Oatmeal, milk water are added to the crock pot ad is cooked for 6 to 9 hours.
2. Spray the crock pot with vegetable spray which will help to prevent the oatmeal from sticking to the sides.

EGG AND BROCCOLI BRUNCH CASSEROLE (CROCK POT)

- Prep Time: 5 mins
- Total Time: 3 hrs 35 mins
- Servings: 6

INGREDIENTS

- 3 Cups Low Fat Cottage Cheese
- 3 Cups Frozen Chopped Broccoli, Thawed And Drained
- 2 Cups Reduced Fat Shredded Cheddar Cheese
- 6 Eggs, Lightly Beaten
- 1/3 Cup All-Purpose Flour
- 1/4 Cup Butter, Melted
- 3 Tablespoons Finely Chopped Onions
- 1/2 Teaspoon Salt
- 1/2 Cup Shredded Cheddar Cheese (Optional)

DIRECTIONS

1. All the INGREDIENTS are mixed well and pour it into the cooker. The cooker should be greased and has to be cooked on high for 1 hour.
2. Then reduce the heat and cook for 2 to 3 hours and then sprinkle with ½ cup of cheese if you need to.

CROCK POT BARLEY PUDDING

- Prep Time: 5 mins
- Total Time: 8 hrs 5 mins
- Servings: 8-10

INGREDIENTS

- 2 Cups Barley
- 2 Teaspoons Salt
- 1 Teaspoon Cinnamon
- 1 Teaspoon Nutmeg
- 1/2 Teaspoon Coriander
- 10 Cups Water
- 1 1/2 Cups Raisins
- 2 Cups Chopped Dried Fruit (Whatever You Feel Like, Some Ideas Are Apples, Apricots, Prunes)
- 1/3-2/3 Cup Honey, Depending On The Sweetness Desired

DIRECTIONS

1. Mix all INGREDIENTS in crock pot and cook it in low temperature overnight.

SLOW COOKER MAPLE BERRY OATMEAL

- Prep Time: 5 mins
- Total Time: 8 hrs 5 mins
- Servings: 8

INGREDIENTS

- 8 Cups Water
- 2 Cups Steel Cut Oats
- 1/2 Cup Dried Blueberries
- 1/2 Teaspoon Salt
- 1 Cup Dried Cranberries
- 1/4 Cup Maple Syrup

DIRECTIONS

1. Combine all the INGREDIENTS with water and put it in the crock pot. Cover and cook for 7 to 8 hours till all the oats are tender.
2. After the cooking is done stir all the INGREDIENTS well and add cranberries and maple syrup.

CROCK POT CHEESY HASH BROWNS PATTIES

- Prep Time: 2 mins
- Total Time: 3 hrs 2 mins
- Servings: 4

INGREDIENTS

- 1 -1 1/4 Lb Hash Brown, Partly Thawed
- 1 (10 3/4 Ounce) Cans Cheddar Cheese Soup
- 6 Ounces Evaporated Milk
- 1 1/2 Ounces French-Fried Onions
- Salt And Pepper, To Taste

DIRECTIONS

1. All INGREDIENTS are mixed and are placed in greased slow cooker. Cover it and cook for nearly 2nd half hours and serve

CROCK POT BREAKFAST

- Prep Time: 15 mins
- Total Time: 4 hrs 15 mins
- Servings: 8

INGREDIENTS

- 1 Lb Sausage, Browned And Drained Or 1 Lb Little Smokies Cocktail Franks
- 6 Eggs, Beaten
- 1 1/2 Cups Milk
- 8 Slices Bread, Cut Into Squares
- 1 Cup Mozzarella Cheese, Shredded
- 1 Dash Salt And Pepper

DIRECTIONS

1. Mix all INGREDIENTS except the cheese. Put all in crock pot. Sprinkle with cheese and cover it. Cook for 2 hours on high and then 1 hour on LOW.

WEIGHT WATCHERS SLOW-COOKER PUMPKIN OATMEAL

- Prep Time: 2 mins
- Total Time: 8 hrs 2 mins
- Serves: 8, Yield: 8 cups

INGREDIENTS

- 6 Cups Water
- 3 Cups Pumpkin, Diced
- 1 1/2 Cups Steel Cut Oats
- 1/2 Cup Honey
- 1 Teaspoon Ground Cinnamon
- 1/2 Teaspoon Salt
- 1/4 Teaspoon Nutmeg

DIRECTIONS

1. Put all INGREDIENTS and mix well. Put in crock pot and cook for 8 hours. Stir it very well before serving.

CROCK POT PEARS AND OATMEAL

- Prep Time: 15 mins
- Total Time: 8 hrs 15 mins
- Servings: 4

INGREDIENTS

- 3 -4 Ripe Pears
- 1 Cup Steel Cut Oats
- 1/2 Cup Brown Sugar
- 1/2 Teaspoon Nutmeg
- 1 1/4 Teaspoons Cinnamon
- 1/2 Cup Butter (Softened)
- 4 Cups Apple Juice
- 1/3 Cup Pecan Pieces
- 1/3 Cup Raisins (Or Craisins)

DIRECTIONS

1. Cut pears in half and mix with the oats sugar raisins, spices, and butter. Actually, stuff the pears.
2. Place in crock pot ad layer it. Pour apple juices over pears and put the crock pot for cooking for 6 to 8 hours. Sprinkle nuts on top. Cool it before serving.

CROCK POT STEAK FOR BREAKFAST BISCUITS

- Prep Time: 15 mins
- Total Time: 12 hrs 15 mins
- Servings: 4-6

INGREDIENTS

- 2 Lbs Round Steaks Or 2 Lbs Cube Steaks
- 3/4 Cup Flour
- Salt And Pepper
- Olive Oil (For Frying)
- 2 Cups Beef Stock (Can Also Use Beef Gravy)

DIRECTIONS

1. Cut the steaks into a smaller portion. The dredges are being added with salt and pepper in flour.
2. Put oil to fry steaks until it is brown. Put browned steak in crock pots and add beef stock.
3. Cook on low heat. Thicken the liquid part and serve in your favorite's biscuits or over rice. They are great meal.

SOUTHWEST CROCK POT BREAKFAST

- Prep Time: 20 mins
- Total Time: 8 hrs 20 mins
- Servings: 12

INGREDIENTS

- 1 Tablespoon Butter
- 1 Lb Bulk Breakfast Sausage (Cooked And Drained)
- 1 Onion, Chopped
- 1 Green Bell Pepper, Chopped
- 4 Ounces Chopped Green Chilies, Drained
- 2 1/2 Cups Grated Monterey Jack Cheese
- 18 Eggs
- Sour Cream (Optional)
- Salsa (Optional)

DIRECTIONS

1. The crock pot is being greased with butter. A layer with the sausages, meat, onions peppers chilies and cheese.
2. Repeat it twice. In another bowl, whisk egg and pour it in the layers. Cover and cook it for 7 to 8 hours.
3. Thus serve with sour cream

COZY COMFORT IN A CROCK POT

- Prep Time: 10 mins
- Total Time: 8 hrs 10 mins
- Servings: 6

INGREDIENTS

- 16 Ounces 90% Lean Ground Turkey Or 16 Ounces Lean Ground Beef
- 1/2 Cup Chopped Onion
- 3 Cups Diced Raw Potatoes
- 1/3 Cup Uncooked Rice
- 1 1/2 Cups Shredded Carrots
- 1 Cup Finely Diced Celery
- 1 1/2 Cups Healthy Request Tomato Juice Or 1 1/2 Cups Any Reduced-Sodium Tomato Juice
- 1 (10 1/4 Ounce) Cans Healthy Request Tomato Soup
- 1/4 Teaspoon Black Pepper
- 1 Teaspoon Dried Parsley Flakes

DIRECTIONS

1. A skillet is being sprayed with butter-flavored cooking spray, brown the meat.
2. Then put it in the slow cooker. Add onions, potatoes, uncooked rice and carrots and celery.
3. Mix well and add tomato juice tomato soup, black pepper and parsley flakes.

4.   Cover and cook for 6 to 8 hours.

****

CROCK POT HOT MULTIGRAIN CEREAL

- Prep Time: 5 mins
- Total Time: 8 hrs 5 mins
- Servings: 4

INGREDIENTS

- 1 Cup Multigrain Cereal (Or 1/2 Cup Multigrain Cereal And 1/2 Cup Rolled Oats)
- 1/4 Teaspoon Salt
- 4 Cups Water
- 2 Apples, All-Purpose, Peeled And Thickly Sliced
- 1/4-1/3 Cup Raisins (Optional)

DIRECTIONS

1.   Combine the multigrain cereals, salt, water and apples. Cover and cook for 8 hours. And in the morning just before serving add raisins and hot cereals. Stir and serve

CROCKPOT COCOA GRANOLA

- Prep Time: 5 mins
- Total Time: 4 hrs 5 mins
- Yield: 5 cups

INGREDIENTS

- 4 Cups Rolled Oats (Quick Or Old Fashioned)
- 1 Cup Bran Flakes
- 1 Cup Wheat Germ
- 2/3 Cup Honey
- 1/2 Cup Sesame Seeds
- 1/4 Cup Vegetable Oil Or 1/4 Cup Canola Oil
- 2 Tablespoons Cocoa
- 1 Teaspoon Cocoa
- 1 Teaspoon Cinnamon

DIRECTIONS

1. Combine and add the dry INGREDIENTS in the crock pot. Stir well when the INGREDIENTS are wet. Stir it on LOW temperature and cook for 2 to 4 hours.
2. Stir the food occasionally

SLOW COOKER BREAKFAST CASSEROLE

- Prep Time: 10 mins
- Total Time: 3 hrs 10 mins
- Servings: 8

INGREDIENTS

- 6 Eggs, Beaten
- 1 Lb Cocktail Franks, Browned And Drained (Lil' Smokies) Or 1 1/2 Lbs Bulk Sausage, Browned, Crumbled And Drained
- 1 1/2 Cups Milk
- 1 Cup Cheddar Cheese, Shredded
- 8 Slices Bread, Torn Into Pieces
- 1 Teaspoon Salt
- 1/2 Teaspoon Dry Mustard
- 1 Cup Mozzarella Cheese, Shredded

DIRECTIONS

1. Mix ingredient and add in greased slow cooker. But don't mix the mozzarella. Sprinkle it instead on the top.
2. Cover and cook for 2 hours on high and 1 hours on low.

HUEVOS IN A CROCK-POT

- Prep Time: 15 mins
- Total Time: 8 hrs 15 mins
- Servings: 8-10

INGREDIENTS

- 1 Dozen Egg, Lightly Beaten With A Little
- Milk
- 1 Dozen Flour Tortilla
- 1 Lb Cheddar Cheese, Grated
- 1 Quart Salsa

DIRECTIONS

1. In a buttered crock pot layer all the INGREDIENTS like 1 four tortilla, 1 ladle egg and 1 handful cheese and ¼ salsa.
2. Cook it overnight and enjoy it the next morning

SPICED CROCK-POT OATMEAL

- Prep Time: 5 mins
- Total Time: 8 hrs 5 mins
- Servings: 4

INGREDIENTS

- 1 Cup Steel Cut Oats
- 4 Cups Water
- 1/2 Cup Half-And-Half
- 1 Teaspoon Ground Cinnamon
- 1/2 Teaspoon Ground Ginger
- 1/8-1/4 Teaspoon Freshly Grated Nutmeg
- 1 Pinch Ground Cloves
- 1/4 Cup Honey

DIRECTIONS

1. Except the honey mix all INGREDIENTS in the crock pot and cook for 6 to 8 hours. Put the honey and stir it using the wooden spoon. Serve hot or cool

5 GRAIN CROCK-POT HOT CEREAL

- Prep Time: 5 mins
- Total Time: 8 hrs 5 mins
- Servings: 12

INGREDIENTS

- 1 Cup Brown Rice
- 1 Cup Rolled Oats
- 1 Cup Steel Cut Oats (Oat Groats)
- 1 Cup Pearl Barley
- 1 Cup Wheat Berries
- 1 Cup Unsweetened Coconut
- 1 Teaspoon Salt
- To Prepare Use 1 Cup Grain Mixture Plus
- 3 Cups Water

DIRECTIONS

---

1. The 7 INGREDIENTS are mixed ad stored in air tight container. When you cook, mix one cup of grain mixture and nearly water of 3 cups. Cook on low for overnight.

CROCKPOT BREAKFAST

- Prep Time: 30 mins
- Total Time: 8 hrs 30 mins
- Serves: 8-10, Yield: 10.0

INGREDIENTS

- 12 Medium Eggs
- 1/2 Cup Milk
- 9 Hash Browns, Potato Patties
- 2 Medium Onions, Sliced And Separated Into Rings
- 2 Medium Green Peppers, Sliced
- 1 (8 Ounce) Packages Shredded Cheese, Cheddar, Swiss Or 1 (8 Ounce) Packages Mozzarella Cheese
- 3 Slices Ham, Chopped

DIRECTIONS

1. Mix egg and milk and put aside. Grease the crock pot. Add onions and green pepper layer and add some cheese on top. A ham piece layer is also added.
2. Repeat this layer for twice or thrice.
3. The egg mixture is then poured over the layers. Cover it and cook on low for 8 to 9 hours.

CROCK POT JOOK

- Prep Time: 10 mins
- Total Time: 8 hrs 10 mins
- Servings: 4-6

INGREDIENTS

- 1 Cup Medium Grain Rice
- 2 Tablespoons Vegetable Oil
- 10 Cups Chicken Broth Or 10 Cups Turkey Broth
- 2 Teaspoons Salt
- 1 Tablespoon Minced Cilantro Stems
- 1 Cup Milk (Optional)
- 1 Tablespoon Chopped Fresh Cilantro Leaves
- 1 Tablespoon Minced Green Onion
- Soy Sauce Or Hot Sauce Or Oyster Sauce
- Vinegar Potato Chips

DIRECTIONS

1. Clear the rice with water. Soak it for 30 minutes. Heat oil ad slow cooker is set to high. Rinse and drain the rice water.
2. Cook the rice in hot oil and stir till the rice is well coated with oil. Add the stocks salt and cilantro stems and stir it well.
3. Cook for 8 to 9 hours in low. If you want the thicker gravy, then put the slow cooker on high and cooks for two and a half hours.

4. Stir it very occasionally. Before serving sprinkle chopped cilantro leaves minced green onions, sliced potato chips, and sauce.

****

CROCKPOT GRANOLA

- Prep Time: 5 mins
- Total Time: 4 hrs 5 mins
- Servings: 12

INGREDIENTS

- 5 Cups Oats
- 1/4 Cup Honey
- 1/4 Cup Melted Butter
- 1 Tablespoon Chia Seeds
- 1/4 Cup Slivered Almonds
- 1/4 Cup Raw Pumpkin Seeds
- 1/4 Cup Raw Sunflower Seeds
- 1/2 Cup Dried Fruit

DIRECTIONS

1. Put all INGREDIENTS in slow cooker melt the butter and add along with honey.
2. Stir it well. Cook but you must have a vent with a chopstick. Cook for 3 to 4 hours and stir it well.
3. Let it cool before serving.

GLUTEN FREE

Gluten Free Waffles

PREP TIME: 8 MINS **TOTAL TIME:** 23 MINS

YIELD: 5 WAFFLES

Ingredients

- 1 Cup Brown Rice Or 1 Cup Rice Flour
- 1/2 Cup Potato Starch (Not Potato Flour)
- 1/4 Cup Tapioca Flour
- 2 Teaspoons Baking Powder
- 1 Teaspoon Salt
- 1/4 Cup Oil
- 2 Eggs (Or Not...See Notes)
- 1 1/2 Cups Buttermilk (Regular Milk Works, Too)
- 1 Teaspoon Sugar

How to make it:

1. First of all, combine all the materials with the help of a spoon or a whisk in a blow.
2. Now, in batches, pour the mix in the waffles. If you feel the mix is too thick, then add milk or extra flour it too liquid.
3. The preparation can be cooked with eggs too; but make sure you add extra liquid in place of them.

Gluten-Free Pancakes

PREP TIME: 10MINS, TOTAL **TIME:** 30 MINS,

YIELD: 12-14 PANCAKES

Ingredients

- 3/4 Cup Gluten-Free Flour
- 1/2 Teaspoon Xanthan Gum Or 1/2 Teaspoon Guar Gum
- 1 1/2 Teaspoons Baking Powder
- 1/2 Teaspoon Salt
- 1 Teaspoon Sugar
- 2/3 Cup Milk
- 2 Eggs
- 2 Tablespoons Cooking Oil

How to make it:

1. Take all the constituents, which are dry into a small pot, then take another pot to mix the eggs with milk and cooking oil. It has to be blended with the dry components.
2. Mix it well and keep it separate for 10mins and then you have to start the oven, Take the batter on a dry frying pan, take a frying pan whose surface doesn't stick, for that matter. When the pan is warm or at medium heat pour the mix on to the pan, pour a full spoon of the mix.

3. Take a spoon to lift the pancake & check whether the pancake is cooked from the side touching the pan, do it when the edges have become dull.

4. When one side has finished, you have to turn it over to the other side.

****

Gluten Free Biscuits

PREP TIME: 10 MINS, **TOTAL TIME:** 30 MINS, **SERVES:** 6-8, **YIELD:** 6.0 BISCUITS

Ingredients

- 4 Tablespoons Butter Or 4 Tablespoons Margarine
- 1 1/3 Cups Cornstarch
- 1 1/4 Teaspoons Xanthan Gum
- 1 Tablespoon Baking Powder
- 1/2 Teaspoon Baking Soda
- 2 Teaspoons Sugar
- 1/2 Teaspoon Salt
- 3/4 Cup Milk (I Used Soy)
- 1 Teaspoon Vinegar (I Used White)

How to make it:

1. Switch on the oven and heat it till the temperature reaches to 375 degrees.

2. Then take a baking sheet or cookie sheet and make it slippery.

3. The components that are waterless have to be mixed with marg or butter in a separate medium sized pot.

4. We have to make light dough by blending it first with milk and also add a little vinegar.

5. The dough has to be transferred to a pan and the thickness of the dough should be around half an inch.

6. Then we have to take a sharp cutting object and cut through the dough to make square biscuits.

****

Gluten Free Danish

PREP TIME: 10 MINS, TOTAL TIME: 25 MINS, SERVES: 6, YIELD: 6 DANISHES

Ingredients

- 2 Tablespoons Shortening
- 1/4 Cup Honey
- 1 Egg
- 1 Tablespoon Yeast
- 1/2 Cup Sour Cream
- 1/4 Cup Potato Starch
- 3/4 Cup Cornstarch
- 1/4 Teaspoon Baking Soda
- 1 Teaspoon Baking Powder

- 1 Teaspoon Xanthan Gum
- 1/2 Teaspoon Salt
- 1/2 Teaspoon Vinegar

FOR TOPPING

- Raspberry Jam (About 1 Tablespoon On Each Danish)
- Powdered Sugar

How to make it:-

1. At first heat up the oven it till the temperature reaches to 375 degrees.
2. Add all the components and make sure there are no chunks.
3. On a non-dry baking sheet, a quarter cup of the mix has to be taken and the dough shouldn't be lumpy.
4. And then a space has to be made in the dough to add the stuffing; it could be made with your finger or a kitchen tool.
5. Then a spoon full of jam has to be added as the filler. The Danish has to be kept in the oven for 15 minutes till the time it turns golden-brown in colour. For a fluidic sugar paste use water and blended sugar.
6. When the Danish has finished, take it out from the oven and apply a little bit of the sugar paste as the icing for each danish, and let it cool down.

Buttermilk Buckwheat Pancakes

PREP TIME: 15 MINS ,**TOTAL TIME:** 25 MINS ,
SERVINGS: 4

Ingredients

- 1 Cup Buckwheat Flour
- 2 Tablespoons Brown Sugar
- 1 Teaspoon Baking Powder
- 1/2 Teaspoon Baking Soda
- 1/2 Teaspoon Salt
- 1/8 Teaspoon Cinnamon
- 1/8 Teaspoon Nutmeg
- 1/8 Teaspoon Clove
- 1 Egg
- 1 Cup Low-Fat Buttermilk
- 1 Tablespoon Butter, Melted

How to make it:

1. In the beginning take all the non-liquid materials in a large circular pot, then mix it with other fluidic ingredients to make it smooth or soft.

2. Then pour the mix measuring it to quarter of a cup on to a heated up pan that doesn't stick, and you could add a lubricant like cooking spray on the pan.

3. Wait till the side touching the pan has become golden brown in colour and turn it over when bubbles are being produced while being heated.

Gluten-Free Buttermilk Donuts

PREP TIME: 30 MINS, **TOTAL TIME:** 40 MINS,
SERVINGS: 16

Ingredients

- 2 Eggs, Beaten
- 2 Cups Buttermilk
- 1/4 Cup Butter, Melted
- 5 Cups Gluten-Free Rice Flour Mix (See Note)
- 1 Cup Sugar
- 1 Teaspoon Nutmeg
- 1/2 Teaspoon Cinnamon
- 2 Teaspoons Baking Soda
- 1 Teaspoon Baking Powder
- 2 Teaspoons Salt
- 2 Teaspoons Xanthan Gum
- 1/2 Cup Sugar, Set Aside In A Bowl

How to make it:

1. Take a large pot and mix melted butter with eggs and add a little buttermilk. All the solid or non-liquid constituents have to be added in a different bowl.

2. Then the process of mixing the materials of both the containers come in and you have to use your hand and a wooden spoon to mix them.

3. To blend it perfectly it has to knead together with hands, make sure your hand is clean. Then the paste has to be left for quarter of an hour and the paste or dough should be rolled into thickness of around one-third of an inch to half an inch.

4. Then we have to heat canola oil till it gets hot enough to fry, then we have to place the dough in the oil, before putting it in the oil you have to make holes in the dough with any cylindrical object.

5. Be careful while putting the dough into the oil, as it will be quite hot. Keep the doughnut in the hot oil till it becomes golden brown in color.

6. Fry only one or two doughnuts at one go. After it's fried take it out with a spoon, which has holes in it, to remove the excess oil in the pot itself.

7. Then you can use soaking paper or brown paper to take out the excess oil, which is still there.

8. Then the sugar coating has to be applied which can be done by putting it in a container full of sugar or any other icing.

9. Now your doughnut is ready to be served!

Cinnamon Rolls

PREP TIME: 1 HR 15 MINS, **TOTAL TIME:** 1 HR 35 MINS, **SERVES:** 8, **YIELD:** 8 ROLLS

Ingredients :-

DOUGH

- 2 Tablespoons Butter
- 1/4 Cup White Sugar
- 2/3 Cup Skim Milk, Warmed
- 1 Tablespoon Yeast
- 1 Large Egg
- 1/4 Cup Canola Oil
- 1/4 Cup Potato Starch
- 3/4 Cup Cornstarch
- 1/2 Cup Millet Flour (Or Rice Or Brown Rice Or Oat)
- 1/4 Teaspoon Baking Soda
- 2 1/2 Teaspoons Xanthan Gum
- 2 Teaspoons Baking Powder
- 1/2 Teaspoon Salt
- 1 Teaspoon Vanilla

FILLING

- 1 Cup Packed Brown Sugar

- 2 1/2 Tablespoons Cinnamon
- 1/3 Cup Butter, Softened

ICING

- 8 Tablespoons Butter, Softened
- 1 1/2 Cups Powdered Sugar
- 1/4 Cup Cream Cheese, Softened
- 1/2 Teaspoon Vanilla
- 1/8 Teaspoon Salt

How to make it:-

1. To start making a cinnamon roll use moderately heated up milk and put the yeast into it, this has to be done in a large pot or container.
2. In the pot add vanilla, butter, oil and sugar and keep on blending it and then put some eggs into.
3. Before putting some flour to the blended mix we have to add potato starch, cornstarch, with an addition baking soda, baking powder.
4. Also add some salt to it. See to it that the mixture is not too thick or slippery, it should be moderate. Then put it in a non-dry pot for an hour or less.
5. The oven has to reach four hundred degrees Fahrenheit. In between two square parchment papers of 13", spread the thick dough.

6. Put some butter on the top and add some cinnamon, brown sugar. You have to roll it properly and separate it in eight different parts with a sharp object.

7. Now in a non-dry baking utensil, where the base is covered in cinnamon and sugar, keep the pieces and leave some gap between the utensil and the pieces, which would allow it to grow if heated. Keep it in the oven for around twenty minutes, till it shows golden brown colour.

8. You could put some more icing on the rolls, by stirring some icing elements, till they become smooth.

Muffins (Gluten Free)

PREP TIME: 10 MINS ,**TOTAL TIME:** 35 MINS,**SERVES:** 6, **YIELD:** 6 LARGE MUFFINS

Ingredients

- 1/2 Cup Brown Rice Flour
- 1/2 Cup Rice Flour (White Rice Flour)
- 1/4 Cup Tapioca Starch Or 1/4 Cup Sweet Rice Flour
- 1/3 Cup Sweet Rice Flour Or 1/3 Cup Potato Starch
- 1/2 Cup Organic Sugar Or 1/2 Cup Brown Sugar
- 2 Teaspoons Gluten Free Baking Powder (Or A Tad More Baking Soda & 1tbs Organic Apple Cider Vinegar In At Last Minute)
- 1 Teaspoon Baking Soda
- 1 Teaspoon Guar Gum (May Substitute Xanthan Gum ~ Corn Derived)
- 1/4 Teaspoon Sea Salt
- 1/3 Cup Bland Oil
- 1 Large Egg (Or Use 2 Ener-G Egg Replacer Eggs)
- Chopped Fruit, Enjoy Life Chocolate Chips, Spices, Etc. (Additions)

How to make it:

1. You could start with heating the oven till it reaches 350degrees. In one small bowl or cup take yogurt/juice/applesauce. Then in a bowl blend all the non-liquid items.

2. After that in an electric mixer, all non-fluidic items are mixed with the liquid constituents.

3. The mix should be thick and some fruits could be added to it later.

4. Then put a full scoop of the mix into a lined muffin tin.

5. Then it has to be kept in the oven for around half an hour.

Pancakes - Gluten Free

PREP TIME: 5 MINS, **TOTAL TIME:** 15 MINS
,SERVINGS: 6

Ingredients :-

- 1 Cup Ultimate Baking And Pancake Mix
- 1 Large Egg
- 3/4 Cup Water
- 1 Tablespoon Oil

How to make it:-

1. At first stir all the ingredients in a bowl so that there are no chunks left.
2. The mix should be moderate in thickness. Heat up the oven till 350 degrees and put quarter of a cup of the mix in the non-dry griddle.
3. The pancakes are ready to served! But to reheat the pancakes remove any covering in which it was kept.

Bananas With Coconut Milk

PREP TIME: 3 MINS, **TOTAL TIME:** 3 MINS, **SERVINGS:** 2

Ingredients :-

- 2 Bananas, Sliced
- 1/4 Cup Organic Coconut Milk (Pretty Thick Consistency)
- 4 Tablespoons Maple Syrup (Or To Taste) Or 4 Tablespoons Local Liquid Honey (Or To Taste)
- Ground Cinnamon (Optional)

How to make it:

1. In two different containers or place diced up bananas, and then coconut milk has to be added to it. Sprinkle or put some maple syrup or honey onto every serving.
2. You could also refrigerate it before serving.

Strawberry Banana Muffins

PREP TIME: 20 MINS ,**TOTAL TIME:** 55 MINS, **SERVES:** 6-12,

YIELD: 12.0 MUFFINS

Ingredients

- 1 1/4 Cups Rice Flour
- 1/4 Cup Potato Starch
- 1/4 Cup Tapioca Flour
- 1/2 Teaspoon Xanthan Gum
- 1/4 Teaspoon Ground Cinnamon
- 1 Teaspoon Baking Soda
- 1 1/2 Teaspoons Baking Powder
- 1/2 Teaspoon Salt
- 1/2 Cup Butter Or 1/2 Cup Margarine, Softened
- 1/3 Cup Sugar
- 2 Eggs
- 1/2 Teaspoon Pure Vanilla Extract
- 1/3 Cup Milk Or 1/3 Cup Soymilk
- 2 Bananas, Peeled
- 1 1/2 Cups Strawberries, Stemmed And Coarsely Chopped

How to make it:

1. First switch on the oven and take it to 350 degrees.

2. Then you grease a paper liner slightly. Mix the rice flour, potato starch, tapioca flour, xanthan gum, cinnamon and baking soda and baking powder and add a pinch of salt in big pot or container. In another bowl we blend the sugar and cream with eggs and milk.

3. There shouldn't be any chunks left. Then we add strawberries to a banana paste and to the wet pot. And then put everything together in one single pot.

4. Take one-third of a cup of the mix and put it into the paper liner. And put it in the oven for less than half an hour. Change sides after quarter of an hour.

5. Use a sharp object to check the muffin's edges to know whether it's done.

6. Then cool it down on a rack and it's ready to be served.

Gluten-Free Doughnut Holes

PREP TIME: 20 MINS ,**TOTAL TIME:** 1 HR, **SERVES:** 6-12,

YIELD: 30.0 DOUGHNUT HOLES

Ingredients :-

- 1 Cup Water
- 1/2 Cup Butter (1 Stick Of Butter) Or 1/2 Cup Margarine (1 Stick Of Butter)
- 1 Cup Potato Starch
- 1 Tablespoon Sugar
- 1/4 Teaspoon Salt
- 4 Eggs
- Oil (For Deep Frying)
- Cinnamon Sugar, For Dusting

How to make it:

1. Put two to three inches of oil in a deep fryer and the temperature should touch 375 degrees.
2. Simultaneously start boiling water in a pot and add some butter.
3. After it has completed put sugar, salt and starch of potato in the dough and blend it thoroughly.
4. Now we take the mix in a electric mixer where we put some eggs in it.

5. The eggs should be mixed properly. Now we put the mix in the deep fryer, keep it in the deep fryer for five minutes and the doughnut will attain a thickness of two inches or less.

6. After the doughnut turns light brown keep it in the oil, use soaking paper to soak the excess oil from the doughnut.

7. Before serving, you could mix the doughnut with a hint of cinnamon icing in a bag.

<u>Easy Gluten Free Banana Bread</u>

PREP TIME: 10 MINS, **TOTAL TIME:** 1 HR 10 MINS,

SERVINGS: 10

Ingredients

- 1/3 Cup Canola Oil
- 2/3 Cup Brown Sugar, Packed
- 2 Large Eggs
- 1 Teaspoon Vanilla Extract
- 1 3/4 Cups All-Purpose Gluten-Free Flour
- 2 Teaspoons Baking Powder
- 1 1/4 Teaspoons Cinnamon
- 1 Teaspoon Xanthan Gum
- 1/2 Teaspoon Salt
- 1 1/2 Cups Mashed Ripe Bananas
- 1/2 Cup Chopped Pecans Or 1/2 Cup Walnuts
- 1/2 Cup Raisins

How to make it:

1. First take the oven temperature to 350 degrees and use a medium or small sized loaf pan. Put sugar, oil, eggs and vanilla in a small container and mix it well to make it smooth and light.

2. In it you have to add salt baking powder xanthan gum, egg mix and most importantly flour has to be added to make the dough.

3. Blend it well and add some raisins and nuts.

4. And cook it in the pan for three quarters of an hour for the small pan and nearly an hour for the bigger pan.

5. Remember, the bigger pan would be around nine inches in length & five inches in width, and the smaller on would be five inches by three inches.

<u>Chocolate Monkey Oatmeal</u>

PREP TIME: 2 MINS ,**TOTAL TIME:** 5 MINS, **SERVINGS:** 1

Ingredients

- 1/3 Cup Rolled Oats (Bob's Red Mill Gluten Free Oats)
- 2/3 Cup Water
- 1 Ripe Sliced Banana
- 1 Tablespoon Cocoa Powder (Hershey's Is Gluten Free)
- 1 Teaspoon Vanilla Extract

How to make it:

1. Take a microwave bowl and put all the materials it. Blend it for some time.
2. Switch on the microwave and heat it in Hot/High mode for three minutes.
3. Mix it well again, add something to sweeten it up and it is ready to be served.

Zucchini Bread

PREP TIME: 10 MINS ,TOTAL TIME: 1 HR 20 MINS ,SERVINGS: 24

Ingredients

- 3 Eggs
- 2 Cups Sugar
- 1/4 Cup Canola Oil
- 1/4 Cup Unsweetened Applesauce
- 1 Teaspoon Vanilla Extract
- 1 1/2 Cups Cornstarch
- 3/4 Cup Rice Flour
- 3/4 Cup Tapioca Flour
- 1 Tablespoon Xanthan Gum
- 1 Tablespoon Cinnamon
- 1 Tablespoon Baking Powder
- 1 Teaspoon Baking Soda
- 2 Cups Fresh Zucchini, Grated
- 1/2 Cup Walnuts (Optional)

How to make it:-

1. First and foremost the oven temperature would be pre set to 350 degrees Fahrenheit.

2. Then take a pot or small container to stir the eggs properly and add sugar, oil and applesauce in it. In another one take the non-wet materials and liquid components from the first container and put it in a electric mixer for around three minutes.

3. To make it a loaf, the mix has to be cooked for over and one hour in two non-dry loaf pans.

4. To make it bread you can put some topping of sugar.

5. And to avoid burning of the loaf you could keep it in a foil. To make muffins from the same, we have to put it in the oven for half an hour in a line muffin tin.

Gluten Free Pumpkin Pancakes

PREP TIME: 10 MINS ,**TOTAL TIME:** 30
MINS,**SERVES:** 6, **YIELD:** 24 PANCAKES

Ingredients

- 2 Cups Gluten-Free Flour, Mix
- 2 Tablespoons Sugar
- 1 Teaspoon Salt
- 1 Teaspoon Ground Cinnamon
- 1 1/2 Cups Skim Milk
- 1 Cup Canned Pumpkin (Not Pumpkin Pie Mix)
- 1/4 Cup Butter, Melted
- 2 Large Egg Yolks
- 4 Large Egg Whites

How to make it:-

1. First take a large pot or container and add the first five dry items.
2. Then in the pot we have to make a hole to add skimmed milk, cup of pumpkin and butter, we keep on blending it and add flour to it. In an electric mixer add some battered eggs whites.
3. Then put it in the earlier mix. Then in a non-stick pan we take quarter cup of the mix and heat it up.

4. See to it that it is turned to the other side after a few minutes, to cook both sides properly.

5. Look for the edges to make sure it has been properly baked.

*****

Delicious Gluten-Free, Dairy-Free, Egg-Free Pancakes

PREP TIME: 15 MINS, TOTAL TIME: 35 MINS, SERVES: 2, YIELD: 6 PANCAKES

Ingredients

- 1 Cup Rice Flour (Brown Or White Or Mix Of Both)
- 3 Tablespoons Tapioca Flour
- 1/3 Cup Potato Starch
- 1 Tablespoon Brown Sugar
- 1 1/2 Teaspoons Baking Powder
- 1/2 Teaspoon Baking Soda
- 1/2 Teaspoon Salt
- 1/2 Teaspoon Guar Gum
- 2 Eggs (May Egg Replacer To Be Egg Free)
- 3 Tablespoons Canola Oil (I Use A Bit Of Both) Or 3 Tablespoons Applesauce (I Use A Bit Of Both)
- 2 Cups Water
- Maple Syrup, For Serving

- Blueberries, A Handful Of (Optional To Add Before Flipping Cakes)

How to make it:

1. Put some rice flour, tapioca flour and add potato starch in a large container, and put all other dry constituents in it.
2. Then we put the wet constituents like water, eggs, and we can also put applesauce in it.
3. Mix it well. Take a greased skillet and heat it up and change the sides till the pancake turns golden brown in colour.
4. Any icing or topping can be added with maple syrup while serving.

Vegan Gluten-Free Buckwheat Pancakes

PREP TIME: 20 MINS ,**TOTAL TIME:** 25 MINS,**SERVES:** 4, **YIELD:** 8 PANCAKES

Ingredients

- 1/2 Cup Buckwheat Flour
- 1/4 Cup Quinoa Flour
- 1/4 Cup Cornflour
- 2 Tablespoons Tapioca Flour (Or Cornstarch Or Arrowroot)
- 1 Tablespoon Ground Flax Seeds (Or Flax Meal)
- 1 Tablespoon Baking Powder
- 1/4 Teaspoon Cinnamon
- 1/4 Teaspoon Salt
- 1/2 Cup Soymilk (Or Other Nondairy Milk)
- 1/2 Cup Water
- 2 Tablespoons Pure Maple Syrup
- 2 Tablespoons Canola Oil
- 1/2 Teaspoon Vanilla Extract

How to make it:

1. Start off with a large container or pot to blend all the dry components, and then we make a hole in the middle where we add the liquid.
2. We use a spoon to stir the mix well and keep it aside for 10 minutes.

3. Then we take a pan and heat it up moderately. Then we use cooking spray to make it greasy and use a scoop to put the mix on to the pan.

4. Keep on heating it for three minutes or less and turn it over and do the same for the other side also.

5. Now it is ready to be served!

<u>Healthy Breakfast Bowl</u>

PREP TIME: 5 MINS ,TOTAL TIME: 5 MINS,SERVINGS: 1

Ingredients

- 1 Apple, Diced
- 150 G Low-Fat Vanilla Yogurt (5 Oz)
- 1/2-1 Teaspoon Ground Flax Seeds

How to make it:

1. Take an apple and slice it up and place it in a medium sized eating bowl.
2. Add half a bowl yogurt in it, and use some seeds of flax in it.
3. Stir it well and it's ready.

Gluten Free Banana Bars

PREP TIME: 20 MINS ,**TOTAL TIME:** 45 MINS,**SERVES:** 12, **YIELD:** 12 BARS

Ingredients

- 3/4 Cup Rice Flour
- 1/4 Cup Potato Starch, Plus
- 2 Tablespoons Potato Starch
- 2 Tablespoons Tapioca Flour
- 1/4 Teaspoon Xanthan Gum
- 2 Teaspoons Baking Powder
- 1/4 Teaspoon Salt
- 1 Cup Mashed Ripe Banana (2 Bananas)
- 3/4 Cup Brown Sugar
- 1/3 Cup White Sugar
- 1/4 Cup Buttermilk
- 1 Egg
- 1 Tablespoon Vegetable Oil
- 2 Teaspoons Vanilla
- 1/2 Cup Chopped Walnuts (Optional)

DRIZZLE TOPPING

- 1/4 Cup Icing Sugar
- 2 Teaspoons Milk Or 2 Teaspoons Juice

How to make it:

1. The oven temperature should be 350 degrees Fahrenheit.

2. Then put some veggie oil to oil up a square griddle.

3. Then take a small container in which xanthan gum, baking powder, salt and essentially flour is added.

4. In another you have to put sugar and banana paste.

5. Stir all the wet items like buttermilk, eggs, oil and vanilla.

6. Mix it well. Now put the nuts in to it and take the mix on to the oiled up griddle and keep it for less than half an hour.

7. After it is cooked we have to take the dough of the cake in the pan.

The sugar paste has to mixed well together and before serving the paste has to be separated in a dozen pieces and the past has to be applied.

Gluten Free Poppy Seed Pound Cake

PREP TIME: 15 MINS ,**TOTAL TIME:** 50 MINS,**SERVES:** 12-20, **YIELD:** 2.0 POUND CAKES

Ingredients

- 2 Cups White Bean Flour
- 3/4 Teaspoon Xanthan Gum
- 1 Teaspoon Baking Soda
- 2 Teaspoons Baking Powder
- 1 Teaspoon Egg Substitute
- 1 Cup White Sugar
- 1 Cup Sour Cream
- 1 (85 G) Packages Vanilla Instant Pudding Mix
- 4 Eggs
- 1/2 Cup Vegetable Oil
- 2 Tablespoons Poppy Seeds
- 3/4 Cup Hot Water

How to make it:

1. Take a large pot or container and mix all the components, leave the poppy seed for later.
2. Blend for two minutes. Now place the poppy seeds into it.
3. Then put the batter in two separate non-dry pans and heat it till it reaches 350 degrees for more than half an hour.
4. For cooling it down use a wire grill.

<u>Dairy-Free, Gluten-Free Pancakes</u>

PREP TIME: 10 MINS ,**TOTAL TIME:** 15
MINS,**SERVES:** 4-6, **YIELD:** 12.0 FLAPJACKS

Ingredients

- 2 Eggs
- 1/4 Cup Agave Nectar
- 1 Tablespoon Vanilla Extract
- 1/2 Cup Water
- 1 1/2 Cups Blanched Almond Flour
- 1/2 Teaspoon Celtic Sea Salt
- 1/2 Teaspoon Baking Soda
- Grapeseed Oil, For Sauteing

How to make it:

1. First make a soft and tender mix of eggs, agave, and vanilla in water.
2. It has to be mixed with baking soda, salt and almond flour to make a mix.
3. Take a big pan, heat it up and add grape seed oil. The dough has to be put in the pan.
4. Pancakes have to be turned over to cook both sides, and observe the bubbles that would form when properly cooked.
5. Again do the same thing for rest of the dough.

Easy & Delicious Apple Crumble

PREP TIME: 10 MINS ,**TOTAL TIME:** 35 MINS,**SERVES:** 4, **YIELD:** 1 CRUMBLE

Ingredients

- 4 Gala Apples, Peeled And Cored
- 6 Tablespoons Brown Sugar
- 1/2 Cup Rice Flour, Mix (1 Cup White Rice Flour To 1/2 Cup Tapioca Starch)
- 1/2 Cup Blanched Almond, Finely Chopped (I Really Like To Add Some Chopped Walnuts As Well)
- 4 Tablespoons Butter
- 2 Teaspoons Cinnamon

How to make it:

1. The oven temperature should be set to 375 degrees. Then the apples have to be sliced into thin pieces.
2. Take a pan that has less depth and put the pieces in it. Cinnamon and some brown sugar can be added to it.
3. Make the crisp layer by combining the mix with nuts and add sugar to it, but not more than four tablespoons.
4. The mixture has to be mixed with hands and butter has to be added to it.
5. Now the mix is put on the pan with the apples.
6. Then heat it for less than an hour till it turns slightly golden.

7. Vanilla ice cream could be added with the slightly heated up crumble before serving it.

****

French Toast

PREP TIME: 10 MINS ,TOTAL TIME: 16 MINS ,SERVINGS: 2

Ingredients

- 4 Slices Gluten Free Bread
- 2 Medium Eggs
- 2 Tablespoons Orange Juice
- 1/4 Cup Almond Milk (Plain Or Vanilla) Or 1/4 Cup Rice Milk (Plain Or Vanilla) Or 1/4 Cup Soymilk (Plain Or Vanilla)
- 1/4 Teaspoon Cinnamon
- 1/8 Teaspoon Nutmeg
- 1/4 Teaspoon Salt
- 1/4 Teaspoon Vanilla Extract
- 2 Tablespoons Ghee Or 2 Tablespoons Margarine

OPTIONAL

- 2 teaspoons honey

How to make it:

1. You start with a small pan where you mix the ghee, butter margarine and bread.

2. Mix it well then put the ghee in a pan, let it absorb for only one or two minutes if the bread is soft and made at home otherwise for a thicker bread you have to keep it for absorption for more than 3-5minutes.

3. Let the extra liquid to fall off the bread and put it in for cooking while mixing it with ghee or margarine.

4. Use some jam, maple syrup or fruit when it's ready to be served.

****

Gluten Free Sausage Crumbles

PREP TIME: 5 MINS , TOTAL TIME: 10 MINS ,SERVINGS: 8

Ingredients

- 1/2 Cup Boiling Water
- 1/2 Teaspoon Liquid Smoke (Optional)
- 3 Tablespoons Braggs Liquid Aminos (Gluten-Free If Needed For Gf Diet) Or 3 Tablespoons Soy Sauce (Gluten-Free If Needed For Gf Diet)
- 1 Teaspoon Maple Syrup
- 1/4 Teaspoon Blackstrap Molasses

- 1/2 Cup Textured Vegetable Protein (Gluten-Free If Needed For Diet)
- 2 Tablespoons Nutritional Yeast
- 1 Teaspoon Garlic Powder
- 1/2 Teaspoon Crushed Sage
- 1/2 Teaspoon Ground Fennel
- 1/4 Teaspoon Black Pepper
- 1/8 Teaspoon Cayenne
- Oil (For Frying)

How to make it:

1. Add maple syrup with soy sauce and molasses with a bowl of boiling water.
2. Now blend TVP with non-wet seasoning, mix it well and allow it to soak the wetness for a bit.
3. Then add some oil in a pan and stir-fry the TVP for five minutes and serve it when it turns brown.

Gluten Free and Vegan Breakfast Bars

PREP TIME: 10 MINS ,**TOTAL TIME:** 30 MINS

,**SERVES:** 8-10, **YIELD:** 12-16 BARS

Ingredients

- 1 1/4 Cups Blanched Almond Flour
- 1/4 Teaspoon Celtic Sea Salt
- 1/4 Teaspoon Baking Soda
- 1/4 Cup Grapeseed Oil
- 1/4 Cup Agave Nectar
- 1 Teaspoon Vanilla Extract
- 1/2 Cup Shredded Coconut
- 1/2 Cup Pumpkin Seeds
- 1/2 Cup Sunflower Seeds
- 1/4 Cup Slivered Almonds
- 1/4 Cup Raisins

How to make it:

1. First in one container take almond flour, baking soda and some salt.
2. Then in a larger one mix vanilla with agave and oil of grape seeds.
3. Mix it well and add almonds, raisins, sunflower and pumpkin seeds with coconut.

4. Take a square dish of 8inches and make it oily by adding some grape seed oil.

5. Then add the batter into the dish and spread it down in the dish properly.

6. It would be ready to be served after baking it for twenty minutes at 350 degrees.

*****

Gluten-Free Sausage Crumbles

PREP TIME: 5 MINSTOTAL TIME: 10 MINSSERVINGS: 8

Ingredients

- 1/2 Cup Boiling Water
- 1/2 Teaspoon Liquid Smoke (Optional)
- 3 Tablespoons Braggs Liquid Aminos (Gluten-Free If Needed For Gf Diet) Or 3 Tablespoons Soy Sauce (Gluten-Free If Needed For Gf Diet)
- 1 Teaspoon Maple Syrup
- 1/4 Teaspoon Blackstrap Molasses
- 1/2 Cup Textured Vegetable Protein (Gluten-Free If Needed For Diet)
- 2 Tablespoons Nutritional Yeast
- 1 Teaspoon Garlic Powder
- 1/2 Teaspoon Crushed Sage

- 1/2 Teaspoon Ground Fennel
- 1/4 Teaspoon Black Pepper
- 1/8 Teaspoon Cayenne
- Oil (For Frying)

How to make it:

1. Molasses has to be added to maple syrup with soy sauce and in a bowl of boiling water.
2. Mix TVP with non-wet seasoning, mix it well and allow it to soak the wetness for a bit.
3. Then add some oil in a pan and stir-fry the TVP for five minutes and serve it when it turns brown.

****

Cinnamon Toast Morning Muffins

PREP TIME: 10 MINS. **COOK TIME:** 20 MINS. **TOTAL TIME:** 30 MINS. **YIELD:** 12 MUFFINS

Ingredients

- 2 Cups + 2 Tbsp Oat Flour (Homemade From Rolled Oats) -- Traditional Wheat Flour Can Also Be Used
- 1 Tbsp Baking Powder
- 1/2 Tsp Salt (Pink Salt Used)
- 2 Tsp Cinnamon
- 1/4 Tsp Vanilla Bean Powder (Or 1/2 Tsp Vanilla Extract)

- 11oz Silken Tofu (Organic + Non-GMO)
- 1/2 Cup Melted Vegan Butter (Earth Balance)
- 1/2 Tsp Apple Cider Vinegar
- 1 Shot Freshly Brewed Espresso
- 1 Cup Coconut Sugar
- Topping: 1 Tbsp Cinnamon Sugar Mix
- 2 Tsp Vegan Butter: For Greasing Muffin Tin

How to make it:

1. At first heat up the oven till the temperature reaches to 400 degrees.
2. Take a paper liner then apply veggie butter not more than two teaspoons.
3. In a large container or pot mix flour, baking powder, salt and cinnamon with rolled oats.
4. Then combine the cider vinegar, espresso with silken tofu and also add sugar & veggie butter in a food mixer.
5. Now add the components from the two and mix it properly, now fill each tin liner with the mix and add some sugar cinnamon icing to it.
6. After that heat it in the oven at the set temperature for over ten minutes then reduce the heat by 50 degrees and heat it for eight minutes.
7. It's ready to be eaten, refrigerate it if you plan to eat or serve it the next day.

Gluten-Free Orange Cranberry Scones

PREP TIME: 20 MINUTES, **TOTAL TIME:** 40 MINUTES ,
YIELD: 8 SCONES

Ingredients

- 1 3/4 Cups Gluten-Free Flour + ¼ More For Sprinkling*
- 1/4 Cup Coconut Palm Sugar
- 2 Tsp Baking Powder
- Zest From 1 Orange
- 1/2 Tsp Salt
- 1/4 Cup Cold Butter, Cubed
- 1/4 Cup Cold 0% Fat Greek Yogurt
- 2 Large Eggs
- 1/4 Cup Orange Juice
- 1 Tsp Vanilla Extract
- 1/2 Cup Dried Cranberries (Unsweetened Preferred)
- Optional: 1/3 Cup White Chocolate Chips, Melted-For Glaze**

How to make it:

1. Switch on the oven and heat it till the temperature reaches to 400 degrees.
2. Add coconut palm sugar, baking powder, orange zest, salt and less than 2 cups of gluten free flour in a large mixing pot.

3. Then mix butter and the yogurt to it, then mix everything with a spatula until becomes granular and it would be more like peas.

4. In another container mix orange juice, vanilla extract with eggs, then we combine everything in one container and it should be properly blended.

5. Put flour on the base where it would take a circular shape of around inch thickness before that it would be round in shape, after that it has to be cut with a sharp object in eight parts.

6. And for the next quarter of an hour it has to kept in the oven over a liner sheet.

7. When it's done, you could apply chocolate on it.

Gluten Free & Grain Free Muffins

PREP TIME 5 MINS ,**COOK TIME:-** 15 MINS ,**TOTAL TIME** 20 MINS **SERVES:** 12 MUFFINS OR 24 MINI MUFFINS

Ingredients

- 1 Cup Nut Butter -
- 2 Medium Sized Bananas
- 2 Large Eggs
- 1 Teaspoon Vanilla (Try Making Your Own!)
- 2 Tablespoons Of Raw Honey(Or Other Sweeteners Such As Maple Syrup, Stevia, Etc.)
- ½ Teaspoon Baking Soda
- 1 Teaspoon Apple Cider Vinegar

TOPPINGS:

- Coconut Flakes,
- Raisins,
- Flaxseed,
- Dark Chocolate Chips Or Cinnamon
- Tupelo Honey
- Apple Butter,
- Strawberry Preserves
- Peanut Butter. Or Carrot Jam

How to make it:

1. You could start with heating the oven till it reaches 400degrees.

2. Take all the material in a food mixer, and start the mixer till the mix is done properly.

3. Then put it onto a buttered tin liner for muffins, and additional icing could be given, make around twenty-four different pieces.

4. Bake it for quarter of an hour or less than it, depends upon the size.

5. It could again be heated in a cake toaster for less than five minutes with temperature set to 350 degrees.

Gluten-Free Banana Muffins

Ingredients

- 2 Teaspoons Baking Powder
- 1/4 Teaspoon Baking Soda
- 1/2 Teaspoon Xanthan Gum
- 1/2 Teaspoon Salt
- 1/2 Teaspoon Cinnamon, Optional
- 1 3/4 Cups King Arthur Gluten-Free Multi-Purpose Flour Or Brown Rice Flour Blend*
- 1/2 Cup (8 Tablespoons) Soft Butter
- 2/3 Cup Sugar
- 2 Tablespoons Molasses Or Honey
- 2 Large Eggs
- 1 1/2 Cup Very Mashed Ripe Bananas (About 2 Medium Bananas)
- 1/2 Cup Chopped Walnuts, Optional

How to make it:

1. First switch on the oven and take it to 375 degrees F.
2. Then butter up a tin liner tray for muffins and keep buttered muffin papers on it.
3. Mix baking powder, baking soda, xanthan gum, salt, cinnamon and flour.

4. Then take molasses with butter and sugar add blend the eggs into it.

5. Now mix everything properly and add banana paste into it but not at once.

6. Blend the ingredients for half a minute and put the walnuts, and then transfer the mixture on the tin liner tray, place the mix into the tray and cook it in the oven for less than half an hour, after it's taken out, let it settle down for five more minutes before serving twelve warm muffins.

Almond Vanilla Scones

Ingredients

- 3 Cups (300 G / 10 ½ Oz)   Almond Meal / Ground Almonds
- 2 Teaspoons Gluten Free Baking Powder   Or ¾ Teaspoon Baking Soda
- ¼ Cup (2 Floz)) Macadamia Nut Oil Or Cold Pressed Olive Oil
- 1 Tablespoon Honey Or Organic Maple Syrup
- 2 Teaspoons Vanilla Bean Paste
- 2 Free Range Eggs
- Strawberry + Vanilla Jam To Serve

How to make it:

1. First and foremost the oven temperature would be pre set to 300 degrees Fahrenheit.
2. Before putting wet items like eggs, oil, honey, and vanilla mix baking powder with almond meal in a bowl.
3. Before making it into circular pieces the mix has to be evenly spread out and make the spread three centimetres in thickness.
4. Cook it in the oven for one-third of an hour or more.
5. Take it out when it turns golden in colour and let it rest for a few minutes before serving it to others.
6. Add some jam as icing to make it better.

7. Some dry fruits like apricot or raisins can be added to it and also some hundred grams of chocolate can be put into it before cooking, to make it more fluidic.

******

Gluten Free Blueberry Muffins

PREP TIME:15MINUTES,**COOK TIME:**20 MINUTES,**SERVINGS:**12 SERVINGS

Ingredients

- **2 Cups** Gluten-Free All-Purpose Flour
- **3/4 Cup** Sugar
- **2 Teaspoons** Baking Powder
- **1 Teaspoon** Xanthan Gum
- **1/2 Teaspoon** Salt
- **1/2 Cup**(1 Stick) Unsalted Butter, Melted And Cooled
- **1/2 Cup** Whole Milk
- **2**large Eggs
- **2 Teaspoons** Grated Lemon Zest
- **1 Teaspoon** Vanilla Extract
- **1 1/2 Cups** Driscoll's Blueberries

How to make it:

1. The temperature of the oven should touch 375 degrees.

2. Then butter up a tin liner tray for muffins and keep buttered muffin papers on it Mix baking powder, baking soda, xanthan gum, salt, cinnamon and flour.

3. Take a big pot and add vanilla to lemon zest, butter, eggs, milk, blend it together to make it .then insert the blueberries in to it, the mix should be thick and transfer the mixture onto the liner tray, fill it till three fourths of the cup is filled.

4. Then cook it in the over for not more than twenty minutes but keep on rotating it to cook it evenly.

5. Take it out and let it rest for around three minutes and top check whether it's' done you could use something small and sharp like a prick to check whether it's done.

6. The proper color of the muffin would be golden brown when cooked properly.

7. Serve and enjoy!

Gluten Free Pumpkin Banana Bread

PREP TIME: 45 MINS ,**TOTAL TIME:** 1 HR 45 MINS ,**SERVINGS:** 12

Ingredients

- 2 Cups All-Purpose Gluten-Free Flour (I Use Bob's Red Mill)
- 1 Teaspoon Baking Soda
- 1/4 Teaspoon Salt
- 1/2 Cup Butter, Softened
- 3/4 Cup Brown Sugar
- 2 Eggs
- 1 Cup Mashed Ripe Banana
- 1 Cup Canned Pumpkin
- 1 Teaspoon Cinnamon
- 1/4 Teaspoon Nutmeg
- 1 Teaspoon Vanilla Extract

How to make it:

1. First switch on the oven and take it to 350 degrees. Remember, to butter up the pan, which would be around nine inches in length & five inches in width and add flour, salt and baking soda in big pot.

2. In another one combine cream together with butter and brown sugar.

3. Then mix Vanilla with eggs, pumpkin, banana paste and spices.

4. Add both the things and make it soft. Then put the combination on the pan and cook it for over an hour but before cooking it keep it aside for half an hour.

*****

Banana-Nut Waffles

PREP TIME: 5 MINS ,**TOTAL TIME:** 10 MINS ,**SERVES:** 6, **YIELD:** 6 WAFFLES

Ingredients

- 1 Large Banana, Mashed
- 1 3/4 Cups Soymilk Or 1 3/4 Cups Rice Milk
- 1/2 Cup Vegetable Oil
- 1 Tablespoon Honey Or 1 Tablespoon Agave Nectar
- 2 Cups Gluten-Free Flour (I Use Bob's Red Mill Gluten-Free All-Purpose Baking Flour)
- 4 Teaspoons Baking Powder
- 1/4 Teaspoon Salt
- 1/2 Cup Chopped Almonds Or 1/2 Cup Walnuts Or 1/2 Cup Pecans

How to make it:

1. Start with an electric waffle iron, which is a hinged grid for waffles.

2. Switch it on and simultaneously blend milk substitute, sweetener, oil and bananas in an electric food mixer.

3. Add some flour, a pinch of salt and baking powder in it. Put the Choco-chips, berries or nuts inside it.

4. Put some of the mix on the waffle iron but put a greasing spray on it before using.

5. Cook it for not more than five minutes and serve with honey, maple syrup or hydrogenated margarine to make it taste better.

6. You could also apply peanut butter, berries or cream on it.

7. Refrigerate any more of the unheated mixture in a bag or bowl to use it later.

****

Gluten Free Pumpkin Muffins

PREP TIME: 15 MINS , **TOTAL TIME:** 40 MINS ,
SERVES: 12, **YIELD:** 12 MUFFINS

Ingredients

PUMPKIN MIX

- 9 Ounces Pumpkin
- 1/3 Cup Maple Syrup
- 1 Teaspoon Gluten-Free Vanilla Extract (I Use A Little Less Vanilla Paste)

DRY MIX

- 2 Cups All Purpose Gluten-Free Flour (Use Your Favorite Mix)
- 1 Teaspoon Guar Gum
- 1 Cup Brown Sugar (You May Use 3/4 Cup If You Prefer It Less Sweet)
- 1 Teaspoon Baking Soda
- 1/2 Teaspoon Salt
- 1 Teaspoon Cinnamon
- 1/2 Teaspoon Powdered Ginger
- 1/4 Teaspoon Ground Allspice

WET MIX

- 2 Eggs (Or Ener-G Egg Replacer)
- 1/3 Cup Canola Oil
- 1/2 Cup Orange Juice

TOPPING

- 1 Cup Granulated Brown Sugar
- 1 Teaspoon Cinnamon

How to make it:

1. Take a pot or container and add all non-wet materials in it.

2. Make a hole in the middle for the liquid elements to come in, use a small spoon to combine it properly.

3. Put the pumpkin in the mix and keep it aside for less than ten minutes and place it in muffin paper after buttering them, cook at 350 degrees for twenty minutes before that put some icing on it.

4. After it's done cool it on a wire grill/ rack.

5. Now it's ready to be served!

****

<u>Gluten Free Muffins</u>

PREP TIME: 10 MINS ,**TOTAL TIME:** 35 MINS
,**SERVES:** 12, **YIELD:** 12 MUFFINS

Ingredients

- 2 1/2 Cups Brown Rice Flour
- 1/2 Teaspoon Baking Soda
- 1/4 Teaspoon Baking Powder
- 1/4 Teaspoon Salt
- 1 Teaspoon Ground Cinnamon
- 1/2 Cup Honey
- 1/3 Cup Vegetable Oil
- 1/3 Cup Milk
- 1/2 Teaspoon Vanilla Extract
- 3 Eggs

- 1 1/2 Cups Blueberries (Fresh Or Frozen)

How to make it:

1. First switch on the oven and take it to 350 degrees &take a muffin liner, which has twelve parts, and place the muffin papers in it.
2. Mix baking powder, baking soda, salt, cinnamon and flour in one place and in another pot mix honey, milk, and eggs with veggie oil.
3. Now mix it well and add the blue berries into it. Place it in the cups and put it in the oven for one-third of an hour or more.

****

Gluten Free Fall Pancakes

PREP TIME: 5 MINS ,**TOTAL TIME:** 25 MINS, **SERVINGS:** 10

Ingredients

- 1/2 Cup Buckwheat Flour
- 1/2 Cup Brown Rice Flour
- 1/2 Cup Garfava Flour (Or Garbonzo Flour)
- 1 Teaspoon Baking Powder
- 1/2 Teaspoon Baking Soda
- 1/2 Teaspoon Salt

- 1/2 Teaspoon Cinnamon
- 1/4 Teaspoon Clove
- 1/8 Teaspoon Nutmeg
- 1 Egg
- 1 1/4 Cups Skim Milk (Rice Or Soy Work Too)
- 1 Large Mashed Banana (Ripe)

How to make it:

1. At first take a non-stick pan, and make it warm and take all the non-wet materials and stir fast for half a minute.
2. You could do it with your hand also; the mix might be chunky or uneven because of the banana, which has to be added.
3. The pan need not be buttered or greased and the size of it would be like that of a regular spatula.
4. While cooking the pancakes it has to be turned over to the other side and to check whether it's done check for the sides it should become dull and you should cook it for two to four minutes and not more than that, for both the sides.
5. See to the colour of the pancake and you can put banana, honey, non-fat yogurt on the pan cake as the topping.
6. Use any of them, it's up to you.

Gluten Free Vegan Banana Bread

PREP TIME: 10 MINS ,**TOTAL TIME:** 55 MINS ,**SERVES:** 12-15, **YIELD:** 1.0 LOAF

Ingredients

- 1 1/2 Cups Brown Rice Flour
- 1 1/2 Cups Millet Flour
- 1/3 Cup Sugar
- 3 Tablespoons Ground Flax Seeds
- 2 Teaspoons Cinnamon
- 3 Teaspoons Baking Powder
- 1 Teaspoon Guar Gum Or 1/2 Teaspoon Xanthan Gum
- 1/2 Teaspoon Salt
- 3 Bananas, Ripe, Mashed
- 1 1/2 Cups Water Or 1 1/2 Cups Rice Milk Or 1 1/2 Cups Soymilk
- 2/3 Cup Walnuts, Chopped (Optional)

How to make it:-

1. In the beginning we start by taking a large mixing pot and adding sugar, seeds of flax, cinnamon, baking powder with flour of millet and rice, you could also put guar gum in it.
2. Blend the water or milk with the bananas with a spoon, spatula or a food mixer but mix it well.

3. Cook it for less than an hour at 350 degrees in a pan, which is a square of eight inches, and it has to buttered or oiled.

4. When the middle portion is properly cooked we take it out from the heat and let it rest for a few minutes, then make it into square pieces after it cools down.

****

Gluten Free Bran Muffins

PREP TIME: 5 MINS ,**TOTAL TIME:** 25 MINS,**SERVES:** 4-6, **YIELD:** 12.0 MUFFINS

Ingredients

- 1/2 Cup Blanched Almond Flour
- 1/2 Cup Flax Seed Meal
- 1 Teaspoon Baking Soda
- 1/2 Teaspoon Celtic Sea Salt
- 6 Dates
- 3 Eggs
- 2 Tablespoons Olive Oil

- 1/4 Cup Water
- 1/4 Cup Sesame Seeds
- 1/4 Cup Sunflower Seeds
- 1/2 Cup Raisins

How to make it:-

1. We start with mixing almond flour with flax meal, baking soda in a large pot and then mix eggs, olive oil, dates and water in a blender.

2. The mixture should be soft and light. Now we add all the components together, i.e. the non-wet and liquid components in to one pot and add seeds of sesame, sunflower and also put some raisins.

3. Then stir the mixture and put into lined tin tray and cook it in the oven for one-third of an hour or more.

4. Then take it out and cool it down.

5. Now your muffin is ready to be enjoyed with your dear ones!

Hot Quinoa Breakfast With Fruits

PREP TIME: 5 MINS ,TOTAL TIME: 13 MINS ,SERVINGS: 2-3

Ingredients

- 1 Cup Quinoa
- 2 Cups Water
- 1/2 Cup Thinly Sliced Apple
- 1/3 Cup Raisins Or 1/3 Cup Sultana
- 1/2 Teaspoon Cinnamon

How to make it:-

1. We start with a rice strainer where we clean the quinoa with water.
2. We can use a small pot where we boil it in water and cook it for five minutes.
3. Fruits like apple, raisin can be added with a hint of cinnamon, we cook till it gets dry.
4. Take it out and put some milk and honey in it before eating.

Baked Double Chocolate Donuts

PREP TIME: 15 MINS ,**TOTAL TIME:** 25 MINS,**YIELD:**
6 DONUTS

Ingredients :-

DONUTS

- 2/3 Cup All-Purpose Flour, Blend Gluten Free
- 2 Tablespoons Tapioca Starch (Expandex)
- 1/4 Cup Cocoa
- 1/2 Cup Sugar
- 1 Teaspoon Xanthan Gum
- 1 Teaspoon Baking Powder
- 1/4 Teaspoon Salt
- 1 Teaspoon Cinnamon
- 3 Tablespoons Dried Dry Buttermilk
- 2 Large Eggs
- 3 Tablespoons Coconut Oil, Melted
- 2 -4 Tablespoons Water, Divided

CHOCOLATE GLAZE

- 1 1/2 Tablespoons Melted Coconut Oil
- 1 1/2 Tablespoons Unsweetened Cocoa
- 1 1/2-2 Tablespoons Hot Water, Divided
- 3/4 Cup Confectioners' Sugar

- 1/2 Teaspoon Vanilla
- Chopped Peanuts (Optional)
- Sweetened Flaked Coconut (Optional)
- Nonpareils (Optional)

How to make it:-

1. First switch on the oven and heat it to 350 degrees. Grease a donut pan, which can make half a dozen donuts at once.
2. Now in a mid-sized container put buttermilk powder with flour, tapioca starch , cocoa, gum, baking powder, cinnamon, sugar and also some salt.
3. In another small mixing container and stir the eggs, oil and two tablespoons of water till it becomes soft but thick. It should be constituent and even.
4. Add some water if needed.
5. But it shouldn't get too liquidly.
6. Transfer the mixture to the donut pan and keep it in the oven for ten minutes or so, then let it stay in the pan for one or two minutes to let it settle down, then take it out and keep it on a wired grill and let it cool down.
7. Then in a small container put coconut oil, cocoa, less than two tablespoons of hot water, vanilla and sugar.
8. Now pour the Chocó liquid on the donuts and add a topping like nonpareils, peanuts or coconut.
9. Now your donut is ready to be served!

Peppered Breakfast Bacon

PREP TIME: 10 MINS ,**TOTAL TIME:** 25 MINS
,**SERVINGS:** 6

Ingredients

- 1 Lb Thick Sliced Bacon
- Brown Sugar
- Fresh Cracked Black Pepper

How to make it:-

1. Fire up the oven till four hundred degrees, then place the bacon on a grill on a roast pan.
2. Put some brown sugar and also some black pepper for taste.
3. Heat it for a quarter of an hour.
4. Serve it fresh and when it turns golden and crunchy.

Mixed Whole-Grain Breakfast

PREP TIME: 5 MINS ,**TOTAL TIME:** 20 MINS,

SERVINGS: 1-2

Ingredients

- 1 Cup Water
- 2 Tablespoons Buckwheat Groats, Rinsed (Raw, Not Toasted)
- 2 Tablespoons Millet, Rinsed
- 3 Tablespoons Rolled Oats Or 3 Tablespoons Quinoa
- 1/2 Cup Chopped Red Apple
- 1/4 Cup Chopped Almonds (Or Fav. Chopped Nuts)
- 1/4 Cup Raisins Or 1/4 Cup Chopped Dates
- 1/4 Teaspoon Ground Cinnamon
- 1/8 Teaspoon Ground Cardamom
- 1/8 Teaspoon Salt
- 2 Teaspoons Ground Flax Seeds
- Milk (Optional) Or Yogurt (Optional)
- Honey, To Taste (Optional)

How to make it:

1. Clean the quinoa with water on a strainer and take a small saucepan or pot where water needs to be heated up.
2. Put cleaned millet and buckwheat, oats or quinoa, apple, almonds, raisins, dates, cardamom and cinnamon.
3. Also add some salt in it.

4. Cover the saucepan and keep it the heat in low mode.

5. Let the liquid to be absorbed and heat for quarter of an hour and put the lid on the saucepan for five more minutes, even after the heat is switched off.

6. Blend some seeds of flax and put yogurt in it before serving it. It would surely add to the taste.

****

Fresh Date Sweet Gluten Free

PREP TIME: 10 MINS ,**TOTAL TIME:** 17 MINS
,**SERVES:** 1, **YIELD:** 1 SERVING

Ingredients

- 7 Fresh Dates (Depending On Size, I Have Used Sweetened Al-Noor Dates Of Tunisia Which Are Normally Soaked In Corn)
- 4 1/2 Tablespoons Butter (A Guess, Please Add As Needed To A Consistency Of A Thick Sauce)
- 3 1/2 Tablespoons Finely Ground Rice Flour Or 3 1/2 Tablespoons All-Purpose Flour
- 2 Dashes Freshly Ground Cardamom

How to make it:-

1. At first take a small dish where deseeded dates are kept then we add melted butter to it in a small pot and the flour is also blended together.

2. Heat it, at medium temperature and blend it continuously till the flour achieves a golden brown color, due to the heat.

3. Add some cardamom in it for taste, and keep it aside to settle down and also for cooling it down.

4. Then when there's still some heat intact put the dates into it and your Bedouin Dates are ready!

5. Serve with a beverage; Coffee or tea would complement your dish!

******

Potato Latkes Gluten-Free

PREP TIME: 20 MINS ,**TOTAL TIME:** 30 MINS,**SERVINGS:** 6-8

Ingredients

- 4 Lbs Russet Potatoes
- 1 Large Onion, Peeled
- 2 Teaspoons Salt
- 1 Tablespoon White Pepper
- 1 Cup Gluten-Free Rice Flour Mix
- 3 Eggs, Beaten
- Olive Oil (For Frying)

How to make it:

1. The oven temperature should be set to 200 degrees.
2. Use a food processor for granulating the potatoes and before doing that you have to take out the skin of the potatoes.
3. Also with that food processor you need to shred the onion into minute pieces.
4. After the skins of the potatoes are taken off the potatoes need to be kept in cold water.
5. Then squash the water of the potatoes with your hands and combine the onions and the potatoes, to stop oxidation do this process quickly.
6. Then take a cast iron pan where olive oil has to be put but do not put more than half an inch of oil in the pan and moderately heat the oil.
7. Then add all the other components in the earlier mix and when it is mixed properly you have put one-fourth of a cup into the oil and take a flat spoon or spatula to make the surface even and it should not be more than one-third of an inch in thickness.
8. You have to keep it in the oil till the colour becomes golden brown and the latkes are crunchy enough.
9. And you would have to turn it over from one side to the other to cook it evenly; observing the edges you could check the crunchiness.

10. Then we have to shift the material onto a dish where soaking paper is kept to soak the excess oil and shift it to a cooling grill to over a cookie sheet and put it in the oven till it's served.

11. Now it's ready to be served with either cream or applesauce.

12. Rest unused latkes can be refrigerated with cookie paper and freezer papers and keep it in a airtight bag or container

****

Guilt Free Scrambled Eggs

PREP TIME: 5 MINS ,TOTAL TIME: 7 MINS,SERVINGS: 2

Ingredients :-

- 4 Large Egg Whites, Whisked
- 1/4 Cup Grated Low-Fat Cheddar Cheese
- 1/2 Tablespoon Red Bell Pepper, Finely Diced
- Salt And Pepper

How to make it:

1. Take a few eggs and beat them up and use one microwave dish and heat for one minute.

2. After that put some cheese, pepper and little bit salt in to it and heat it again for half a minute.

3. You can use red peppers as topping.

Honey Oatmeal Bread

PREP TIME: 45 MINS ,**TOTAL TIME:** 1 HR 15 MINS,

YIELD: 1 LOAF

Ingredients

- 1 (7/8 Ounce) Package Yeast
- 1 Cup Oats
- 1 1/2 Cups Oat Flour
- 1/4 Cup Rice Flour
- 1/4 Cup Cornstarch
- 1/2 Cup Tapioca Flour
- 1/2 Cup Sorghum Flour
- 2 Teaspoons Xanthan Gum
- 1 Teaspoon Salt
- 1 Egg
- 1/3 Cup Honey
- 1 Tablespoon Canola Oil
- 1 Teaspoon Apple Cider Vinegar
- 1 1/4 Cups Warm Water
- 1 Tablespoon Warm Water

How to make it:

1. Take a midsized container and mix non-wet materials and another container add the wet items.

2. Now we add the non-wet materials into the wet materials and keep on blending for about three minutes. Then we take an oiled up nine inches by five inches wide pan where flour is also added.

3. Then we butter a wrap and put it on the side of the cake facing down.

4. We keep it aside for half an hour in room temperature or in a slightly hot area.

5. Then we heat up the oven to 350 degrees F, we take out the wrap and place it in the oven for more than half an hour.

6. The temperature of the bread should be above 200 degrees, see to this point before taking it out.

7. For ten minutes the bread can be kept uncovered but a foil has to be placed to stop the bread from becoming darker in colour.

Apple Cinnamon Muffins With Crumble Topping

PREP TIME: 30 MINS, **TOTAL TIME:** 56 MINS, **YIELD:** 5 LARGE MUFFINS

Ingredients

MUFFINS

- 1/2 Cup Brown Rice Flour
- 1/2 Cup Rice Flour (White Rice Flour)
- 1/4 Cup Tapioca Flour
- 1/3 Cup Potato Starch
- 1/2 Cup Brown Sugar
- 2 Teaspoons Baking Powder (Gluten Free)
- 1 Teaspoon Baking Soda
- 1 Teaspoon Guar Gum (Xanthan Gum May Be Substituted ~ Corn Derived)
- 1/4 Teaspoon Sea Salt
- 1/3 Cup Canola Oil
- 1 Egg (If You Use Ener-G Egg Replacer Use 2)
- 1 Cup Unsweetened Applesauce
- 1 1/2 Apples, Pealed And Chopped (Organic Are Better)
- 1 Teaspoon Cinnamon

CRUMBLE TOPPING

- 1/2 Cup Ground Cashews Or 1/2 Cup Almond Meal
- 1 Tablespoon Brown Rice Flour
- 2 Tablespoons Brown Sugar
- 1 Tablespoon Canola Oil

How to make it:-

1. The oven temperature should be set to 350 degrees.
2. Use a fine mesh grill to put white rice flour, tapioca starch, starch of potato, a half cup brown sugar, baking powder, baking soda, guar gum, one teaspoon cinnamon, salt with half cup brown flour.
3. All these have to be put in a midsized container. It has to be blended quite nicely and we put some eggs, applesauce, diced apples and one-third cup canola oil in it.
4. We blend it slightly to mix all materials and add some juice to make it liquidized, do it if needed.
5. Take line muffin tray and put some grease on it, and take muffin cups and fill it properly. You can add almond meal or cashews into a tiny container with one tablespoon of brown rice flour, two tablespoon of sugar, ne tablespoon of canola oil and half teaspoon cinnamon.
6. Blend it perfectly and put it as icing on the muffins.
7. Then cook it in the oven for less than half an hour. Remove it and let it cool down and your muffins are ready to be consumed at any point of time.

Gluten Free - High Fiber

PREP TIME: 5 MINS ,**TOTAL TIME:** 15 MINS

,**SERVINGS:** 8

Ingredients

- 1/2 Cup Buckwheat Flour
- 1/2 Cup Brown Rice Flour
- 1/2 Cup Garfava Flour (Or Garbonzo Flour)
- 1 Teaspoon Baking Powder
- 1/2 Teaspoon Baking Soda
- 1/4 Teaspoon Salt
- 2 Egg Whites (Or 1 Egg)
- 1 1/4 Cups Skim Milk (Rice Or Soy Work Too)
- 1 Mashed Banana (Very Ripe)
- Banana, And Honey For Topping

How to make it:

1. Take all the non-wet materials at first in a pot for mixing then take another pot for mixing and add two egg whites and banana paste and place it on the non-wet mixture.

2. Then you put milk in it and keep on whisking and blending it constantly till the point of time it is not thin anymore.

3. Then take a non-stick pan and heat it up moderately and put around one-third of the mixture in the pan.

4. After heating for a while the edges would start to look dull and it cook it for less than two minutes, and turn it over side to side to cook it evenly.

5. Then you put honey on top of it with some pieces of banana. You have to place the dish in the microwave so to make the banana soft.

Sugar, Dairy, Wheat Free Muffins

PREP TIME: 10 MINS ,TOTAL TIME: 35 MINS ,SERVES: 4, YIELD: 8 MUFFINS

Ingredients

- 1/4 Cup Ground Flax Seeds
- 3/4 Cup Buckwheat Flour
- 1 Teaspoon Baking Powder
- 1/4 Teaspoon Salt
- 1 Teaspoon Cinnamon
- 1 Egg
- 1/2 Cup Almond Milk
- 2 Apples, Peeled Then Grated
- 3 Tablespoons Coconut Oil, Melted
- 1/2 Cup Walnuts, Chopped
- 3 Tablespoons Coconut Oil
- 1 Tablespoon Raw Honey

How to make it:

1. We start with taking a small container and add the first five non-wet materials in it.

2. Then we take another container and we put eggs and use a stirrer, along with that we put some milk, coconut oil and finally some apple pieces.

3. Blend it properly to make a proper mix of components from both the containers.

4. Then add the nuts and put the mixture on the pan, which has to be oiled slightly. Heat it at 350 degrees and for less than half an hour.

5. Place a sharp but thin prick like object to test whether it's done.

6. To cool it down you have to keep it on a cooling grill for around ten minutes.

7. When it's in the oven take honey with coconut oil and added together, the coconut oil should be refrigerated to make it hard, and only hard coconut oil has to be used.

8. It could be put when the muffins are taken out from the oven and should be put before the muffins get cold.

9. Do remember that children below one year should not be given honey.

Gluten-Free Moist Mango and Nut Bread

PREP TIME: 15 MINS ,TOTAL TIME: 1 HR 15 MINS ,SERVES: 6-8, YIELD: 2.0 SMALL LOAVES

Ingredients

- 1 Cup Bob's Red Mill Gluten-Free All-Purpose Baking Flour (You Can Substitute With All Purpose Baking Flour For A Regluar Recipe, And If You Can Tolerate Glute)
- 3 Teaspoons Baking Powder
- 1/2 Cup Brown Sugar
- 2 Teaspoons Coconut Oil
- 1/4 Teaspoon Salt
- 2 Large Eggs
- 1/2 Cup Macadamia Nuts Or 1/2 Cup Walnuts, Chopped

- 300 G Raw Mangoes, Pureed Or 2 -3 Mangoes, Depending On The Size
- 2 Teaspoons Vanilla Extract
- 1 Teaspoon Cinnamon (Optional)

How to make it:-

1. The oven temperature should be set to 350 degrees. And in a big container or pot mix flour, salt, baking powder and mix it well.

2. In another one put separated egg whites and blend it with a electric blender and combine the yolks with vanilla, sugar, and oil.

3. In the flour mixture we can put the egg yolk mix and then put the egg whites into that and make it soft and light.

4. Add the mangoes and nuts into it then transfer the mix in two different buttered loaf pan and cook for one hour and to check whether it's done with a sharp prick like object in middle.

5. If done then take it out and it's ready to be eaten with delight.

Breakfast Hash Browns

PREP TIME: 15 MINS ,**TOTAL TIME:** 25 MINS,**SERVINGS:** 4

Ingredients

- 1 Lb Russet Potato
- 1/4 Teaspoon Salt
- Pepper
- 1/2 Cup Cheddar Cheese (Mild, Medium Or Aged Your Choice)
- 2 Slices Bacon, Cooked &Crumbled,Optional
- 2 Green Onions

How to make it:-

1. First take some potatoes and heat them in water, they should become slightly soft and mince the potatoes after cooling it down.
2. Take a non-stick pan and add vegetable oil and take half of the potatoes and put it in it.
3. Add some pepper and salt. Then put green onions, bacon and cheddar above it then let the rest of the potatoes to be placed above it.
4. Let the heat be increased and move the pan constantly to keep it loose.

5. Then see to it with a spoon whether the lower half has turned golden brown or not, the put a lid over the pan and twist it on the other side to take out the cake with the side which was on the pan surface above.

6. And again put some more oil in the pan and cook the uncooked side. Serve it fresh after cutting it into thin pieces.

Brown Rice Breakfast Cereal

PREP TIME: 10 MINS ,**TOTAL TIME:** 10 MINS,**SERVES:** 4, **YIELD:** 4 CUPS

Ingredients

- 2 Cups Brown Rice, Cooked
- 1 Cup Nonfat Milk
- 1 Cup Apple, Chopped
- 1 Cup Cashews
- 1/4 Cup Dried Cranberries
- 1 Teaspoon Cinnamon
- 1 Teaspoon Vanilla
- 1 Teaspoon Salt

How to make it:-

1. Take all the materials in a container and add boiled brown rice.
2. Refrigerate it in the night to settle the constituents.
3. Then heat it in the morning and serve it with yogurt.

Gluten, Dairy & Cane Sugar Free Blueberry Muffins

PREP TIME: 20 MINS ,**TOTAL TIME:** 40 MINS

,**SERVES:** 12, **YIELD:** 12 MUFFINS

Ingredients

- 1 Cup Unsweetened Rice Milk
- 1 Tablespoon Apple Cider Vinegar
- 1 1/2 Cups Brown Rice Flour
- 3/4 Cup Sweet Rice Flour
- 1/2 Cup Tapioca Flour
- 1 Teaspoon Guar Gum
- 1 Teaspoon Baking Soda
- 1 Tablespoon Gf Baking Powder
- 1/2 Teaspoon Sea Salt
- 1/3 Cup Raw Honey
- 2 Teaspoons Gf Vanilla
- 2 Organic Eggs
- 1/4 Cup Olive Oil (Or Safflower)
- 1 Cup Frozen Blueberries

How to make it:-

1. First we take a cup full of rice milk and mix it with vinegar.
2. Simultaneously the oven has to have temperature of around 400 degrees.

3. Now in a large pot mix all the non-wet components and in another one we add the liquid materials.

4. Then we blend everything together till its proper.

5. Then we add the refrigerated blueberries to the mix.

6. And now we stir it and take it on a non-dry muffin tins and put it in the oven for quarter of an hour.

W/Sausage - Gluten Free

PREP TIME: 5 MINS ,**TOTAL TIME:** 25 MINS
,**SERVINGS:** 2

Ingredients :-

- 2 Small Breakfast Sausage Links (I Use Safeway Maple Breakfast Sausage)
- 1 Teaspoon Finely Minced Or Pureed Onion (Optional)
- 1 Tablespoon Butter Or 1 Tablespoon Margarine
- 1 1/2 Tablespoons Cornstarch
- 1 Cup Milk
- 1/8 Teaspoon Salt
- 1 Pinch Ground Black Pepper (A Little Less Than 1/8 Tsp)
- 2 Large Gluten-Free Biscuits (I Use Recipe #152283)

How to make it:-

1. First take a pot and heat it at moderate temperatures then put two sausages with one teaspoon of onions, heat till the pinkness vanishes.
2. When it's done move the sausage from there.
3. Now at lower heat put some butter and make the sausage into pieces.
4. After the melting of the butter is done take cornstarch not more than one and half tablespoon and mix butter.
5. Now the heat has to be taken up and milk has to put in it.

6. Stir the mix until flour is mixed properly.

7. Once the thinness is gone add the sausage and put one-eighth teaspoon of salt and pepper.

8. And let the heat be at its lowest and blending has to be done constantly.

9. And remember to put a lid on it when not stirring or blending.

10. Then on a plate put the gravy over the biscuit. And your 'biscuit and gravy' is ready!

Tomato Breakfast

PREP TIME: 3 MINS ,**TOTAL TIME:** 11 MINS ,**SERVES:** 3, **YIELD:** 3

Ingredients

- Cooking Oil (Vegetable, Canola)
- Cooking Onion, Chopped
- Fresh Tomato, Chopped
- Sea Salt, To Taste
- Fresh Ground Black Pepper, To Taste
- Sweet Butter (Optional)
- Fresh Cilantro, Chopped (Optional)
- Unrefined Extra Virgin Olive Oil
- Pita Bread, To Serve (We Eat With Rice Cakes Or Rice Crackers To Be Gluten Free)

How to make it:-

1. Take some small tablespoons of cooking oil in a pan and heat it, put onions that are chopped, fry instantly and till it softens.
2. Then place tomatoes with salt and pepper. Use some butter & cilantro (while taking it out from the heat) and fry it till it becomes soft.
3. Take a near flat pot or dish and put some olive oil on it.

4. For beverages tea is preferred and also you could use some pita bread and cheese, which is plated with eggs for better presentation and taste.

5. Now it's ready to be served!

Arab Breakfast With Gluten Free

PREP TIME: 15 MINS ,**TOTAL TIME:** 25 MINS,**SERVES:** 3-4, **YIELD:** 3.0

Ingredients

BREAKFAST TEA

* 3 Orange Pekoe Tea Bags (I Use Tetley Tea Bags)
* 2 1/2 Cups Water
* Heavy Cream (Or Half-And Half)
* 6 Teaspoons White Sugar (To Taste)
* 7 Cardamom Pods, Crushed Slightly

CHEESE PREPARATION

* 1 Tablespoon Olive Oil (A Good Quality Please!)
* Halloumi Cheese (Haloom, Arabic, Hellim -Turkish)
* 1/4 Cup All-Purpose Flour (To Be Gluten Free I Use White Rice Flour Or A Mix With Tapioca Starch In 1/2 The Amount)
* 1 Lemon, Cut In Half

THE REST

* 1 Large Pita Bread (1 Bag, Do NOT Use If Gluten Free)
* Rice Crackers (Optional, For The Gluten Free)
* 1/4 Cup Butter, Sliced

- Cream Cheese (Not Sliced!!! Called Puck, Buck In Arabic, Danish Cream Cheese, No Substitute) Or Yogurt Cheese Balls In Oil Or Goat Feta Cheese, Sliced
- Assorted Gourmet Olive

- Hummus (Homemade Or Store Bought, Ours Tends To Be The Later)
- Assortment Fresh Fruit, Cut Up Into Chunks (Lovely Sprinkled With Orange Blossom Water & Sugar If Needed)

How to make it:

1. Take a pot or pan and heat water in it, put cardamom in it but don't boil the water.
2. Add the tea and let it be kept for less than two minutes and add in the sugar for taste and cream can be added as to how much colour you want.
3. The Haloumi cheese is made in to thin pieces and cleaned with water let it be moist.
4. Now the flour has to be added on a flat base and the cheese is added to it.
5. Take only half of it, now take the oil in a pan and fry the pieces till the colour becomes golden brown.
6. When it's done take it aside on a dish and add lemon on it, place some butter hummus, olives, cheese in a separate dish.
7. Also put fruits, cheese and the bread on a separate plate and spoons have to be laid out for serving purposes. Place these

dishes on a blanket or small table, which has very less height to eat in a traditional Islamic fashion.

****

Pomegranate, Honey & Quinoa Breakfast

PREP TIME: 10 MINS ,**TOTAL TIME:** 25 MINS ,**SERVES:** 1, **YIELD:** 1 BOWL

Ingredients

- 1/3 Cup Quinoa
- 1/3 Cup Milk, Substitute
- 1/3 Cup Water
- 1/4 Teaspoon Cinnamon, Powder
- 1 Pinch Ginger Powder
- 1 Tablespoon Flax Seed, Ground (I Use Ground Sunflower Seeds!!)
- 1 Tablespoon Unpasteurized Honey (Raw)
- 1/4 Cup Fine Desiccated Coconut (I Left This Out But It Would Probably Be Good)
- Handful Whole Almond, Chopped And Toasted In A Dry Frying Pan
- 1/2 Pomegranate, Seeds Of

How to make it:-

1. First take a sieve and clean the quinoa. Put it in a moderately sized heating bowl and add milk with water and cinnamon.
2. You can also try adding ginger powder but proportionately.
3. After heating it for quarter of an hour, throw the excess liquid. Then we blend it with honey, diced coconut pieces and seeds of sunflower & flax. Pomegranate and almonds can be used as final toppings.

****

Banana Maple Pecan Bread Muffins (Gluten-Free)

PREP TIME: 15 MINS ,**TOTAL TIME:** 35 MINS ,**SERVES:** 18, **YIELD:** 18 MUFFINS

Ingredients

BATTER

- 3 Ripe Bananas, Coarsely Mashed
- 1/3 Cup Pure Maple Syrup
- 1/2 Cup Pecans, Chopped
- 2 Cups Flour
- 1 Teaspoon Xanthan Gum
- 1 Cup Packed Brown Sugar
- 1 Teaspoon Baking Soda
- 1/2 Teaspoon Salt

- 1 Teaspoon Pumpkin Pie Spice
- 2 Tablespoons Dry Buttermilk
- 2 Eggs, Beaten
- 1/3 Cup Vegetable Oil
- 1/2 Cup Water

MAPLE PECAN TOPPING

- 3/4 Cup Chopped Pecans
- 1/4 Cup Pure Maple Syrup

CREAM CHEESE TOPPING

- 6 Ounces Cream Cheese (Optional)
- 1/4 Cup Brown Sugar (Optional)
- 1/4 Cup Pure Maple Syrup (Optional)

How to make it:

1. Take bananas at first then put some maple syrup and pecans. Let flour be mixed with sugar, xanthan gum, baking soda, salt, pie spice, pumpkin and buttermilk, which is dry.
2. You can also try cinnamon, ginger instead of pumpkin pie. Make a hole in the center and put all the liquid stuff in it, which are oil, water and eggs. Blend it with a wooden spoon, till its mixed properly.
3. Take a sharp object and four parts of the mix and put banana mixture in it.

4. Then put the mixture in muffin cups and add pecan maple syrup as frosting before cooking and also you can add cream cheese but only after it has been cooked. Take the oven temperature to 375 degrees and heat it for one-third of an hour.

EGGS FOR BREAKFAST

Frittata With Ham and Roasted Pepper

- **Prep Time:** 15 Mins
- **Total Time:** 37 Mins
- **Servings:** 4

Ingredients

- 5 Eggs
- 1/2 Cup Milk Or 1/2 Cup Half-And-Half Cream
- 1 Tablespoon Dijon Mustard
- 1 Cup Crouton
- 1/4 Cup Ham, Chopped
- 1/2 Cup Fontina Or 1/2 Cup Provolone Cheese, Grated
- 1/4 Cup Roasted Red Pepper, Drained And Chopped
- 1/4 Cup Green Onion, Finely Chopped (Green Part Only)

How to make it

1. First take a nice clean bowl, whip eggs in them.
2. Then pour in the milk and the Dijon mustard. Now put in the ham, the half cheese, half green onions, croutons and pour the mix over an oiled 9 inch pie plate.
3. Put in rest of the cheese, the green onion and the pepper.
4. Start by preheating your oven, and then cook at 350 F for around 20 minutes.

5. Till then the eggs should be set.

6. Cook for further 2 minutes to make sure the frittata is lightly risen.

7. Let it cook for 5 minutes and then use a spatula to cut the wedges.

*****

Sublime Scrambled Eggs

- **Prep Time:** 5 mins
- **Total Time:** 10 mins
- **Servings:** 3

Ingredients

- 6 Large Eggs
- 3 Tablespoons Butter, Diced (Ice-Cold)
- 2 Tablespoons Creme Fraiche
- Freshly Ground Sea Salt And Pepper (You Can Use Regular Salt If You Need To)
- 3 Chives, Snipped (Substitute With Green Onion If Necessary)
- 3 Slices , Rustic Bread To Serve (Such Aspain Polaãƒ Ne)

How to make it

1. Start by breaking the eggs over a pan and cook it with low heat.

2. Now add in half the butter and stir the whole package.

3. Mix up the whites with the yellows.

4. Just before you feel the mix is about to set in, pour in rest of the butter. In 5 minutes, the eggs will be lumpy and soft, just make sure they do not get extra hot by taking it off and on from the stove.

5. Get the sourdough breads toasted.

6. Now pour in the crème and then season up the eggs by putting in chives.

7. Place the bread over plates, put eggs over them and eat them hot.

****

Grilled Breakfast Burrito

- **Prep Time:** 30 mins
- **Total Time:** 45 mins
- **Servings:** 5

Ingredients

- 1/4 Cup Vegetable Oil
- 2 Large Potatoes, Diced
- 1 Onion, Diced
- 1/2 Bell Pepper, Diced
- 1/4 Cup Butter Or 1/4 Cup Margarine
- 8 Eggs, Beaten

- 1 Lb Breakfast Sausage Or 1 Lb Chorizo Sausage, Cooked And Drained
- 1 Teaspoon Salt
- 1/2 Teaspoon Fresh Ground Black Pepper
- 1 Cup Monterey Jack Cheese, Shredded
- 1 Cup Sharp Cheddar Cheese, Shredded
- 10 Large Flour Tortillas
- Nonstick Cooking Spray

How to make it

1. Get a big pan ready and pour and heat quarter cup of vegetable oil over it on mid flames.
2. Just make sure your fry the potatoes in them till they are cooked.
3. After this, put in the peppers and the onions; and let it cook till they are soft. When done, drain the water from it, put it aside.
4. Over in the same pan, put in margarine or butter at mid flames.
5. Put in some eggs and then put in the potatoes, sausage and the vegetables right before it's done.
6. Put pepper or salt as per taste. Put cheese and egg mix over every tortilla and then roll them over a burrito.
7. Pour in hot grill (preferably George Foreman) with grill cooking spray and grill it for 10 minutes.
8. Eat with sour cream, salsa, pico de Gallo, fried beans or even Spanish rice.

Fried Eggs With Dill

- **Prep Time:** 0 mins
- **Total Time:** 5 mins
- **Servings:** 1

Ingredients

- 3 Eggs
- 1 -3 Tablespoon Dried Dill
- Salt
- Pepper

How to make it

1. Start by frying your eggs scrambled or sunny side top.
2. Over it, dash in some pepper and salt.
3. Finally add in dried dill, as per your taste.

Egg Salad Sandwiches

- **Prep Time:** 25 mins
- **Total Time:** 25 mins
- **Servings:** 8

Ingredients

- 4 Pieces Bacon, Cooked And Crumbled
- 1/2 Cup Cheddar Cheese, Shredded
- 1/2 Cup Sour Cream
- 1/3 Cup Mayonnaise
- 2 Tablespoons Chives, Minced
- 1/4 Teaspoon Salt
- 1/4 Teaspoon Pepper
- 10 Hard-Cooked Eggs, Chopped
- 8 Lettuce Leaves
- 8 Croissants, Split

How to make it:

1. Take a large and a big bowl; mix up the 1st seven materials before putting in the eggs as well.
2. Fridge it for 2 hours at least whilst covering it.
3. Use lettuce croissants whilst eating.

Ricotta, Tomato and Basil Torte

- **Prep Time:** 20 mins
- **Total Time:** 1 hr 20 mins
- **Servings:** 8

Ingredients

- 500 G Low Fat Fresh Ricotta
- 100 G Low-Fat Feta, Crumbled
- 3 Eggs
- 2 Garlic Cloves, Crushed
- 1 Bunch Fresh Basil, Finely Shredded
- 375 G Grape Tomatoes Or 375 G Cherry Tomatoes, Halved

How to make it

1. Begin with preheating the oven at 360 F or 180 C on the oily side. Put baking papers over its base of 20 centimeter spring form tin.
2. Whip eggs, ricotta, garlic and feta before adding in the basil.
3. Put the mix over the tin and smooth out the top layer, also put in tomatoes.
4. Preheat the oven and bake it for 60 minutes.
5. Cool it and then fridge it up for 60 minutes to firm it.

Baked Eggs in Bread

- **Prep Time:** 5 mins
- **Total Time:** 30 mins
- **Servings:** 6

Ingredients

- 6 Crusty Dinner Rolls
- 6 Large Eggs
- 6 Teaspoons Chives
- 6 Teaspoons Heavy Cream
- Salt And Pepper
- 6 Teaspoons Parmesan Cheese

How to make it

1. Take out the top of every single dinner roll and eradicate bread till you can make a hole to put in the egg.
2. Put the rolls over a baking paper, reserve the top.
3. Break an egg into them, and bit cream and herbs over it.
4. Dash in a bit of pepper and salt on the dish; before putting in the parmesan.
5. Heat the dish at 350 and toast the bread for 25 minutes. After the eggs have been done for 20 minutes, bake the bread and keep it for 5 minutes.
6. Put the tops over the rolls and eat them up!

Tamale Hash

- **Prep Time:** 10 mins
- **Total Time:** 13 mins
- **Servings:** 2

Ingredients

- 1 Tablespoon Vegetable Oil
- 1/2 Small Onion, Chopped
- 1/2 Jalapeno Pepper, Chopped
- 1 Garlic Clove, Finely Chopped
- 3/4-1 Cup Black-Eyed Pea Salsa, Black-Eyed Pea Salsa (Cowboy Caviar) (Cowboy Caviar)
- 2 Tamales, Large Cut Into Bite-Size Pieces (Any Flavor Really Good Quality Tamale Works, We Like Pork)
- 2 Large Eggs
- 1/4 Cup Cheddar Cheese, Finely Greated
- 1 Tablespoon Fresh Cilantro, Chopped And Sprinkled On Top
- Sour Cream (Optional)

How to make it

1. Begin with heating oil at medium over a big pan.
2. Put in the onion, garlic, thee-fourth or one cup of pea salsa (the caviar), tamales pieces and jalapeño.
3. Cook for 3 minutes, and as it's cooking ready the eggs (yellow side up). Whilst eating, distribute the hash into 2 plates.

4. Put eggs over each of them.

5. Garnish with cilantro and cheese—place in sour cream if you like it.

****

Smoked Paprika Egg Salad Sandwich

- **Prep Time:** 15 mins
- **Total Time:** 15 mins
- **Servings:** 4

Ingredients

- 2/3 Cup Mayonnaise
- 2 Tablespoons Dijon Mustard
- 1 Tablespoon White Wine Vinegar
- 1 Tablespoon Smoked Spanish Paprika (Or Sweet Paprika)
- Salt & Freshly Ground Black Pepper
- 2 Green Onions, Thinly Sliced (Green And Pale Green Part)
- 3 Tablespoons Finely Chopped Flat Leaf Parsley
- 1 Cup Diced Celery
- 8 Hard-Boiled Eggs, Peeled And Coarsely Chopped
- 3 Tablespoons Olive Oil (For Brushing The Bread Slices)
- 8 Slices Whole Grain Or 8 Slices Whole Wheat Bread
- 1/2 Small Red Onion, Thinly Sliced
- Fresh Parsley Leaves, For Garnish (Optional)

How to make it

1. Whip in Dijon, mayo, Spanish paprika and wine vinegar over a large dish. Keep quarter of the mayo for the bread.

2. Now add in celery, eggs, parsley and the green onion with rest of the mayo.

3. Mix it well and then dash in pepper and salt. Cover both sides of the bread with some oil and grill it (or even pan grill it) over a baking paper for 45 seconds each sides.

4. Cover the bread with leftover mayo.

5. Finally distribute the egg salad over the slices of bread (should be 8) and garnish with parsley leaves and onion. Keep it open.

*****

<u>Perfect Soft Boiled Eggs</u>

- **Prep Time:** 2 mins
- **Total Time:** 7 mins
- **Servings:** 2

Ingredients

- 4 Large Eggs
- 1 Teaspoon Salt
- 6 Cups Water

How to make it

1. Boil up some water, and punch in some salt whilst boiling.

2. Prick the wider end part of the egg and dip it inside the boiled water for 5 minutes or so.

3. Put in cool water, crack the egg and eat it!

****

Biltmore Goldenrod Eggs

- **Prep Time:** 10 mins
- **Total Time:** 20 mins
- **Servings:** 4

Ingredients

- 3 Eggs, Hard Cooked And Peeled
- 1 Cup Medium White Sauce, Hot
- 6 Slices Bread, Toasted
- Parsley, For Garnish (Optional)

How to make it

1. Take the eggs, separates the whites from the yellows.

2. Cut up the whites and put in white sauce to it.

3. Put this sauce over the 4 pieces of bread toast. Push the yellows through the strainer and pour it over the top.

4. Triangle up the toasts and serve it with parsley.

Deviled Eggs

- **Prep Time:** 15 mins
- **Total Time:** 35 mins
- **Servings:** 12

Ingredients

- 12 Hardboiled Egg, Peeled
- 1 Tablespoon Mayonnaise
- 1/2 Teaspoon Worcestershire Sauce
- 1/2 Tablespoon Prepared Mustard
- 2 Teaspoons Apple Cider Vinegar
- 1 Dash Salt
- Paprika

How to make it

1. Piece up the eggs in straights, take out the yellows keep the whites. Mash the yolks quite well.
2. Mix the mayo, yolk, Worcestershire sauce, one teaspoon of vinegar and mustard in a bowl.
3. Pour in extra vinegar and mash it till you get 2 teaspoons.
4. If the mix does not become moist, then put in extra mayo. Put in salt to the mix and then put the mix over hollow egg whites.
5. Garnish with paprika and eat cold.

Egg and Cheese Sandwiches

- **Prep Time:** 5 mins
- **Total Time:** 10 mins
- **Yield:** 1 sandwich

Ingredients

- 2 -3 Tablespoons Butter (Or To Taste) Or 2 -3 Tablespoons Margarine (Or To Taste)
- 1 -2 Large Egg (I Use 2 Eggs For One Sandwich)
- Salt And Black Pepper (To Taste)
- 2 Slices Whole Wheat Bread Or 2 Slices White Bread
- 1 -2 Tablespoon Mayonnaise
- 1 Slice American Cheese

How to make it

1. Start by toasting the bread and spread button on side and mayo on the other as per your wish.
2. Put in one cheese slice over any side before heating nearly 2 tablespoons of butter over a pan at mid heat.
3. Make the eggs in the pan with pepper and salt.
4. Cover up the pan and let the eggs cook but do not harden the yellows. Put the egg mix over the bread top cheese and place another toast over it. Your dish is ready to serve and eat.

Egg & Mushroom Breakfast

- **Prep Time:** 5 mins
- **Total Time:** 15 mins
- **Servings:** 2

Ingredients

- 3 Slices Bacon
- 3/4 Cup Mushroom (Roughly Diced)
- 1/2 Cup Red Pepper (Diced)
- 1/3 Cup Onion (Diced)
- 1/4 Cup Mexican Blend Cheese
- 4 Eggs
- Salt & Pepper

How to make it

1. Start with cooking the bacon over a 10 inch pan till they crisp up.
2. Piece up the bacons and drain it over half slices.
3. Take out the grease and give back 1 to two tbsp bacon grease (or less) to the pan.
4. Slightly fry up the peppers and onions for 5 minutes then add the mushrooms.
5. Cook at low flames till you feel the veggies are done. Put in veggie over a plate and clear the pan. Pour in some olive oil and make egg scrambles in it.

6. Whilst the eggs are still tender, put in the cheese and cook again. Now add in the veggies and fold up the bacon pieces before serving it.

7. Serve the dish in plates.

****

Cluckerberries Eggs

- **Prep Time:** 20 mins
- **Total Time:** 40 mins
- **Servings:** 12

Ingredients

- 12 Eggs
- 1 Large Yellow Onion, Sliced Into Thin Rings
- Pickle Juice
- 5 Garlic Cloves, Smashed
- 4 Teaspoons Crushed Red Pepper Flakes (Optional)
- 4 Tablespoons Hot Sauce (Optional)

How to make it

1. Start by boiling eggs for 5 minutes (use cold water at first) and then let it cool for 20 minutes.

2. Now place in the eggs on the coldest water you can find and chill them out till they are absolutely cold.

3. It can take about 20 minutes.

4. The eggs should now peel off easily.

5. Whilst you do the eggs, take a juice jar and put some onion slices in it. Put smashed up garlic in the jar it by first cutting them up and then mashing it with your arm.

6. Use red pepper or pepper flakes if you want to make the eggs spicy. You can also use Tobasco sauce.

7. Now put in the eggs. Chill them in the fridge let them soak up well before eating.

8. Now if you want your pickle to be extra spicy and really hot then throw in a can of pickle jalapenos and its juice with the eggs.

9. There you go—your pickle is ready, but make sure you cool it well before eating!

Spinach Mushroom Quiche

- **Prep Time:** 15 mins
- **Total Time:** 55 mins
- **Servings:** 6

Ingredients

- 4 egg whites, beaten slightly
- 1 egg, beaten slightly
- 1/2 cup plain fat-free yogurt
- 1 (4 ounce) jars mushrooms, sliced
- 10 ounces spinach, frozen cooked and drained very well
- 1 1/2 ounces French-fried onions (half a small can)
- 3/4 cup reduced-fat swiss cheese, shredded (I use Alpine Lace)
- 1 pie shell

How to make it

1. Start up by mixing all the materials first and make sure the spinach is moisture less.
2. Pour the mix over the crust of pie.
3. Now bake the crust for 45 minutes at 350 or till you feel it's set.
4. Cover it with a foil after half an hour if you see that the crust has become extra dark.

Microwave Poached Eggs

- **Prep Time:** 2 mins
- **Total Time:** 4 mins
- **Servings:** 1

Ingredients

- 1 Tablespoon Water Or 1 Teaspoon Butter
- 1 Egg
- Salt
- White Pepper
- Grated Parmesan Cheese (Optional)

How to make it

1. Begin with heating up butter or even water over a custard bowl or cup. Put in the egg and poke it well before dashing in pepper, salt and parmesan if you like it.
2. Put a lid and on mid heat in the microwave cook it for nearly 1 and quarter minutes.
3. Let it for 60 seconds before serving.

Spanish Potato Omelet

- **Prep Time:** 15 mins
- **Total Time:** 1 hr
- **Servings:** 6

Ingredients

- 1/2 Cup Olive Oil
- 1/2 Lb Potato, Thinly Sliced
- Salt And Pepper
- 1 Large Onion, Thinly Sliced
- 4 Eggs
- Salt And Pepper
- 2 Tomatoes, Peeled, Seeded, And Coarsely Chopped
- 2 Green Onions, Chopped

How to make it

1. Take a large pan and at mid heat pour some olive oil.
2. Put in the potatoes and dash in salt and pepper.
3. Cook the mix till it's crisp and golden in color.
4. Now the time is right to put in the onions.
5. Stir regularly, whilst beating the eggs with pepper and salt in a bowl. Now pour the egg mix to the pan and lower the flames.
6. Cook till the eggs are brown in color at the bottom.
7. Loosen the base of the omelet and turn it over.
8. Now cook the uncooked side.
9. Serve the omelet with green onions and tomato. Eat warm.

Eggs & Rice

- **Prep Time:** 2 mins
- **Total Time:** 7 mins
- **Servings:** 2-10

Ingredients

- Rice (Left Over)
- 1 -2 Tablespoon Butter
- 3 -4 Eggs
- Salt And Pepper

How to make it

1. Start by melting the butter over a pan before putting in the rice.
2. Mix them up well before pouring in whipped eggs to the pan.
3. Scramble and mix well and serve.

<u>Scotch Eggs</u>

- **Prep Time:** 10 mins
- **Total Time:** 15 mins
- **Servings:** 12

Ingredients

- 12 Hard-Boiled Eggs, Well Chilled
- 2 Lbs Sausage Meat
- 1/2 Cup Flour
- 4 Eggs, Beaten
- 1 1/2 Cups Panko Breadcrumbs
- Vegetable Oil, Frying (About A Cup)

How to make it

1. Begin with peeling eggs and distributing the sausages to twelve same parts. Roll up the eggs with flour and cover it with sausage.
2. Cover the sausage-egg with whipped eggs and Panko crumbs. With oil, cook the eggs at 350 F for 5 minutes or so.
3. Remove the excess oil with a paper napkin and eat the dish warm or cold as per your choice.

Egg and Chive Tea Sandwiches

- **Prep Time:** 5 mins
- **Total Time:** 11 mins
- **Serves:** 4, **Yield:** 4 Rounds Sandwiches

Ingredients

- 4 Medium Free Range Eggs
- 1 Tablespoon Salad Cream
- 2 Tablespoons Mayonnaise
- 1 Tablespoon Finely Chopped Fresh Chives
- 8 Slices Thin Sliced Brown Bread
- Butter, Softened, For Spreading
- Salt And Pepper

How to make it

1. Take a tiny pan and pour a bit of water in it to cover the surface along with the eggs. Boil the eggs for 6 minutes before draining the water and cooling the eggs down.
2. Take the skin off and mash the eggs in a bowl. Combine the mix with mayo, salad cream, chives and with salt-pepper.
3. Take out the crust of bread with a knife and place them towards one side for making breadcrumbs.
4. Spread butter over the bread and distribute the egg mix over 4 pieces. Top it up with rest of the breads.

5. Pile up two sandwiches with each and piece them into three before serving.

Tips:-

- Pierce off the rounded side of each egg with the help of a pin so that the shell does not crack up.
- Cooling down the eggs with cold water halts the extra cooking and also stops the formation of the dark circle.
- If you need to peel off the eggs quickly, then place it under cold water in a colander to gather up all the shell pieces.
- The water halts the shell from fixing to your hands and also to the egg.

Huevos Rancheros

- **Prep Time:** 10 mins
- **Total Time:** 30 mins
- **Servings:** 4

Ingredients

- 4 (6 Inch) Corn Tortillas
- 1 Cup Canned Refried Beans
- 2 Tablespoons Unsalted Butter Or 2 Tablespoons Vegetable Oil
- 8 Large Eggs
- Salt And Black Pepper, Freshly Ground
- 1/2 Cup Monterey Jack Cheese, Grated
- 1 Avocado
- 2 Teaspoons Lime Juice, Fresh
- 1/2 Cup Prepared Salsa
- 1/2 Cup Sour Cream
- 1/4 Cup Fresh Cilantro, Coarsely Chopped
- 1 Green Onion, White And Green Parts (Thinly Sliced On The Bias)

How to make it

1. Start by preheating up the broiler and placing in the tortillas for toasting then each on a pan or over the naked flame.

2. Put in a baking sheet, cover each of the tortillas with quarter cup of re-fried beans and cover it to keep it hot and warm.

3. You will have batches to work with.

4. Now take a large pan or skillet, put butter in it and at mid-high flames heat it.

5. Break the eggs in over the pan and lower the flames to mid-low or even low. Cook the eggs and shake it well so that the eggs do not stick up. Dash in pepper and salt and cook as per your liking but keep the yellow side up.

6. For sunny side the time should be 2 minutes, for medium yolks 3 minutes and for hard, 4. Or if the whites have become opaque, flip over the eggs and let it heat for further half a minute for easy; a full minute for medium and 2 for hard.

7. Make sure to top up each tortilla with two fried and made eggs along with two tablespoons of cheese (grated).

8. Put the tortillas inside the broiler so that the cheese can melt.

9. Finally, piece up the avocado and mix it with lime juice to make sure that the avocado keeps it color.

10. Make sure that you top each of the serve with two tablespoons of sour cream and two table spoons again of salsa.

11. Distribute the avocado over the tortillas.

12. Serve each of the tortilla with one table spoon of cilantro and also one table spoon worth of green onion.

Egg Salad

- **Prep Time:** 10 mins
- **Total Time:** 10 mins
- **Servings:** 4

Ingredients

- 4 Tablespoons Tahini
- 4 Tablespoons Fresh Lemon Juice
- 4 Garlic Cloves, Crushed
- 1/4 Cup Fresh Parsley, Finely Chopped
- Salt And Pepper, To Taste
- 6 Hard-Boiled Eggs, Mashed
- 2 Tablespoons Water
- 1/2 Teaspoon Paprika

How to make it

1. Put the lemon juice and the tahini over a blender and let it rip for few seconds.
2. Then shift the mix to a bowl (use an immersion blender). Now put in parsley, pepper-salt, garlic, water and eggs to the mix and combine them up well.
3. Put the mix in a plate and garnish with paprika and serve it well.

Hamburgers With Eggs

- **Prep Time:** 8 mins
- **Total Time:** 23 mins
- **Servings:** 4

Ingredients

- 1 1/2 Lbs Ground Sirloin, Shaped Into 4 Patties
- 4 Teaspoons Butter
- 4 Tablespoons Butter
- 4 Eggs
- 6 -12 Anchovy Fillets (Optional)
- 2 Tablespoons Capers, Drained
- 1 Tablespoon Parsley, Finely Chopped
- Salt & Freshly Ground Black Pepper

How to make it

1. Start with dashing in the salt-pepper over the patties and grill up the burgers.
2. Shift the patties to a plate, and then begin with the eggs.
3. Warm up butter worth four teaspoons over a pan/skillet and break the eggs in them.
4. Cook them, with the tops on the front, till they get white.
5. Take out the eggs from the pan and put each egg over the pattie.

6. Put in some pepper and salt over the eggs. Put anchovies on the front if desired.

7. Warm up four tablespoons over a pan and put in the parsley and capers when they become hot.

8. As soon as the butter gets brown, put in sauce equally over the pattie and eat.

****

Egg Curry

- **Prep Time:** 10 mins
- **Total Time:** 55 mins
- **Servings:** 4

Ingredients

- 1 Spanish Onion, Chopped
- 2 Tablespoons Grated Fresh Ginger
- 2 Garlic Cloves, Crushed
- 2 Tablespoons Light Oil
- 2 Tablespoons Good-Quality Curry Powder
- 1/2 Teaspoon Ground Turmeric
- 1 Cinnamon Stick
- 10 Fresh Curry Leaves
- 425 G Diced Tomatoes
- 8 Hard-Boiled Eggs
- 1/3 Cup Red Lentil

- 1 Cup Peas (Frozen Are Fine)
- 2 Tablespoons Chopped Fresh Coriander
- Cooked Rice, To Serve

How to make it

1. Begin with putting in the garlic, ginger and the onion in a processor and make a paste.
2. Now take a saucepan, heat oil over it, place i n the paste and let it sauté for 3 minutes or so.
3. Then put in the spices and cook a minute further.
4. The mix will emit the flavors. Pour 2 cups of water and the tomatoes; boil it.
5. Now shell the eggs up and put in the pan with peas and lentils.
6. If the mix becomes thick, pour in half a cup of water.
7. Cook the mix at low for quarter of an hour. Place in the coriander and eat with rice.

Eggs and Onions

- **Prep Time:** 10 mins
- **Total Time:** 20 mins
- **Servings:** 4

Ingredients

- Olive Oil
- 1/2 Large Onion, Chopped
- 1/2 Red Bell Pepper, Cut Into Bite Size Pieces
- 8 Eggs, Scrambled
- 6 Ounces Smoked Salmon, Cut Into Bite Size Pieces (Lox)

How to make it

1. Slightly fry the onions and the pepper with the olive oil. Fry till they are done well.
2. Put in the lox pieces and cook further 5 minutes till they become opaque.
3. Toss the eggs and scramble them.
4. Cook the eggs as per you like it. You can also use egg beaters along with couple of eggs with great results.

Eggs Poached in Tomato Sauce

- **Prep Time:** 10 mins
- **Total Time:** 30 mins
- **Servings:** 2-4

Ingredients

- 1 1/2 Tablespoons Olive Oil Or 1 1/2 Tablespoons Butter
- 1 Small Onion, Finely Chopped
- 1 Garlic Clove, Finely Chopped
- 4 -5 Medium Tomatoes, Peeled, Seeded And Chopped
- Salt (To Taste)
- Pepper (To Taste)
- 4 Eggs
- 1 Tablespoon Chives, Finely Chopped

How to make it

1. Begin with putting in the oil over a non sticky pan and heat it at mid-hi flames.

2. Put the garlic and the onions and let it fry a bit before lowering the heat to mid flames. Cook the veggies till the onions are colored.

3. Now add tomatoes and cook for 10 minutes before dashing in the pepper and the salt.

4. If the sauce is done, take a spoon to make four circular wells, over in every quarter of the skillet.

5. Break every egg and put them in the holes. Put the lid on partially, so that moisture and heat can go through and cook your eggs till your own preferred density.

6. Take out the eggs and add it and sauce over the plates. Serve with chives.

7. Eat with hot pita or even flatbreads.

Tip:

- You can make this dish extra spicy by just dashing in a bit of chili over the onions.
- If you do this, then you might as well not use the chives too as parsley will be a better option.

<u>Breakfast Club Sandwich</u>

- **Prep Time:** 15 mins
- **Total Time:** 35 mins
- **Servings:** 6

Ingredients

- 18 Slices Bacon (About A 1 Lb Package)
- 12 Eggs, Lightly Beaten
- 3/4 Cup Mayonnaise
- Salt And Pepper
- 18 Slices Tomatoes
- 12 Leaves Boston Lettuce
- 12 Slices Sandwich Bread
- Toothpick

How to make it

1. Place the rake right at the middle of the oven and preheat it to 425 F or 220 C.
2. Put a 15 into 10 inch of a dish with a paper of parchment sheet and make sure the sheet cover the whole plate and beyond.
3. Grease up the sheet with oil and also the sides of the plate. Now put in the bacon over the plate.
4. Now cook the plate for quarter of an hour till they crisp up. Remove the extra fat of the bacon and keep it aside.

5. Now take a bowl combine the eggs and 60 milliliter of mayo, before dashing in the pepper and salt.

6. Put the mix over a dish and bake it for 12 minutes or so. Piece up the omelet in six pieces and keep it aside.

7. Heat the bacon again.

8. For serving, prepare 3 pieces of bread and put mayo over its top. Over one slice, place in the eggs and 3 pieces of bacon.

9. Cover it with bread before putting in lettuce leaves (2) and tomatoes (3) over it.

10. Put in the final bread piece to complete the whole sandwich.

11. Place in a toothpick over all the corners and piece it on triangles.

12. Do the same with rest of the materials.

Baked Eggs in Tomato Cups

- **Prep Time:** 0 mins
- **Total Time:** 25 mins
- **Servings:** 8

Ingredients

- 8 Large Tomatoes
- 1/3 Cup Fresh Grated Parmesan Cheese
- 8 Medium Eggs
- 1 Teaspoon Herbs, Of Your Choice See Note
- 4 Slices Cheddar Cheese Or 4 Slices American Cheese, Sliced Into Four Pieces
- Salt
- Fresh Ground Pepper

How to make it

1. You should first make sure that the tomatoes should absolutely be fresh and you should be able to make holes in them.
2. But the top should be buttery on the next day.
3. Herbs you need: Chervil, Oregano, Sage, Basil and of course Mrs Dash.
4. Start by preheating the over at 425 F whilst slicing up the tomatoes. Take out the top, and remove the pulp and the seeds of the fruit.

5. Put in a deep baking plate, dash in bit of salt (or even Mrs Dash, preferably Italian), a bit of parmesan and even freshly ground pepper.

6. Break up the eggs straight inside the tomatoes.

7. Put in Mrs Dash or salt, pepper, parmesan and the herbs. Cook for 20 mins or so for softening the yellow, 35 mins to make them hard.

8. During the final minutes (5 mins before) put in the 2 cheddar cheese pieces and form a cross pattern with it.

9. Let them melt and put in a bit of chives over the top of the cheese.

10. This dish will easily serve eight people.

<u>Migas Lite</u>

- **Prep Time:** 10 mins
- **Total Time:** 20 mins
- **Servings:** 2

Ingredients

- 4 Teaspoons Olive Oil, Divided
- 3 Corn Tortillas, Cut In Strips
- 1/2 Small Onion, Chopped
- 1 Raw Jalapeno Pepper, Seeded And Diced
- 1 Small Plum Tomato, Diced
- 1 Cup Egg Substitute
- 2 Ounces Left Over Shredded Pork Or 2 Ounces Beef Roast
- Salt And Pepper
- 1/4 Cup Reduced-Fat Monterey Jack Cheese Or 1/4 Cup Cheddar Cheese, Grated
- Salsa
- Avocado, Slices

How to make it

1. Start by warming the oil over a pan before adding in the tortilla strips and frying them till they become brown but not crispy.
2. Place in the jalapeno and the onion, cook for 2 minutes, and pour a bit more oil if require. Now add the tomato and cook for 2 minutes.

3. Put in the shred meat and the eggs substitute and stir and let it cook before adding in pepper-salt.

4. Place in the cheese over the egg mix and put a lid on before switching off the heat till the cheese gets melted.

5. Eat the dish with your best salsa, extra corn tortillas or even avocados if needed.

*****

All-In-One Egg Casserole

- **Prep Time:** 15 mins
- **Total Time:** 35 mins
- **Servings:** 4-6

Ingredients

- 10 Bacon, Strips Diced
- 1 Cup Sliced Fresh Mushrooms
- 1/2 Cup Sliced Green Onion
- 1/4 Cup Butter, Cubed
- 1/4 Cup All-Purpose Flour
- 1/4 Teaspoon Salt
- 1/4 Teaspoon Pepper
- 2 Cups Milk
- 1 1/2 Cups Shredded Cheddar Cheese

SCRAMBLED EGGS

- 8 Eggs
- 1/2 Cup Milk
- 1/2 Teaspoon Pepper
- 1/4 Teaspoon Salt
- 4 English Muffins, Split, Toasted And Lightly Buttered
- 2 Tablespoons Fresh Parsley, Minced

How to make it

1. Take a big pan, cook the bacon in it till they become crispy and then take out the bacon.
2. Throw away all but two tablespoons worth of drippings.
3. Now slightly fry the onions and the mushrooms till they become soft. Now take a large pan, put in the butter before adding the salt, pepper, flour and cook till they smooth out.
4. Pour in the cheese and the milk slowly and thicken up the mix. Put in the mushroom, bacon and the onions before turning off the heat.
5. To prepare the scrambled eggs, first whip in the eggs with pepper-salt and the milk.
6. Put the mix over an oily pan and cook it well till the eggs are done. Now piece up the English muffins in quarters and put them over an eleven into 7 inch of cooking plate.
7. Now pour in half of the sauce of cheese and put in the eggs over the top and again pour in the sauce.
8. Dash in parsley on top.

9. Let it bake now (without any cover) for roughly 25 minutes at 325, till the dish become bubbly.

*****

Poached Eggs Florentine

- **Prep Time:** 10 mins
- **Total Time:** 30 mins
- **Servings:** 2

Ingredients

CHEESE SAUCE

- 2 Teaspoons Cornstarch
- 1/3 Cup 2% Low-Fat Milk
- 2 Tablespoons Butter
- 3 Tablespoons Gruyere Cheese, Grated
- 1 Dash Kosher Salt, To Taste
- 1 Dash Black Pepper, To Taste
- 1 Dash Nutmeg (Optional)

SPINACH

- 1/2 Tablespoon Olive Oil
- 2 Green Onions, Chopped Or 1/4 Cup Thinly Sliced Leek
- 2 Cups Fresh Baby Spinach
- 1/4 Teaspoon Dill Weed

- 1 Dash Kosher Salt, To Taste
- 1 Dash Black Pepper, To Taste

EGGS

- 1 Teaspoon Vinegar
- 2 Eggs Or 1 Cup Egg Beaters Egg Substitute
- 2 Slices Whole Wheat Bread, Toasted
- 1 Dash Paprika, Garnish

How to make it

1. First the Cheese sauce:
2. Combine the cornstarch to a paste with around quarter cup of milk. Now take a pan, put in the remaining milk and the butter in it and boil them up.
3. Pour in the boiled milk over the cornstarch mix and pour the lot back in to the pan. Boil again till it is thick.
4. Now take off the pan from the heat, put in the gruyere cheese, pepper, nutmeg and the salt.
5. Now put parchment sheet over the top of the sauce so that the cover does not skin up.

For the Spinach:

1. Now heat up the oil over a large pan, place in the onions (or the leeks) and slightly fry it for 3 minutes or so.

2. Put in the spinach and combine it well for 3 minutes over mid flames. Check if the spinach has become wilted or not and if the leeks are soft.

3. Throw away the water, put the veggies in a strainer or a sieve and totally take out the any moisture with the help of a spoon.

4. Get back to the pan and put in some dill, pepper and salt. Put the lid on and keep it hot.

Now the eggs:

1. Half fill in a midsized pan with clear water and boil it.

2. Pour in vinegar over it before breaking in the eggs and cooking it for four minutes. Spoon up the boiled water over the yellows.

3. Take the eggs out and get them dry with paper. Heat up the broiler and put in the wheat based toast slices over the baking paper. Put the spinach mix over them.

4. Make some space over the spinach with a spoon and put in the eggs over them.

5. Spoons up the cheese over the eggs; top it with paprika. Broil it well till they brown up.

Breakfast Pita Pizza

- **Prep Time:** 5 mins
- **Total Time:** 17 mins
- **Servings:** 2

Ingredients

- 1 Tablespoon Olive Oil
- 1/4 Cup Finely Chopped Red Onion
- 1 Small Finely Chopped Red Bell Pepper
- 2 Large Eggs, Beaten
- 1/2 Teaspoon Salt
- 14 Teaspoons Ground Black Pepper, To Taste
- 1 (6 Inch) Whole Wheat Pita Bread, Cut In Half And Lightly Toasted
- 1/4 Cup Grated Sharp Low-Fat Cheddar Cheese
- 4 Slices Pancetta Or 1 Slice Bacon, Cooked And Cut Into Small Pieces

How to make it

1. Start with heating olive oil over a non sticky skillet or pan. Slightly fry the onions over it for couple of minutes.
2. Dash in the red pepper and cook it for 3 minutes. Now put the eggs and scramble them well.
3. Put in salt-pepper and turn off the heat. Preheat the broiler or your oven and distribute the egg mix over the pitas.

4. Full up and top every pita with half cheese and half bacon or pancetta. Toast it or broil it till you see the cheese is melting.

5. Eat warm!

****

Fluffy Omelet

- **Prep Time:** 5 mins
- **Total Time:** 5 mins
- **Servings:** 2

Ingredients

- 3 -4 Large Eggs
- 1/8 Teaspoon Baking Powder (This Will Create A Fluffy Omelet)
- 2 Tablespoons Whipping Cream (Unwhipped)
- Salt And Pepper
- 2 Tablespoons Butter (Can Use More Or Less!)
- 1/4 Cup Monterey Jack Cheese, Shredded (Can Use More)
- 1 Green Onion, Finely Chopped (Optional)

How to make it

1. Take a bowl whip the eggs and put in the cream, baking powder, salt, green onion, pepper, and salt.

2. Heat up an eight inch pan at mid flames, put in the butter and cover the surface of it well.

3. Now break in the eggs over the pan, let them place. Use a spatula, move the eggs from the edge towards the middle and let the eggs fill up the blocks.

4. Make a good omelet and lift up the pan if needed. Throw in some cheese over the middle of the omelet.

5. Now take the spatula and fold up the omelet over the cheese. Now take the pan and remove the eggs to a plate.

6. Make sure your eggs do not break up that much.

******

Hidden Eggs

- **Prep Time:** 5 mins
- **Total Time:** 25 mins
- **Servings:** 3-4

Ingredients

- 6 -8 Slices Bread, Tore Into Bite Size Pieces
- 4 Tablespoons Butter, Melted And Divided
- 6 Eggs
- Salt And Pepper
- 1 -2 Cup Cheddar Cheese, Shredded

How to make it

1. Begin with preheating the oven at 350 F.

2. Now take a large pan, cover it with broken bread and add 2 tablespoon of butter over it.

3. Break the eggs over the bread and give pepper-salt. Give more bread over the eggs.

4. Give rest of the butter and top it with the cheese pieces.

5. Cook it for 20 minutes or so till they eggs are good to eat.

****

Egg Salad Sandwich

- **Prep Time:** 5 mins
- **Total Time:** 15 mins
- **Servings:** 3

Ingredients

- 6 Hard-Boiled Eggs
- 3 Tablespoons Mayonnaise (I Use Light Mayo On Mine, Don't Care For Salad Dressing, Use More Mayo If Needed)
- 1 Tablespoon Mustard (I Use Regular Yellow Mustard)
- 1 Tablespoon Relish
- Pepper (Optional)
- Lettuce (Optional)
- 6 Slices Whole Wheat Bread (Any Type Will Do)

How to make it

1. Piece up the boiled eggs well.

2. After this combine one 1 tablespoon mayo each, so that the quantity can be maintained.

3. Combine pepper, relish and the mustard.

4. Place the egg mix over the bread (toasted) and over the rolls for finger snacks. Do remember to put lettuce over the sandwich.

****

Cheese Scrambled Eggs

- **Prep Time:** 5 mins
- **Total Time:** 15 mins
- **Servings:** 4

Ingredients

- 3 Ounces Cream Cheese, Softened
- 1/4 Cup Milk
- 4 Eggs, To 6
- 1 Teaspoon Chives, Chopped
- 1 Teaspoon Salt
- 2 Tablespoons Butter
- 4 Slices Bread, Crusts Removed, Buttered

How to make it

1. Whip cream cheese well before it smoothens up.

2. Pour milk, put salt, chives and the eggs.

3. Whip or whisk it well till it's dense.

4. Now take a pan, melt some butter over it, when it's hot enough put the egg mix over it.

5. Cook it at mid flames and keep stirring the eggs from the middle and the sides.

6. Make sure they are cooked well. Shift the eggs in toast cups and top it with chives.

To ready the toast cup:

1. Butter up both fronts of the bread.

2. Put the bread over greased muffins cups.

3. The edges will make points. Bake them at 350 till they get brown in color.

4. The cups can be made beforehand but remember to reheat them before you serve it.

Basted Eggs

- **Prep Time:** 15 mins
- **Total Time:** 40 mins
- **Servings:** 4

Ingredients

- 2 Tablespoons Olive Oil
- 1 Onion, Chopped
- 1/2 Red Bell Pepper, Chopped
- 1/2 Green Bell Pepper, Chopped
- 4 Tomatoes, Chopped
- 4 Eggs

How to make it

1. Get a lid equipped pan, heat oil over it before adding the peppers and the onions.
2. Cook for a minute before adding the tomatoes and covering the pan for a cook of 10 minutes.
3. Put in pepper-salt and break the eggs over the sauce top.
4. Cook till you feel the eggs are done. Eat and enjoy!

Cheese Strata

- **Prep Time:** 24 hrs
- **Total Time:** 24 hrs 50 mins
- **Servings:** 6

Ingredients

- 1 Lb Cheddar Cheese, Grated
- 9 Slices White Bread, Crusts Removed
- Salt, To Taste
- Black Pepper, To Taste
- 1 1/2 Tablespoons Dried Onion
- 4 Eggs
- 3 Cups Milk
- 1 Teaspoon Worcestershire Sauce
- 1 Teaspoon Dry Mustard

How to make it

1. Take grease casserole, and then preheat the oven at 325 F.
2. Piece up three slices of bread in three strips.
3. Put it inside the casserole. Put one-third onion, pepper and salt.
4. Add in one-third of cheese and repeat the layers twice. Whip eggs; pour milk, sauce and the mustard over it before putting all of it over the bread. Cool it overnight in the fridge.
5. Take the mix out 2 hours before baking it. Bake for an hour or so at 325 F.

Frittata

- **Prep Time:** 5 mins
- **Total Time:** 25 mins
- **Yield:** 6 wedges

Ingredients

- 3 Tablespoons Extra Virgin Olive Oil (EVOO)
- 1/4 Lb Chorizo Sausage, Casing Removed And Chopped
- 2 Large Boiling Potatoes, Cut In Half And Thinly Sliced (White)
- 1 Small Onion, Thinly Sliced
- 4 Garlic Cloves, Chopped
- 12 Extra-Large Eggs (Or 1 Quart Of Pasteurized Egg Yolks)
- 1/3 Cup Half-And-Half (Eyeball It)
- 1 Teaspoon Salt
- Black Pepper
- 1/4 Lb Manchego Cheese, Grated
- 1/2 Cup Flat Leaf Parsley, Chopped (A Couple Of Handfuls)

How to make it

1. Being with preheating the oven at 400 F.
2. Take an oven proof 12 inch pan and heat it at mid-hi flames.
3. Put in the chorizo and the EVOO and let it cook till the Chorizo is crispy. Put in the potatoes and the onions and cook it for 5 minutes till the potatoes are soft.

4. Put the garlic in. Now put in the eggs along with half & half and put salt-pepper.

5. Put the eggs in and let it set.

6. Take a spatula and remove the bottom of the pan; allowing the egg's liquid to settle it.

7. As soon as the frittata is positioned, dash it with cheese and shift it to the oven. Cook for 12 minutes further, till it becomes golden.

8. Take it off and let it stay for 5 minutes. Serve with parsley and cut as per your wish.

****

Cheese Special

- **Prep Time:** 10 mins
- **Total Time:** 10 mins
- **Servings:** 1

Ingredients

- 2 Slices Bacon, Cooked And Crumbled
- 2 Eggs
- 1 Slice American Cheese Or 1 Slice Cheddar Cheese
- 1 Slice Bread, Toasted
- Salt And Pepper

How to make it

1. Start with the putting Pam on a pan and pre heat it at mid flames, till you feel the water is gone.

2. Put in the eggs (keep the yellow part in tact). Put a lid on it and cook for 5 minutes at mid heat, or as per your yolk preference.

3. Toast your breads and put in cheese slices before adding the eggs, pepper-salt and the bacon over it.

Tip: You can also break the eggs over a bowl and whip it before putting it in the pan.

******

<u>Eggs and Bacon</u>

- **Prep Time:** 20 mins
- **Total Time:** 40 mins
- **Servings:** 6

Ingredients

- 2 Tablespoons Butter Or 2 Tablespoons Margarine
- 1/4 Cup Chopped Onion
- 2 Tablespoons All-Purpose Flour
- 1 1/2 Cups Milk
- 1/2 Cup Shredded Swiss Cheese
- 1/2 Cup Shredded American Cheese
- 6 Hard-Boiled Eggs, Sliced

- 12 Slices Crisp Bacon, Cooked And Crumbled
- 1 1/2 Cups Packaged Fried Onions

How to make it

1. Begin with pre heating the oven to 350 F degrees. Melt up butter over a large enough pan or skillet at mid flames.
2. Put in the finely chopped onion and slightly fry it.
3. Put flour and mix it well before pouring in the milk. Now add the cheeses and let them melt.
4. Put half of the eggs over the end of a dish.
5. Put in half of the cheese mix over it.
6. Put half bacon and half of the sautéed onions. Repeat it again for the next layer.
7. Bake the dish without any lid for 20 minutes.

<u>Smoky Hard Boiled Eggs</u>

- **Prep Time:** 1 min
- **Total Time:** 14 mins
- **Servings:** 12

Ingredients

- 1 Dozen Egg
- 1 Cup Soy Sauce
- 2 Tablespoons Liquid Smoke

How to make it

1. Boil up the eggs and then cool then under water before peeling.
2. Put in the soy sauce over the eggs and liquid smoke them all over a bowl.
3. Put a lid on it and let it fridge up.
4. Flip the eggs till all the sides golden up.
5. Eat it fresh!

Italian Egg Sandwiches

- **Prep Time:** 5 mins
- **Total Time:** 10 mins
- **Servings:** 1

Ingredients

- 2 Slices Good Quality Bread, Toasted Pretty Crunchy, Per Person
- 1 Tablespoon Pizza Sauce, Per Slice
- 2 Eggs, Per Person
- Garlic Salt
- Parmesan Cheese

How to make it

1. Begin first by toasting your bread (you can use D'Annuzios).
2. Use a good cibatta, French or Italian. Sauté the eggs as per your own taste and then dash in some salt and garlic over it.
3. Fire up the pizza sauce over a microwave and cover it over the toasts. You can use more than 1 tbsp of sauce as per your preference.
4. Put your eggs over the sauce and top it with parmesan.
5. You can also use spaghetti, marina or even tomato sauce. But you can also use good pizza sauce!

<u>Creamy Baked Egg</u>

- **Prep Time:** 5 mins
- **Total Time:** 25 mins
- **Servings:** 2

Ingredients

- 1 Tablespoon Butter
- 4 Eggs
- 2 Tablespoons Parmesan Cheese
- Salt, To Taste
- Pepper, To Taste
- 1/4 Cup Heavy Cream

How to make it

1. Start with preheating the oven at 325 degrees.
2. Now butter up 2 eight OZ Ramekins and break two eggs over each side. Keep the yellows intact.
3. Throw in the parmesan over the top and then the pepper-salt.
4. Pour in 2 table tablespoons of the cream on top of the eggs mix at every ramekin.
5. Now put the ramekins over the cookie paper and let it bake for 20 minutes.

Egg in the Basket

- **Prep Time:** 1 min
- **Total Time:** 4 mins
- **Servings:** 1

Ingredients

- Egg
- Bread
- Butter
- Salt And Pepper

How to make it

1. Make a round at the center of the bread.
2. If you do not have cookie cutter, then use a glass to do it. Heat up a pan and pour in Mazola or the pam.
3. Put the bread on the pan.
4. Place half of the butter over the holes of the bread. Now heat up the butter, till it melts.
5. Now break up the eggs and move the whites to get it done.
6. When the eggs are done, flip the bread and the egg over to the other side. Keep the yellow intact.
7. Whilst doing this, toast up the holes from the bread, so that the dipping can be accommodated. Now put in the pepper-salt.
8. You can also try to toast up the breads before you pan it up.

Ham and Eggs Benedict

- **Prep Time:** 7 mins
- **Total Time:** 17 mins
- **Servings:** 4

Ingredients

- 4 Frozen Biscuits
- 2 Tablespoons Butter, Melted
- 3 Tablespoons Fresh Chives, Chop And Divide
- 1 (1 Ounce) Package Hollandaise Sauce Mix (Or Make Your Own)
- 1 Cup Milk
- 1 Tablespoon Lemon Juice
- 3/4 Cup Cooked Ham, Chopped
- 1/4-1/2 Teaspoon Ground Red Pepper (Optional)
- 1/2 Teaspoon White Vinegar
- 4 Large Eggs

- 2 Cups Loosely Pack Arugula (Optional)
- 1 Small Avocado, Sliced (Optional)
- Black Pepper, To Taste

How to make it

1. Start with baking the biscuits as per the instructions.

2. Mix up the butter, 1 tbsp of chives and split the biscuits and brush up with the mix.

3. Put the biscuits (keep the buttered side on top) over a baking paper and bake it for 5 minutes at 375F.

4. In the mean time, get the hollandaise ready; make use of the milk and the lemon liquid but leave out the butter.

5. Slightly fry up the ham in a pan at mid-flames for 3 minutes. Add red pepper over the Hollandaise and keep it warm.

6. Pour in the water till two inches over a pan.

7. Boil it up and lower the heat. Put in half a teaspoon of white vinegar.

8. Break the eggs one each over big serving spoon and put it in the water. Boil it for 5 minutes or till desired.

9. Now take out the slotted spoon and trim the edges over a sharp knife.

For serving purpose:

- Put the bottom of the biscuit at half and butter it up and put on the four plates.

- Prep it with arugula, pieces of avocado and over the eggs. Put in the hollandaise mix over the eggs.

- Top it with chives and pepper.

- Serve with the biscuits.

<u>Eggs and Beets</u>

- **Prep Time:** 15 mins
- **Total Time:** 15 mins
- **Servings:** 6

Ingredients

- 1 Cup Cider Vinegar
- 1 Cup Beet Juice (Add Water, If Necessary, To Make 1 Cup)
- 1/2 Cup Brown Sugar (Packed)
- 1 Teaspoon Salt
- 6 Hard-Boiled Eggs, Shelled
- 1 (15 Ounce) Cans Small Round Beets

How to make it

1. Firstly boil the 4 materials for 5 minutes.
2. Now let the liquid cool down and put in the eggs and the beets.
3. Now keep it in the fridge for one night at least or 3 days maximum. Serve with eggs.

Bacon and Egg Sandwich

- **Prep Time:** 5 mins
- **Total Time:** 20 mins
- **Servings:** 1

Ingredients

- 2 Slices White Bread
- 3 Slices Crisp Bacon
- 1 Fried Egg
- Sliced Tomatoes
- Miracle Whip

How to make it

1. Start with spreading a bread piece with miracle Whip. Put in the fired egg now.
2. Whilst the egg is under the heat, break up the yellow with a metal or steel spatula.
3. Cover the eggs with the miracle whip.
4. Now put the bacon over the layer and then tomatoes.
5. Finally put the miracle whip layered bread.

No Brainer Cheese and Egg Souffle

- **Prep Time:** 10 mins
- **Total Time:** 40 mins
- **Servings:** 3

Ingredients

- 6 Eggs
- 1/3 Cup Milk
- Garlic Salt
- Fresh Ground Black Pepper
- Mozzarella Cheese, Shredded

How to make it

1. Take a bowl, combine milk, eggs, garlic salt and the pepper.
2. Put three ramekins with non-sticky oil spray and half fill with the cheese.
3. Put the egg mix over it now.
4. Now put the ramekins over the sheet and let it bake for 375 for half an hour. Eat warm and hot.

<u>VEGAN RECIPES</u>

<u>NEW Vegan Pancakes</u>

- **Prep Time:** 5 mins
- **Total Time:** 15 mins
- **Serves:** 2, **Yield:** 6-8 pancakes

Ingredients :-

- 1 Cup Flour (Whichever Kind You Prefer)
- 1 Tablespoon Sugar (I Used Organic Cane Sugar)
- 2 Tablespoons Baking Powder
- 1/8 Teaspoon Salt
- 1 Cup Soymilk
- 2 Tablespoons Vegetable Oil

How to make it:

1. Put a medium pan on stove for preheating.
2. Mix the flour, sugar, baking powder and salt in a bowl as per measurement.
3. When mixed, add the vegetable oil and the soy milk to it.
4. When the batter is smooth, take one spoon of batter and put it on the preheated pan.
5. As the edges stiffen and bubbles appear in the middle, flip the pancake carefully.

<u>Vegan Bacon</u>

- **Prep Time:** 5 mins
- **Total Time:** 25 mins
- **Servings:** 3-4

Ingredients

- 1 Lb Firm Tofu, Cut Into Strips Shaped Like Bacon
- 2 Tablespoons Nutritional Yeast
- 2 Tablespoons Soya Sauce
- 1 Teaspoon Liquid Smoke
- 1 Tablespoon Oil, Something Neutral, Not Olive Oil

How to make it:

1. Place the tofu strips in a pan with a little oil, for 10 minutes on each side and fry them until crispy.
2. Mix together the liquid smoke and soya sauce and add it to the tofu.
3. When coated on all sides, sprinkle the yeast so that a sticky consistency is achieved.

<u>Easy Vegan Pancakes</u>

- **Prep Time:** 10 mins
- **Total Time:** 20 mins
- **Servings:** 4

Ingredients :-

- 2 1/2 Cups All-Purpose Flour
- 2 Tablespoons Sugar
- 2 Tablespoons Baking Powder
- 1 Tablespoon Vegetable Oil
- 1 Teaspoon Salt
- 2 1/2 Cups Soymilk Or 2 1/2 Cups Water
- 1 Dash Cinnamon (Optional)

How to make it:

1. Lightly mix all the ingredients in a large bowl.
2. Let the mixture rest for 3 to 5 minutes.
3. Fold it a few times, but do not over-mix or over-fold.
4. On a medium sized griddle or skillet, cook the pancakes on medium heat.
5. Flip over and serve hot.

<u>Vegan French Toast</u>

- **Prep Time:** 2 mins
- **Total Time:** 7 mins
- **Servings:** 4-6

Ingredients :-

- 1 Cup Vanilla-Flavored Soymilk
- 2 Tablespoons Flour
- 1 Tablespoon Sugar
- 1 Tablespoon Nutritional Yeast
- 1 Teaspoon Cinnamon
- 4 -6 Slices Bread (Slightly Stale Is Best)

How to make it:-

1. Add the first 5 ingredients.
2. Take a piece of bread and dip it in the mixture.
3. Cook until golden-brown in a skillet.

Bacon with a Vegan

- **Prep Time:** 5 mins
- **Total Time:** 30 mins
- **Servings:** 4

Ingredients :-

- 1 Tablespoon Oil, Neutral Tasting (Don't Use Extra Virgin Olive Oil-Too Strong)
- 1 (14 Ounce) Packages Firm Tofu, Cut Into Strips (To Resemble Bacon)
- 2 Tablespoons Soy Sauce (I Use Bragg's Aminos)
- 1 Teaspoon Liquid Smoke
- 2 Teaspoons Brown Sugar (I Might Try Molasses Next Time)
- 2 Tablespoons Nutritional Yeast
- Fresh Ground Black Pepper (Optional)

How to make it:

1. Let oil heat up in a large skillet.
2. Fry bacon strips until crispy. Make sure to do it on low flame and when they are firm, turn them.
3. Mix together the soy sauce, brown sugar and the liquid smoke, stir until the sugar dissolves.
4. Removing the skillet from heat, add the soy sauce mix to the tofu and coat it properly. Place the skillet back to heat.

5. On the tofu, sprinkle freshly ground black pepper and the nutritional yeast.

****

<u>Vegan Banana Muffins</u>

- **Prep Time:** 10 mins
- **Total Time:** 30 mins
- **Serves:** 12, **Yield:** 12 muffins

Ingredients :-

- 4 Ripe Bananas
- 1/2 Cup Brown Sugar Or 1/2 Cup Pure Maple Syrup
- 1/2 Cup Vegetable Oil
- 1 Teaspoon Cinnamon
- 1 Teaspoon Cardamom Powder
- 3/4 Teaspoon Salt
- 1 Cup Whole Wheat Flour
- 1 1/2 Cups White Flour
- 1 Teaspoon Baking Powder
- 1 Teaspoon Baking Soda

How to make it:-

1. Grease12 muffin tins.
2. Preheat oven to 350°F.

3. Mix maple syrup or sugar, oil, cinnamon, salt and cardamom.

4. Mash bananas and add the previous mixture to it.

5. Mix flour, baking soda and baking powder to it.

6. Fill the muffin tins with this mix and bake until browned, or for 20-25 minutes.

****

<u>Vegan Pumpkin Pie Pancakes</u>

- **Prep Time:** 15 mins
- **Total Time:** 30 mins
- **Yield:** 10-12 medium-sized pancakes

Ingredients:-

- 1 1/2 Cups Unbleached All-Purpose Flour
- 3 Tablespoons Sugar
- 1 Tablespoon Baking Powder
- 1/2 Teaspoon Salt
- 1/4 Teaspoon Pumpkin Pie Spice
- 1 1/4 Cups Soymilk
- 1/3 Cup Canned Pumpkin
- 1 Tablespoon Vegetable Oil

How to make it:-

1. Mix flour, baking powder, pumpkin pie spice, sugar and salt.

2. Separately mix canned pumpkin, soy milk, and corn oil.

3. Add the wet mix to the dry mix and lightly fold them together.

4. Use this batter to make pancakes.

******

Vegan Breakfast Sausage

- **Prep Time:** 10 mins
- **Total Time:** 20 mins
- **Servings:** 4

Ingredients

- 1 Cup Cooked Brown Rice
- 3/4 Cup Rolled Oats
- 2 Tablespoons Whole Wheat Flour
- 1 Tablespoon Ground Flax Seeds
- 3 Tablespoons Water
- 1 Teaspoon Molasses
- 2 Tablespoons Canola Oil (Divided)
- 2 Tablespoons Nutritional Yeast
- 1 1/2 Tablespoons Tamari
- 1/2 Teaspoon Red Pepper Flakes (Or More If Desired)
- 1 Teaspoon Black Pepper
- 1 1/2 Teaspoons Ground Sage
- 1/4 Teaspoon Nutmeg

- 1/4 Teaspoon Thyme

How to make it:

1. Mix water and flax together.
2. Break the oats in a food processor and also add the pulse and rice to it.
3. Add water and flax mix to it, with 1 table spoon canola oil.
4. When mixed together, make little patties about 1/4" thick, with dampened hands and flatten them.
5. Add 1 table spoon canola oil to a non-stick frying pan.
6. Cook until they are browned.

******

Waffles Perfect

- **Prep Time:** 30 mins
- **Total Time:** 30 mins
- **Serves:** 8-10, **Yield:** 8.0 waffles

Ingredients:-

- 4 Cups Water
- 3 Tablespoons Olive Oil
- 1/4 Cup Natural Cane Sugar
- 2 Teaspoons Vanilla
- 1 Teaspoon Salt

- 3 Cups Rolled Oats
- 3/4 Cup Cornmeal Or 3/4 Cup Millet Flour
- 3/4 Cup Whole Wheat Flour

How to make it:

1. Blend all ingredients in a food processor or blender and make it smooth, by adding a little water. (You can also blend banana)
2. Pour enough batter to cover the nonstick and preheated waffle iron.
3. Bake for 7 to 14 minutes, or until golden.

******

Oatmeal Cookies (Raw Vegan)

- **Prep Time:** 20 mins
- **Total Time:** 12 hrs 20 mins
- **Yield:** 12 cookies

Ingredients

- 2 Cups Oats (Groats, Whole)
- 1/2 Cup Almonds
- 1/2 Cup Raisins
- 1/2 Cup Agave Nectar (Or Maple Syrup)
- 1/4 Cup Cashews

How to make it:

1. Blend the whole groat oats and almonds in a food processor and empty it into a bowl.
2. Add raisings and the nectar to this mix.
3. Grind some cashews to coat your palm, so that the cookie batter does not stick to your hands.
4. Make small chunks of the dough and flatten them.
5. Set them on a mesh sheet of a dehydrator tray.
6. Dehydrate the dough for about 12 hours on 110 degrees.

****

Vegan Pancakes

- **Prep Time:** 5 mins
- **Total Time:** 20 mins
- **Servings:** 4

Ingredients

- 2 cups flour
- 1 teaspoon baking soda
- 1 teaspoon baking powder
- 2 cups soymilk
- 2 tablespoons oil

How to make it:

1. Mix flour, baking powder and baking soda.
2. Add soymilk and oil lightly to it.
3. Fold in the blueberries and chocolate chips etc.
4. Heat skillet and grease it.
5. Make pancakes with a little batter.
6. Flip the pancakes, when bubbles appear in the middle.
7. In a 200 degree oven, keep the ready pancakes, until all are finished. Serve with syrup or fruits.

****

Tomatoes Toast

- **Prep Time:** 3 mins
- **Total Time:** 5 mins
- **Servings:** 1

Ingredients :-

- 1 Slice Toast, Preferably Rye,But Whole Wheat Will Work (White Bread Is NOT Recommended)
- Peanut Butter (Creamy Is Preferable, But Crunchy Will Do)
- Thick Slices Of Real Tomatoes, The Homegrown Kind (The Pink Plastic Rocks In Grocery Stores Will NOT Work, They Have Absolutely No Flavor Of Their Own)
- Pepper (Required)
- Salt (Optional)

How to make it:-

1. Make hot toasts and spread peanut butter (as much as you want) on them.
2. Cover the toasts completely with tomato slices.
3. Sprinkle a bit of salt and black pepper.

*****

<u>Creamy Fruit Salad</u>

- **Prep Time:** 35 mins
- **Total Time:** 35 mins
- **Serves:** 10, **Yield:** 10 cups

Ingredients

- 2 Medium Bananas, Diced
- 2 Medium Apples, Diced
- 1 Lemon, Juice Of
- 1 (20 Ounce) Cans Pineapple Tidbits, Drained, Juice Reserved
- 2 Cups Sliced Strawberries
- 2 Cups Grapes
- 1/4 Cup Pecans, Chopped
- 1 (1 1/2 Ounce) Boxes Sugar-Free Instant Vanilla Pudding Mix Or 1 (1 1/2 Ounce) Boxes Vegetarian Sugar-Free Instant Vanilla Pudding Mix
- 1/2 Cup Water

How to make it:

1. In large mixing bowl, toss all the fruits together with lemon juice.
2. Separately mix water, pudding mix and the pineapple juice and whisk it.
3. Spread the pudding mix on the fruits.

****

Crock Pot Oatmeal

- **Prep Time:** 5 mins
- **Total Time:** 10 hrs 5 mins
- **Servings:** 4

Ingredients

- 2 Cups Old Fashioned Oats (I Get This In Bulk From My Food Co-Op, If You Used The Quick Cooking Ones, It Might Be Even Creamier)
- 6 Cups Water, I Think You Need More Than Usual Because Of The Long Cooking Time
- Cinnamon (Optional)
- Dried Fruits (Optional)
- Spices (Optional)

How to make it:

1. Mix all ingredients together in a crock pot.

2. Put in on low heat, overnight.

3. Have it with blueberry syrup, soy milk, maple syrup or pourable fruit.

4. To add texture to it, use raisins or dried cranberries.

*****

'Get Up & Go' Bars

- **Prep Time:** 5 mins
- **Total Time:** 10 mins
- **Servings:** 24

Ingredients

- 1/2 Cup Sugar
- 1 1/2 Cups Light Corn Syrup
- 1 Cup Peanut Butter
- 4 Cups Grape-Nuts Cereal (Wheat And Barley Nugget Cereal)
- 1 Cup Rolled Oats
- 1 Cup Sliced Almonds
- 1 Cup Dried Cranberries

How to make it:

1. Coat a 9" x 13" baking dish with foil.

2. Spray with nonstick cooking spray or simply use ungreased parchment paper.

3. Mix corn syrup, sugar and peanut butter in a saucepan, on medium heat.

4. When brought to a boil, add all other ingredients and let it cool.

5. Spread on the baking tray and cut into bars.

****

Spicy Hash Browns

- **Prep Time:** 15 mins
- **Total Time:** 45 mins
- **Servings:** 5

Ingredients:-

- 2 Tablespoons Olive Oil
- 1 Teaspoon Paprika
- 3/4 Teaspoon Chili Powder
- 1/2 Teaspoon Salt
- 1/4 Teaspoon Red Pepper, Ground
- 1/8 Teaspoon Black Pepper
- 6 1/2 Cups Baking Potatoes, Diced (About 2-1/2 Lbs)
- Cooking Spray

How to make it:

1. Preheat an oven to 400 degree Fahrenheit.

2. Mix paprika, black pepper, olive oil, chili powder, salt, red peppers.

3. Coat the diced potatoes in this mix and place them on a cooking sheet.

4. Bake for 30 minutes at 400 degrees Fahrenheit or until browned.

******

African Banana Coconut Bake

- **Prep Time:** 0 mins
- **Total Time:** 10 mins
- **Servings:** 6

Ingredients

- 5 Medium Bananas
- 1 Tablespoon Margarine, Low-Fat
- 1/3 Cup Orange Juice
- 1 Tablespoon Lemon Juice
- 3 Tablespoons Brown Sugar, Packed
- 2/3 Cup Shredded Coconut

How to make it:

1. Preheat an oven to 375°F.

2. Cut bananas crosswise into halves and then lengthwise into halves.

3. Arrange them in a greased pie plate.

4. Drop a few dollops of butter or margarine and drizzle with lemon and orange juice.

5. Sprinkle brown sugar and coconut on top and bake for 8 to 10 minutes.

*****

Pumpkin Oatmeal

- **Prep Time:** 1 min
- **Total Time:** 4 mins
- **Servings:** 1

Ingredients

- 1/2 Cup Old Fashioned Oats (Example Quaker Oats)
- 1 Cup Water
- 1/8 Cup Pumpkin
- 1 Teaspoon Pumpkin Pie Spice
- 1 Tablespoon Brown Sugar
- 1 (1 G) Packet Splenda Sugar Substitute

How to make it:

1. Mix all ingredients in a bowl with some chopped nuts.

2. Microwave for 2-3 minutes.

3. Put it in a slow cooker and keep stirring occasionally.

4. Serve with flavored coffee.

****

Apple Oatmeal

- **Prep Time:** 8 mins
- **Total Time:** 15 mins
- **Servings:** 1

Ingredients

- 1/2 Cup Diced Golden Delicious Apple
- 1/3 Cup Apple Juice
- 1/3 Cup Water
- 1/8 Teaspoon Salt (Optional)
- 1/4 Teaspoon Ground Cinnamon
- 1/4 Teaspoon Nutmeg
- 1/3 Cup Old Fashioned Oats, Uncooked
- Brown Sugar (Optional)
- Milk (Optional)

How to make it:

1. Mix the juice, apples, and spices with some water and bring it to a boil.
2. Add the rolled oats and cook for 7 minutes.
3. Serve hot with brown sugar and milk.

*****

Easy Caramelized Bananas

- **Prep Time:** 5 mins
- **Total Time:** 10 mins
- **Servings:** 2

Ingredients:-

- 2 -3 Bananas
- 4 -6 Tablespoons Granulated Sugar (Or More)
- Cooking Spray (Regular Or Butter Flavor)

How to make it:-

1. Cut the bananas in a shape as you may desire.
2. Roll and coat bananas in sugar, spread on a plate.
3. Put them in a medium size nonstick pan.
4. Cook for 4-5 minutes or until light to golden brown.
5. Flip bananas to cook thoroughly and serve with ice cream.

Oatmeal Breakfast Bars

- **Prep Time:** 10 mins
- **Total Time:** 40 mins
- **Servings:** 12

Ingredients :-

- 2 Cups Rolled Oats, Uncooked
- 1 Cup Oat Flour (Can Be Made By Pulverising Rolled Oats In A Blender Or Food Processor)
- 1 Cup Packed Currants Or 1 Cup Raisins Or 1 Cup Chopped Prunes Or 1 Cup Other Dried Fruit
- 1 Cup Apple Juice Or 1 Cup Orange Juice (You Could Also Use 1/4 Cup Molasses And 3/4 Cup Water)
- 1/4 Cup White Sugar Or 1/4 Cup Brown Sugar
- 1/2 Teaspoon Cinnamon
- 1/2 Teaspoon Salt
- 1/2 Cup Vegetable Oil
- 1/4 Cup Sesame Seeds Or 1/4 Cup Nuts, Pieces

How to make it:-

1. Preheat an oven to 375 degrees F.
2. Grease a baking dish.
3. Mix all ingredients in a bowl.
4. It should have a wet texture, but not too liquidy.

5. Spread evenly in the baking dish.

6. Bake for 30 minutes.

7. Remove from oven and let it cool a little.

8. Cut into squares while still hot.

****

Oat bran-Banana Breakfast

- **Prep Time:** 2 mins
- **Total Time:** 5 mins
- **Servings:** 1

Ingredients :-

- 1/2 banana, chopped
- 1/3 cup oat bran
- 1 dash salt
- 3/4 cup water
- 1 teaspoon sugar (or honey)

How to make it:

1. Mix oat bran, chopped banana, water, salt and sugar in a microwave-safe bowl.

2. Microwave it for 3 minutes.

3. Keeping stirring it after each minute.

4. Add honey to it and serve with milk.

Icy Pumpkin Smoothie

- **Prep Time:** 5 mins
- **Total Time:** 35 mins
- **Serves:** 2, **Yield:** 2 cups

Ingredients

- 1 Medium Banana, Frozen
- 1 Cup Soymilk
- 1/2 Cup Canned Pumpkin Puree Or 1/2 Cup Fresh Pumpkin, I Guess
- 1/2 Teaspoon Cinnamon
- 1/4 Teaspoon Ground Ginger
- 1/4 Teaspoon Allspice
- 1/4 Teaspoon Nutmeg
- 1 Tablespoon Maple Syrup

How to make it:

1. Blend the banana in a blender until creamy-smooth.
2. Add spices, pumpkin puree and pour into cups.
3. Refrigerate it for 1/2-1 hour or until firm.

Oatmeal Cooked in a Rice Cooker

- **Prep Time:** 5 mins
- **Total Time:** 30 mins
- **Servings:** 2-3

Ingredients:-

- 1 1/4 cups large flake rolled oats
- 2 tablespoons wheat bran
- 1 pinch salt
- 1/3 cup raisins or 1/3 cup other dried fruit or 1/3 cup fresh fruit (optional)
- 2 1/2 cups water

How to make it:

1. Add all ingredients in a rice cooker and cook for 25 to 30 minutes.
2. Stir and serve hot with a little sugar, ground flaxseed and light cream.

Fruit Salsa with Cinnamon Tortilla Chips

- **Prep Time:** 35 mins
- **Total Time:** 41 mins
- **Servings:** 6

Ingredients

- 2 Medium Granny Smith Apples, Chopped
- 2 Teaspoons Lemon Juice
- 1 Cup Fresh Strawberries, Chopped
- 3 Medium Kiwi, Peeled And Chopped
- 1 Small Orange
- 2 Tablespoons Brown Sugar
- 2 Tablespoons Apple Jelly, Melted
- 8 8-Inch Flour Tortillas
- Water
- 1/4 Cup Granulated Sugar
- 2 Teaspoons Cinnamon

How to make it:

1. In a large bowl, toss in the fruits one after the other and add the lemon juice.
2. Add one tablespoon of orange peel.
3. Add 3 tablespoons of the orange juice.
4. Add the jelly and the brown sugar.

5. Brush the tortillas with a little water.

6. Sprinkle sugar and cinnamon mix on watered tortillas, so that they stick to the tortillas.

7. Cut tortillas into wedges.

8. Bake them in a 400 degree preheated oven for 6 minutes or until browned.

9. Cool until crisp.

10. Serve with apple salsa.

Low Carb Bread

- **Prep Time:** 10 mins
- **Total Time:** 3 hrs 10 mins
- **Yield:** 12 slices

Ingredients

- 4 Teaspoons Bread Machine Yeast
- 1/2 Teaspoon Sugar
- 1 1/4 Cups Water (90-100 F)
- 3 Tablespoons Olive Oil
- 3/4 Teaspoon Baking Powder
- 1 Teaspoon Salt
- 1 Tablespoon Splenda Sugar Substitute
- 1 Cup Vital Wheat Gluten Flour
- 1/4 Cup Oat Flour
- 3/4 Cup Soy Flour
- 1/4 Cup Flax Seed
- 1/4 Cup Wheat Bran

Alterations Add

- 2 Tablespoons Sunflower Seeds (Optional)
- 2 Tablespoons Flax Seeds (Optional)
- 2 Tablespoons Sesame Seeds (Optional)

Rye Add

- 2 Tablespoons Caraway Seeds (Optional)
- 1 Teaspoon Instant Coffee (Optional)
- 1 Teaspoon Cocoa (Optional)
- 1/2 Cup Dark Rye Flour (Optional)

How to make it:

1. Mix all the dry ingredients, without the yeast and baking powder in a bowl.
2. Add water, oil, and sugar in a bread machine pan.
3. Take 1/4 cup of the dry mix and add the yeast and baking powder to it.
4. Add everything together in the bread machine pan.
5. Gently lift the dough out after 55 minutes.
6. Put it back again, this time, removing the paddle; so that large holes don't form.
7. Let it cool and put in the refrigerator in a Ziploc bag.

Crumpets

- **Prep Time:** 1 hr
- **Total Time:** 1 hr 13 mins
- **Yield:** 24 crumpets

Ingredients

- 4 Cups Flour
- 2 Tablespoons Baking Powder
- 1 1/2 Teaspoons Salt
- 1 1/2 Teaspoons Sugar
- 3 Cups Water, Lukewarm
- 1/2 Ounce Compressed Yeast

How to make it:

1. Mix baking powder, salt, sugar and flour into a large bowl.
2. Dissolve yeast in water.
3. Mix it to the dry ingredients.
4. Grease a pan (you can use traditional frying pan or electric frying pan).
5. For electric fry pan, pre-heat it to 260 F.
6. Cook for 10 minutes.
7. Serve hot.

Crispy Potatoes

- **Prep Time:** 15 mins
- **Total Time:** 1 hr
- **Servings:** 2

Ingredients

- 1 Lb Potato (Yukon Gold, Yellow Finn, Or New Potatoes)
- 2 Tablespoons Olive Oil
- 1 Garlic Clove, Minced
- 1/2 Teaspoon Fresh Rosemary Or 1/2 Teaspoon Dried Rosemary
- 1/2 Teaspoon Salt
- Fresh Ground Black Pepper

How to make it:

1. Boil salted water in a skillet.
2. Without peeling, cut the potatoes in halves and boil them in the salted water.
3. When boiled, immediately put those in icy cold water and drain them.
4. Place them on a kitchen towel to absorb any excess water.
5. Cut them into 1/2 inch thick large crosswise slices.
6. Heat a skillet and add olive oil to it.
7. When hot, quickly add the potatoes.
8. Add salt and pepper.

9. Cook for about 5 minutes or until golden.

10. Sprinkle with garlic and rosemary.

11. Serve hot.

****

Apple Almond Oatmeal

- **Prep Time:** 10 mins
- **Total Time:** 20 mins
- **Servings:** 2

Ingredients

- 2 Cups Water
- 1/4 Teaspoon Salt
- 1 Cup Quick Oats (Or Old Fashioned Oats)
- 1 Cup Almond Milk (Use Amount Desired.....Or Soy Milk Or Cow's Milk)
- 1 Granny Smith Apple, Diced (Or Apple Of Choice)
- 3 Tablespoons Real Maple Syrup
- 6 Tablespoons Sliced Almonds, Roasted

How to make it:

1. Boil water and salt and add the oats.
2. After a minute or so, add the apples when the oats are halfway cooked.

3. After a few minutes, cover the pan and remove from heat.

4. Serve with maple syrup, diced apple, milk and sliced almonds.

5. You can roast the almonds for 7-10 minutes in a 350°F oven.

******

Fresh Fruit Fiesta Bars

- **Prep Time:** 15 mins
- **Total Time:** 45 mins
- **Yield:** 36 bars

Ingredients

BASE

- 1 3/4 Cups All-Purpose Flour
- 1 1/2 Cups Old Fashioned Oats
- 1/2 Teaspoon Ground Cinnamon
- 3/4 Cup Butter Or 3/4 Cup Margarine, Softened
- 1 Cup Packed Brown Sugar

TOPPING

- 10 Ounces Canned Mandarin Oranges, Drained
- 1 Banana, Sliced
- 1 Apple, Cubed And Peeled
- 1/2 Cup Raisins

- 1/4 Cup Orange Juice
- 1 Teaspoon Ground Cinnamon

How to make it:

1. Preheat the oven to 375 degrees.
2. Mix flour, oats and cinnamon in one bowl and set aside 1 ¼ cups of mixture.
3. Beat butter and sugar in a creamy batter.
4. Fold the flour mixture in this batter.
5. Place the 1 ¼ cups of mixture in an ungreased 13 by 9 inch cake pan.
6. Mix banana, oranges, raisins, apples, orange juice and cinnamon.

*****

Breakfast Porridge

- **Prep Time:** 5 mins
- **Total Time:** 45 mins
- **Servings:** 4

Ingredients

- 1/2 Cup Barley (I Prefer Hulled To Pearled)
- 1/2 Cup Quinoa
- 1 Pinch Salt

- 4 Cups Water
- Dried Fruits (Optional, Such As Raisins, Cranberries Or Cherry)
- Honey (Optional) Or Maple Syrup (Optional) Or Sugar (Optional)
- Spices, Such As Cinnamon, Nutmeg, Cardamom (Optional)
- Milk (Optional) Or Yogurt (Optional)

How to make it:

1. Crock pot method: Mix quinoa, barley, salt and water and cook overnight on low heat.
2. Stovetop method: Mix quinoa, barley, salt and water in a saucepan and bring it to a boil. Cover for 40 minutes and cook until water is absorbed.
3. Fluff with a fork.
4. Serve on plate and place the dried fruits and spices, and sweetener as desired.
5. Serve with milk or yogurt.
6. You can substitute the milk with soy milk.

Pumpkin Pie Oatmeal

- **Prep Time:** 10 mins
- **Total Time:** 10 mins
- **Servings:** 2

Ingredients

- 1/2 Cup Old-Fashioned Oatmeal, Uncooked
- 1/2 Cup Canned Pumpkin
- 1 Cup Water
- 1 Pinch Ground Cardamom
- 1/4 Teaspoon Pumpkin Pie Spice
- 1 Tablespoon Splenda Sugar Substitute

How to make it:

1. Mix all ingredients.
2. Cook for 20 minutes over low heat, or until thick.
3. Add skim milk instead of water, if you want it thick.
4. Do not use milk if you want it Vegan.

Tortilla Wraps

- **Prep Time:** 5 mins
- **Total Time:** 5 mins
- **Servings:** 4

Ingredients

- 1 (15 Ounce) Cans Black Beans, Rinsed And Drained
- 2 Tablespoons Lime Juice
- 2 Tablespoons Orange Juice
- 2 Cloves Garlic, Coarsely Chopped
- 1/8 Teaspoon Salt
- Cayenne Pepper
- 3 Scallions, Finely Chopped
- 1/4 Cup Red Bell Peppers Or 1/4 Cup Green Bell Pepper, Finely Chopped
- 4 Flour Tortillas Or 4 Corn Tortillas
- Salsa

How to make it:

1. Blend lime juice, beans, garlic, orange juice, salt and cayenne pepper in a blend.
2. Empty the smooth mix in a bowl.
3. Add the bell peppers and scallions.
4. Spread 1/4th of the mix on tortilla and top with salsa.

Egyptian Fava Bean Dip

- **Prep Time:** 5 mins
- **Total Time:** 35 mins
- **Servings:** 4

Ingredients

- 1 (15 Ounce) Cans Cooked Fava Beans Or 1 1/2 Cups Cooked Fava Beans
- 1 Small Onion, Chopped
- 3 Garlic Cloves, Chopped
- 1 Large Tomatoes, Chopped
- 1/2 Teaspoon Chili Powder
- 1/2 Teaspoon Curry Powder
- 1/2 Teaspoon Cumin (But Season To Your Own Taste!)
- 1 Dash Cinnamon (But Season To Your Own Taste!)
- 1 Dash Clove (But Season To Your Own Taste!)
- 1 Dash Turmeric (But Season To Your Own Taste!)
- 1 Dash Cayenne (But Season To Your Own Taste!)
- 1 Tablespoon Lemon Juice (Or To Taste)
- Salt
- 1 Small Potato, Peeled And Cooked, Added When Onion Is Cooking (Optional)

How to make it:

1. Sauté onion in a little vegetable oil.
2. Add garlic, chopped tomato one after the other and cooking a little.
3. Stir in the spices and lemon juice.
4. Add the fava beans.
5. Add salt to taste.
6. Leave for about 15-20 minutes on low heat.
7. Put the mix in a blender and make a smooth puree.
8. Empty in a serving dish and drizzle olive oil.
9. Serve with Carol's pita bread or French bread.

Cinnamon Toast

- **Prep Time:** 5 mins
- **Total Time:** 5 mins
- **Serves:** 1, **Yield:** 2 slices

Ingredients

- 2 Slices Whole Wheat Bread (Use Raisin Bread For A Special Treat)
- 1 Small Banana
- 2 Teaspoons Ground Flax Seeds
- 2 Teaspoons Brown Sugar
- 1/2 Teaspoon Cinnamon (Generous)

How to make it:

1. Toast the bread.
2. Mash the banana to make "banana butter".
3. Mix sugar, flax and cinnamon.
4. Spread "banana butter" on bread toasts and sprinkle the sugar mix.
5. Enjoy with fruit bowl, soy milk or rice milk.

<u>Oven Hash Browns</u>

- **Prep Time:** 10 mins
- **Total Time:** 55 mins
- **Servings:** 8-10

Ingredients

- 6 Large Potatoes, Peeled,Cut Int 1/2 " Pieces And Cooked Until Almost Tender Apprx 5 Minutes,Drain Well
- 1 Teaspoon Paprika
- 1 Teaspoon Chili Powder
- 1 Teaspoon Cajun Seasoning (Tony Chachere's Or Other Cajun Spice And If Not Available Use Additional Tsp Chili Powder)
- 1/4 Cup Lite Olive Oil

How to make it:

1. Preheat oven to 400 degree F.
2. Spread potatoes on a baking sheet.
3. Sprinkle chili, paprika, cajun spice to evenly coat the potatoes.
4. Season with salt.
5. Bake potatoes for 40 minutes or until crisp, turning the potatoes in every 10 minutes.

Oatmeal with Spices

- **Prep Time:** 5 mins
- **Total Time:** 10 mins
- **Servings:** 2

Ingredients

- 2 Cups Water
- 1 1/2 Cups Rolled Oats
- 1/3 Cup Raisins
- 1 Pinch Salt
- 1 Teaspoon Vanilla
- 1/2 Teaspoon Ground Cinnamon
- 1/4 Teaspoon Ground Nutmeg
- 2 Tablespoons Brown Sugar

How to make it:

1. Cook oats with the raisins and salt, as per the directions on the oat box.
2. Remove from heat and add cinnamon, vanilla, and nutmeg.
3. Sprinkle brown sugar on top of each bowl.

Scrambled Tofu

- **Prep Time:** 5 mins
- **Total Time:** 10 mins
- **Servings:** 1

Ingredients

- 4 Ounces Extra-Firm Silken Tofu
- 1 Tablespoon Nutritional Yeast
- 1 Tablespoon Water
- 1/2 Teaspoon Soy Sauce
- 1/8 Teaspoon Turmeric
- 1/8 Teaspoon Onion Powder
- 1 Pinch Garlic Powder
- Salt And Pepper, To Taste

How to make it:

1. Crumble tofu with fingers and add nutritional yeast to it.
2. Mix turmeric, soy sauce, garlic powder and onion powder together.
3. Add to the crumbled tofu.
4. Add cooking spray to a skillet.
5. Add the crumbled tofu and add salt and pepper to it.
6. To make Vegetable Scrambled Tofu: Saute 2 sliced mushrooms, 1 tb sp chopped green pepper, 1 tb sp chopped onion.
7. You can add a little turmeric.

Larabar Copycat

- **Prep Time:** 10 mins
- **Total Time:** 10 mins
- **Servings:** 6

Ingredients

- 1 Cup Dates
- 3 Cups Cashews

How to make it:

1. Blend dates and pulse to make a smooth blend.
2. Chop the cashews and spread on the blended mix.
3. When date and cashews are evenly mixed, form a rope from eh dough and cut into car shapes.

*****

Everyday Scrambled Tofu

- **Prep Time:** 10 mins
- **Total Time:** 25 mins
- **Servings:** 6

Ingredients :-

- 1 Lb Firm Tofu

- 1 Tablespoon Soy Sauce (I Use The Healthier Bragg Liquid Aminos)
- 1 Tablespoon Onion Powder Or 2 Green Onions, Chopped
- 1/2 Teaspoon Salt
- 1/4 Teaspoon Turmeric
- 1 Tablespoon Italian Seasoning
- 1 Green Bell Pepper, Chopped
- 1 -2 Tomatoes, Chopped
- 1 Tablespoon Canned Green Chilies (Optional) Or 2 Tablespoons Dried Green Pimientos (Optional)
- Black Salt, To Taste (This Sulferic Salt Is Optional But Makes A Huge Difference In Making The Tofu Taste More Like Eggs,)

How to make it:

1. Crumble tofu with your fingers.
2. Mix all ingredients except for tomatoes in a skillet. Cook for 5 to 8 minutes.
3. Now add the tomatoes and cook for another 5 to 8 minutes.

Bagels

- **Prep Time:** 0 mins
- **Total Time:** 2 hrs
- **Yield:** 12 Bagels

Ingredients :-

- 4 1/4-4 3/4 Cups All-Purpose Flour
- 2 (1/4 Ounce) Package Active Dry Yeast
- 1 1/2 Cups Water (110: To 115)
- 3 Tablespoons Sugar
- 1 Tablespoon Salt
- 1 Tablespoon Sugar

How to make it:

1. Mix half cup of flour and yeast.
2. Separately mix warm water with the sugar and salt. Pour it over the flour mix.
3. Beat for about 30 seconds in low speed and for 3 minutes at high speed.
4. Fold in the remaining flour.
5. Taking it out of the processor, knead it for 6-8 minutes total to make a moderately stiff dough.
6. Cover it and let it rest for 10 minutes.
7. Cut 12 portions and make smooth balls and make holes in the center.

8. Place them on greased baking sheet and let it rise for 20 minutes.

9. Broil for 3-4 minutes.

10. Mix 1 Tbsp sugar to 1 gallon of water and let it boild.

11. Reduce heat and cook 4 or 5 bagels for 7 minutes.

12. Turn them once and drain.

13. Bake them on a greased baking sheet for 25-30 minutes in a 375 degree oven.

14. To make Light Rye Bagels: Mix 1 1/2 cups of rye flour for the first 1 1/4 cups of all-purpose flour.

15. For Herb Bagels: Follow the same method. But, also add crushed or 1 tsp dried dill, 1 tsp. dried tarragon, 1/2 tsp. garlic powder and also 2 tsp. dried marjoram to the yeast.

16. To make Onion Bagels: Cook 1/2 cup of finely chopped onion in 3 Tbsp butter. Brush it on the bagels and bake.

17. To make Poppy or Sesame Seed Bagels: Brush the tops of the bagels with beaten egg and sprinkle with the poppy or sesame seed.

Cream of Oat Bran

- **Prep Time:** 5 Mins
- **Total Time:** 8 Mins
- **Servings:** 1

Ingredients

- 1/2 Cup Unsweetened Soymilk
- 1/4 Cup Cold Water
- 1/4 Cup Oat Bran
- 1 Pinch Salt
- 1 Dash Ground Cinnamon
- 2 Tablespoons Chopped Walnuts
- 1 Tablespoon Ground Flax Seed
- Sliced Banana (Optional)

How to make it:

1. Mix water, soymilk, oat bran and salt together and microwave the mix on high for 3 minutes. You can also cook it on stovetop, until you get a desired consistency.
2. Top it with walnuts, cinnamon and flaxseeds.
3. You can also add sliced bananas on top.

Apple Pineapple Crisp w/o Sugar

- **Prep Time:** 10 mins
- **Total Time:** 35 mins
- **Servings:** 4

Ingredients

- 4 Medium Tart Apples (I Used Granny Smith)
- 1 Cup Canned Crushed Pineapple In Juice
- 1/2 Cup Quick Oatmeal Or 1/2 Cup Regular Oatmeal (Not Instant)
- 1/8 Teaspoon Ground Nutmeg
- 1 Banana, Frozen

How to make it:

1. Preheat oven to 375 degrees.
2. Spray a square baking dish with oil.
3. Slice the apples after peeing and coring.
4. Place them in the baking dish.
5. Add canned pineapple.
6. Microwave and defrost the frozen banana and add to the oatmeal.
7. Add nutmeg to it.
8. Spread the oatmeal on top of the apples.
9. Spray olive oil on top and bake for 20-25 minutes
10. Serve warm or cold.

Mashed Brown Potatoes

- **Prep Time:** 5 mins
- **Total Time:** 15 mins
- **Servings:** 1

Ingredients

- 3/4 Cup Mashed Potatoes
- 1/2 Teaspoon Flour
- 1/8 Teaspoon Parsley (Or Herb Of Your Choice)
- 1/8 Teaspoon Garlic Powder
- Salt And Pepper, To Taste
- Flour, For Coating
- 2 Teaspoons Olive Oil Or 2 Teaspoons Butter, For Frying

How to make it:

1. Heat up a small fry pan.
2. Mix mashed potato, herbs, 1/2 teaspoons of flour, garlic powder, salt and pepper.
3. Make patty and flatten it.
4. Sprinkle flour on each side of the patty, by holding it in hands.
5. Add olive oil or butter to the heated pan.
6. Gently place the patty into the pan.
7. Let it cook for 3-5 minutes, do not move it.
8. When browned on one side, flip it and cook for another 3 to 5 minutes.

9. Again, do not move!

10. Omit the butter if you want it Vegan.

*****

Fried Plantain

- **Prep Time:** 10 mins
- **Total Time:** 25 mins
- **Yield:** 16 Patacones

Ingredients

- 4 Green Plantains (Do Not Use Yellow, Or Yellowish Green. It Vastly Changes The Taste)
- Vegetable Oil
- Salt

How to make it:

1. Peel Plantain, and cut it into 3 or 4 pieces.
2. Heat vegetable oil in a pan.
3. Fry plantain pieces for about 3 minutes, or until golden.
4. Remove on a kitchen towel and drench the excess oil.
5. Flatten the fried plantain about 1/4" thick with your hands and not with anything else, as excess pressure will stick the plantains to that surface.
6. Deep fry the flattened plantains again, until golden brown.

7. Remove on kitchen towel and sprinkle with salt.

8. Serve hot with queso blanco or salty white cheese.

******

Pan Fried Potatoes

- **Prep Time:** 10 mins
- **Total Time:** 40 mins
- **Servings:** 6

Ingredients

- 2 Kg Potatoes
- 2 Onions
- 4 Garlic Cloves
- 150 Ml Canola Oil

How to make it:

1. Cut very thin slices of the potatoes after washing and peeling.

2. Chop onions and garlic.

3. Place the potato slices in heavy iron, oiled casserole.

4. Add onion and garlic as seasoning.

5. Cover the casserole and cook the potatoes.

6. When steam comes out, turn the potatoes and cook on the other side.

7. Cook for 25-30 mins. Do not add any liquid to cook the potatoes, turn the heat on low.

8. Serve hot!

Scrambled "eggs"

- **Prep Time:** 15 mins
- **Total Time:** 15 mins
- **Servings:** 2

Ingredients

- 1 Lb Firm Tofu
- 1 Tablespoon Nutritional Yeast
- 1/2 Teaspoon Turmeric
- 1/2 Teaspoon Onion Powder
- 2 Tablespoons Low Sodium Soy Sauce
- Pepper

How to make it:

1. Crumble tofu and add all the other ingredients to coat the tofu.
2. Cook the mixture on a skillet, until brown.

Strawberry Pancakes

- **Prep Time:** 5 mins
- **Total Time:** 15 mins
- **Serves:** 4, **Yield:** 16 pancakes

Ingredients

- 2 Cups Unbleached Flour
- 1/4 Cup Cornstarch
- 2 Tablespoons Sugar
- 1 Teaspoon Salt
- 1 Tablespoon Baking Powder
- 1/4 Teaspoon Cinnamon
- 2 Cups Fresh Strawberries, Chopped
- 2 1/2 Cups Soymilk
- 2 Tablespoons Canola Oil

How to make it:

1. Mix all the dry ingredients and chopped strawberries.
2. Add soymilk and oil and blend well.
3. Make the consistency appropriate by adding more soy milk and flour.
4. Pour batter on a griddle and flip.
5. When dried on the wedges, serve warm.

Orange-Lime Dressing

- **Prep Time:** 40 mins
- **Total Time:** 40 mins
- **Servings:** 8

Ingredients

- 2 Limes, Juice And Rind Of
- 1/4 Cup Frozen Orange Juice Concentrate, Thawed
- 1/2 Teaspoon Vanilla
- 1 Cantaloupe
- 1 Honeydew Melon
- 2 (32 Ounce) Cups Red Seedless Grapes

How to make it:

1. Mix lime juice, lime zest, vanilla and orange juice concentrate.
2. Cut melon and trim away the rind and cut into 1-inch wedges.
3. Mix with fruits and dressing.

<u>Simple Blueberry Muffins</u>

- **Prep Time:** 5 mins
- **Total Time:** 35 mins
- **Servings:** 12

Ingredients

- 1 1/2 Cups Flour
- 1/2 Cup Sugar
- 1 Teaspoon Salt
- 2 Teaspoons Baking Powder
- 3/4 Cup Soymilk
- 1/4 Cup Oil
- 1 Cup Frozen Blueberries

Directions

1. Mix flour, salt, baking powder and sugar in a bowl
2. Add soy milk and oil.
3. Fold in the blueberries.
4. Pour into muffin pan, in paper cups and bake for 25-30 minutes at 400 degrees.

SOUTHERN BREAKFAST

FLORIDA STRAWBERRY BREAD

PREP:15 M COOK:1 H 15 M READYIN: 1 H 30 M

INGREDIENTS:

- 3 Cups All-Purpose Flour
- 1 Teaspoon Salt
- 1 Tablespoon Ground Cinnamon
- 1 Teaspoon Baking Powder
- 1 Cup White Sugar
- 4 Eggs
- 1 1/4 Cups Vegetable Oil
- 1 1/2 Cups Frozen Strawberries, thawed and drained
- 1 1/2 Cups chopped Walnuts

DIRECTIONS:

1. Begin by pre-heating the oven to 350 degrees F.
2. Grease two 9 x 5 inch loaf pans.
3. In a big bowl and mix the flour, cinnamon, salt, white sugar and baking powder.
4. In new bowl, mix the eggs along with oil, and then mix it with the dry materials.
5. Throw in the walnuts and the strawberries and spoon the batter over the loaf pan.

6. Bake for an hour in a preheat hot oven.

7. Bread is done when a toothpick inserted in the center comes out clean.

8. Let it cool for 10 minutes over the pans and then keep it aside.

BEIGNETS

PREP: 30 M , COOK:30 M, READYIN:3 H

INGREDIENTS:

- 2 1/4 Teaspoons Active Dry Yeast
- 1 1/2 Cups Warm Water (110 Degrees F)
- 1/2 Cup White Sugar
- 1 Teaspoon Salt
- 2 Eggs
- 1 Cup Evaporated Milk
- 7 Cups All-Purpose Flour
- 1/4 Cup Shortening
- 1 Quart Vegetable Oil for Frying
- 1/4 Cup Confectioners' Sugar

DIRECTIONS:

1. Begin by taking big bowl and immersing the yeast in it along with warm water.
2. Now add in the eggs, salt, sugar, evaporated milk and mix them well. Then add in the flour (four cups) and beat it again.
3. Add the shortening and then rest of the flour (should be three cups).
4. Put a lid on the whole mix and chill it for a whole day (24 hours)

5. Then, when done, begin to make balls of the dough about one-eight thick in size.

6. Cut them into two half inch squares and fry them at 360 F in hot oil.

7. Drain on paper napkins and garnish with sugar confectioners at the top.

PANHANDLE GRITS

PREP: 30 M COOK:15 M READYIN:45 M

INGREDIENTS:

- 1/2 Pound Smoked Sausage, thinly sliced
- 1 Cup Diced Cooked Ham
- 1/2 Pound Sliced Bacon, diced
- 1 Onion, finely chopped
- 1/2 Cup chopped Green Bell Pepper
- 3 Cups chopped Fresh Tomato
- 1 Teaspoon Garlic Powder
- 1 Teaspoon Garlic Powder
- 4 Cups Water
- 1 Tablespoon Worcestershire Sauce
- 1 Teaspoon Ground Black Pepper
- 1 Teaspoon Salt
- 1 Tablespoon Hot Pepper Sauce (E.G. Tabasco™)
- 1 Cup Yellow Stone-Ground Grits
- 1 Cup Shredded Cheddar Cheese

DIRECTIONS:

1. In a big sauce-pan cook sausage, bacon and the ham.
2. Remove from the heat and save 2 tablespoon worth of grease from the pan.

3. Then, return heat to medium and add in the onion, bell pepper, garlic and the tomatoes.

4. Cook well and then pour in the water and the salt, the worcestershire, pepper sauce and bring to a boil.

5. Finally, put in the grits and the lid on the pan, lower the heat and cook for 10 minutes.

6. Put the meat back in and add cheese after that.

7. Cook until the cheese is melted.

MILK GRAVY FOR BISCUITS

PREP:10 M COOK:25 M READYIN:35 M

INGREDIENTS:

- 1/4 Cup Bacon Drippings
- 1/4 Cup All-Purpose Flour
- 1 Teaspoon Salt, or to taste
- 1 Teaspoon Ground Black Pepper, or to taste
- 4 Cups Milk, divided

DIRECTIONS:

1. Start by heating the bacon drippings in a pan over medium heat. Mix some flour with the drippings until you have a smooth paste.
2. Lower the heat and cook carefully until the mix is caramel in color (about 15 minutes).
3. Put black pepper and the salt before adding in the half cup milk.
4. Add milk half cup at a time and mix it well.
5. Cook the gravy well.

QUICHE (SOUTHERN EGG PIE)

PREP:30 M **COOK:** 1 H **READY**IN: 1 H 30 M

INGREDIENTS:

- 1 Tablespoon Butter
- 1/2 Onion, chopped
- 1 (12 Ounce) Package Spicy Ground Pork Sausage
- 4 Eggs
- 1/2 Cup Ranch-Style Salad Dressing
- 1/2 Cup Milk
- 1 (8 Ounce) Package Cheddar Cheese, shredded
- 1 Dash Hot Pepper Sauce (optional)
- Salt and Pepper to taste
- 1 Pinch White Sugar
- 1 (9 inch) Un-baked Deep Dish Pie Crust

DIRECTIONS:

1. Begin by pre-heating the oven to 425 F.
2. Ina large skillet, melt butter over medium heat.
3. Slightly Sauté the onions before adding in the sausages and cooking them until they turn brown.
4. After this, drain the mix, crumble it and put it aside.
5. In a large bowl, mix the eggs, ranch dressing and pour in the milk.

6. Add in the cheese and sprinkle on the salt and pepper, sauce and the sugar.

7. Spread the sausage at the bottom of the crust and put the egg mix over it. Shake it well, so that no air is left.

8. Bake for 20 minutes and then lower the heat to 350 F and again bake for 50 minutes.

9. Cool it for 10 minutes and then eat it!

MONTE CRISTO SANDWICH

PREP: 10 M **COOK:** 5 M **READY** IN: 15 M

INGREDIENTS:

- 1 Quart Oil For Frying, Or As Needed
- 2/3 Cup Water
- 1 Egg
- 2/3 Cup All-Purpose Flour
- 1 3/4 Teaspoons Baking Powder
- 1/2 Teaspoon Salt
- 8 Slices White Bread
- 4 Slices Swiss Cheese
- 4 Slices Turkey
- 4 Slices Ham
- 1/8 Teaspoon Ground Black Pepper
- 1 Tablespoon Confectioners' Sugar For Dusting

DIRECTIONS:

1. Begin by heating five inches of edible oil in a deep-fryer at 365 F.
2. Prepare the batter by whipping the egg and water together in a large bowl.
3. Mix the flour, baking powder, pepper and the salt and add it to the egg mix and cool it in the fridge.

4. Ready the sandwich by placing1 piece of Swiss cheese between 1 slice of turkey and 1 slice of ham Swiss cheese in the center of two pieces of bread.

5. Cut the sandwich to 4 pieces and put toothpicks on top.

6. Deep fry the sandwiches until they brown.

7. Take out the picks and arrange them

8. Make sure to put sugar confectioners on top.

OKLAHOMA CHEESE GRITS

PREP: 15 M **COOK:** 1 H 11 M **READY** IN: 1 H 30 M

INGREDIENTS:

- 6 Cups Water
- 1 1/2 Cups Quick-Cooking Grits, Dry
- 3/4 Cup Butter
- 1 Pound Processed Cheese, Cubed
- 2 Teaspoons Seasoning Salt
- 1 Tablespoon Worcestershire Sauce
- 1/2 Teaspoon Hot Pepper Sauce
- 2 Teaspoons Salt
- 3 Eggs, Beaten

DIRECTIONS:

1. Begin by pre-heating the in at 350 F.
2. Greasea 9 x 13 inch baking sheet or dish.
3. Then take pan, boil water and put in the grits.
4. Lower the heat and cover and cook for 5 minutes.
5. Combine in the butter now, along with the seasoning salt, cheese, the worcestershire, pepper sauce and the normal salt. Cook for 5 minutes again.
6. Remove from the heat and cool.
7. Fold the eggs in.
8. Put the mix in the baking sheet and bake for an hour.

SAUSAGE GRAVY

PREP: 5 M COOK:25 M READYIN: 30 M

INGREDIENTS:

- 1 Pound Ground Pork Sausage
- 3 Tablespoons Bacon Grease
- 1/4 Cup All-Purpose Flour
- 3 Cups Milk
- 1/2 Teaspoon Salt
- 1/4 Teaspoon Ground Black Pepper

DIRECTIONS:

1. Begin by browning the sausage in a large pan over medium-high heat.
2. Put the sausages aside and use the dripping in the pan again and put in the bacon.
3. Lower the heat and mix in the flour, cook until it turns golden.
4. Pour in the milk and thicken it and put the sausages back in.
5. Sprinkle on the pepper and salt and cook for 15 minutes over low heat.

SWEET POTATO PANCAKES

PREP: 10 M **COOK:**15 M **READY**IN: 45 M

INGREDIENTS:

- 3/4 Pound Sweet Potatoes
- 1 1/2 Cups All-Purpose Flour
- 3 1/2 Teaspoons Baking Powder
- 1 Teaspoon Salt
- 1/2 Teaspoon Ground Nutmeg
- 2 Eggs, Beaten
- 1 1/2 Cups Milk
- 1/4 Cup Butter, melted

DIRECTIONS:

1. Cook sweet potatoes in a medium sized pan of boiling water.
2. Cook for15 minutes and drain. Cool and peel, if desired.
3. Mash potatoes.
4. In a new bowl, combine flour, baking powder, nutmeg and salt.
5. Combine mashed potatoes, milk, butter and eggs in another new bowl.
6. Add in flour.
7. Grease a griddle and pre-heat to medium-high heat.
8. In a tablespoonful of the mix at a time and drop them onto griddle. Cook until golden brown, flipping once.

SOUTHERN-STYLE CHOCOLATE GRAVY

PREP: 10 M COOK:10 M READYIN:20 M

INGREDIENTS:

- 1/4 Cup Cocoa
- 3 Tablespoons All-Purpose Flour
- 3/4 Cup White Sugar
- 2 Cups Milk
- 1 Tablespoon Butter, softened
- 2 Teaspoons Vanilla

DIRECTIONS:

1. Mix in the cocoa, sugar and the flour inside a bowl
2. Now pour in the milk over it and combine well.
3. Take the mix to a pan and cook it over medium heat settings for 10 minutes stirring regularly.
4. Remove from heat; add in the vanilla and butter.

FLORIDA STRAWBERRY MUFFINS

PREP: 10 M **COOK:**20 M **READY**IN: 30 M

INGREDIENTS:

- 1 1/2 Cups chopped Fresh Strawberries
- 1/2 Cup White Sugar
- 1/4 Cup White Sugar
- 1/4 Cup Butter, Softened
- 2 Eggs
- 1 Teaspoon Vanilla Extract
- 1 3/4 Cups All-Purpose Flour
- 1/2 Teaspoon Baking Soda
- 1/4 Teaspoon Salt
- 1/4 Teaspoon Ground Nutmeg

DIRECTIONS:

1. Begin by taking a large bowl and mixing the half cup sugar and the strawberries. Keep it aside for an hour and then drain it and keep both the berries and the liquid individually.

2. Now pre-heat oven to 425 F.

3. Greasea twelve-cup muffin tin and line it with paper liners.

4. In medium-sized bowl, cream together the butter and quarter cup sugar.

5. Mix the eggs and put the vanilla in.

6. Mix the flour now with salt, nutmeg and the baking soda.

7. Put it in the cream mix along with berries' juice.

8. Now put in the berries too and pour the batter into the cups; fill 2/3 of the way.

9. Bake for 20 minutes.

10. Cool on the wire rack

PAIN PERDU II

PREP: 10 M **COOK:**10 M **READY**IN:20 M

INGREDIENTS:

- 5 Eggs
- 1/2 Cup White Sugar
- 1/2 Cup Milk
- 2 Tablespoons Orange Liqueur
- 1 Teaspoon Orange Zest
- 12 Slices White Bread

DIRECTIONS:

1. Take big bowl, mix in the eggs, milk, sugar, zest and the brandy and combine well.
2. Soak in the bread pieces in the mix for couple of minutes.
3. Heat a griddle or even a pan over medium-heat and cover it with cooking spray.
4. Put the bread in it for couple of minutes and eat hot!

COUNTRY SAUSAGE GRAVY

PREP: 15 M COOK:20 M READYIN:35 M

INGREDIENTS:

- 1 Pound Pork Sausage
- 1 Onion, finely chopped
- 1 Green Bell Pepper, finely chopped
- 1 Teaspoon Crushed Red Pepper Flakes
- 2 Tablespoons Garlic, minced
- 4 Tablespoons Unsalted Butter
- Salt and Pepper to taste
- 4 Tablespoons All-Purpose Flour
- 1 Teaspoon minced Fresh Sage
- 1 Teaspoon minced Fresh Thyme
- 2 Cups Milk, Divided
- 2 Cubes Chicken Bouillon
- 1/4 Cup minced Fresh Parsley

DIRECTIONS:

1. In a pan and over medium heat cook the onion, green pepper, pork, red pepper and the garlic until the meat is crumbles. Drain grease but store it for later use.

2. Mix in the salt, pepper and the butter with the meat and cook until the butter melts.

3. Flour the mix now and cook for 5 minutes; be careful it can burn.

4. Now add in the sage and the thyme.

5. Pour in the milk (half cup at a time) and mix it well; when it's thick, add more milk.

6. Don't boil again.

7. Now add in the chicken bouillon and cook for 5 minutes; add extra milk if you feel like it.

8. Sprinkle on salt and pepper if you need it.

9. Before turning off the heat, put in the parsley and the remaining milk.

10. Cool it to thicken it.

BEST BUCKWHEAT PANCAKES

PREP: 5 M COOK:10 M READYIN: 15 M

INGREDIENTS:

- 1 Cup Buttermilk
- 1 Egg
- 3 Tablespoons Butter, melted
- 6 Tablespoons All-Purpose Flour
- 6 Tablespoons Buckwheat Flour
- 1 Teaspoon White Sugar
- 1/2 Teaspoon Salt
- 1 Teaspoon Baking Soda
- 3 Tablespoons Butter

DIRECTIONS:

1. Take medium-sized bowl and mix the buttermilk, butter and the egg.

2. In a new bowl, combine flour, sugar, buckwheat flour, salt and the soda.

3. Put the dry materials in the egg mix and stir for couple of minutes.

4. Heat a griddle or a pan over medium heat and put 1 tablespoon of butter, oil or margarine in it.

5. Pour ¼ cup of batter at a time onto hot griddle and cook until sides firm up and top bubbles.

6. Flip them and cook for 3 minutes.

7. Continue until all batter has been used.

BANANA BREAD

PREP: 15 M **COOK:**1 H **READY**IN:1 H 15 M

INGREDIENTS:

- 2 1/4 Cups All-Purpose Flour
- 1 Teaspoon Baking Soda
- 1/2 Teaspoon Ground Cinnamon
- 1/2 Teaspoon Ground Nutmeg
- 1 Cup White Sugar
- 2 Eggs
- 1/3 Cup Unsweetened Applesauce
- 4 Ripe Bananas, Mashed
- 1 Tablespoon Vanilla Extract
- 1 Cup Raisins (optional)
- 1 Cup chopped Walnuts (optional)

DIRECTIONS:

1. Preheat oven to 375 F
2. Grease and floura 9 x 5" inch loaf pan.
3. In a big bowl, mix flour, baking soda, nutmeg, cinnamon and white sugar.
4. Add the eggs, along with bananas, apple sauce and the vanilla extract.
5. You can also put in the nuts and raisins if using.
6. Pour the mix in the pan.

7. Bake for an hour. Bread is done when a knife inserted through the center comes out clean.

APPLE COBBLER

PREP: 20 M COOK:45 M READYIN: 1 H 5 M

INGREDIENTS:

- 2 (8 Ounce) Cans Refrigerated Crescent Rolls
- 2 Large Granny Smith Apples - peeled, cored, and cut into 8 Wedges each
- 1 Cup Butter, melted
- 1 1/2 Cups White Sugar
- 1 Tablespoon Ground Cinnamon
- 1 (12 Fluid Ounce) Can or Bottle Caffeinated Citrus-Flavored Soda (Such as Mountain Dew®)

DIRECTIONS:

1. Pre-heating the oven 350 F and 350 F
2. Grease a 9 x 13 inch type baking sheet
3. Unroll the crescent dough and individually take out the sheets into triangles.
4. Roll the apple wedge to the dough and put them in the baking dish or plate.
5. Take new bowl and mix butter, cinnamon and sugar in it.
6. Add mix on top of the apple pieces.
7. Dash the soda over the roll.
8. Bake for 45 minutes, the apples will be done by that time.

SOUTHERN GRITS CASSEROLE

PREP: 15 M COOK:45 M READYIN:1 H

INGREDIENTS:

- 6 Cups Water
- 2 Cups Uncooked Grits
- 1/2 Cup Butter, divided
- 3 Cups Shredded Cheddar Cheese, divided
- 1 Pound Ground Pork Sausage
- 12 Eggs
- 1/2 Cup Milk
- Salt and Pepper to taste

DIRECTIONS:

1. Preheat oven to 350 F.
2. Greasea big baking sheet
3. Boil water in a saucepan, add in the grits and lower the heat instantly.
4. Put a cover on and let it cook for 5 minutes before mixing in half the butter and 2 cups cheese.
5. Heat a pan over medium-high heat and cook the sausages over it. Drain grease and then combine with the grits.
6. Mix the eggs and the milk in a bowl and to the pan.
7. Scramble a bit and then combine it with the grits.

8. Now put the grits mix into the baking sheet and put in rest of the butter along with the cheese.

9. Sprinkle on the salt and pepper

10. Bake for half an hour in the oven.

SAUSAGE GRAVY

PREP: 10 M COOK:20 M READYIN:30 M

INGREDIENTS:

- 1 Pound Ground Pork Sausage
- 3 Tablespoons All-Purpose Flour
- 3 Cups Milk

DIRECTIONS:

---

1. Add the sausage in a big pan and cook it over medium-high heat.
2. Take out the sausage, drain it well and keep it aside.
3. Take the fat out from the pan, but keep 3 tablespoons of it.
4. Put flour to the pan over medium-light heat and make a roux.
5. Let the roux cook for 5 minutes—you can even burn it a bit (just a bit).
6. Pour in the milk, about two and half cups, and raise the heat to medium and boil it. Add extra milk if needed.
7. Add the crumbled sausage to the gravy.

SOUTHERN FRIED APPLES

PREP: 10 M COOK:10 M READYIN:20 M

INGREDIENTS:

- 1/2 Cup Butter
- 1/2 Cup White Sugar
- 2 Tablespoons Ground Cinnamon
- 4 Granny Smith Apples - peeled, cored, and sliced

DIRECTIONS:

1. Melt the butter in a big skillet pan over medium heat
2. Add the cinnamon and the sugar before putting in the apples and cooking it for 8 minutes or until soft.

TASTY BUCKWHEAT PANCAKES

PREP: 10 M **COOK:**15 M **READY**IN: 25 M

INGREDIENTS:

- 1/2 Cup Whole Wheat Flour
- 1/4 Cup Buckwheat Flour
- 1/4 Cup All-Purpose Flour
- 1/4 Cup Quick Cooking Oats
- 3 Teaspoons Baking Powder
- 1 Cup Skim Milk
- 3 Tablespoons Safflower Oil
- 2 Tablespoons Honey
- 1 Egg, Lightly Beaten

DIRECTIONS:

1. In a big bowl, mix flour, baking powder and the oats.
2. Add in milk, honey, egg and the oil.
3. Heat the griddle or the pan over medium high and pour the mix in (about quarter cup) to form pancakes.
4. Brown both sides and eat warm

BELGIAN WAFFLES

PREP:25 M **COOK:** 15 M**READY**IN:40 M

INGREDIENTS:

- 1 1/3 Cups All-Purpose Flour
- 3/4 Teaspoon Baking Soda
- 2 Teaspoons White Sugar
- 1/4 Teaspoon Salt
- 3 Eggs
- 1 1/2 Teaspoons Vanilla Extract
- 1 1/3 Cups Milk
- 1/3 Cup Melted Butter
- 2 Teaspoons Baking Powder
- 1/4 Cup Butter
- 2/3 Cup Brown Sugar
- 2 Teaspoons Rum Flavored Extract
- 2 Teaspoons Vanilla Extract
- 1/2 Teaspoon Ground Cinnamon
- 1/4 Cup Whole Pecans
- 1/2 Cup Pancake Syrup (I.E. Mrs. Butterworth's®)
- 3 Bananas, cut into 1/2 inch Slices
- 1 Cup Heavy Cream
- 1/4 Teaspoon Vanilla Extract
- 1 Tablespoon Confectioners' Sugar

DIRECTIONS:

1. Start by pre-heating the waffle iron.
2. In a bowl, mix and combine flour, soda, sugar, baking powder and salt.
3. Take another bowl and mix the eggs, one and half teaspoons of vanilla extract and milk.
4. Add the flour mix and the butter.
5. Mix well and pour into waffle iron (follow manufacturer's instructions.
6. Melt ¼ cup of butter in a sauce pan over medium heat.
7. Mix the brown sugar, 2 teaspoons of the vanilla extract, the rum extract and cinnamon.
8. Cook, stirring, for three minutes.
9. Add in the pecans.
10. After one minute pour the syrup and the bananas and cook for another 4 minutes.
11. Mix cream, ¼ teaspoon of vanilla and confectioners in a mixer.
12. Top cooked waffles with banana foster sauce and whipped cream.
13. Serve hot.

CREAMY SOUTHERN SHRIMP AND CHEESE GRITS

PREP: 25 M **COOK:**25 M **READY**IN:50 M

INGREDIENTS:

- 3 1/2 Cups Water
- 1 Cup Quick-Cooking Grits
- 3 Ounces Farmers Cheese
- 2 Ounces Goat Cheese
- 1 Slice American Cheese
- 2 Tablespoons Butter
- 2 Teaspoons Vegetable Oil
- 1 Large Tomato, diced
- 2 Green Onions, sliced
- 1 Clove Garlic, minced
- 1 Teaspoon Bacon Drippings, or to taste (optional)
- 1 Pound Fresh Shrimp - peeled, deveined, and tails remove
- Salt and Ground Black Pepper to taste
- 1/4 Cup Half-and-Half, or more to taste
- 1 Tablespoon Dry Sherry
- 1 Green Onion (Green Tops Only), sliced

DIRECTIONS:

1. Begin by boiling the water in a big sauce pan before putting in the grits slowly.

2. Lower the heat to medium-low and let it cook for7 minutes.

3. Add the all three types of the cheese. Now place the grits aside.

4. Take big skillet or pan and melt the butter with veggie oil over medium heat.

5. Cook the tomato, two green onions and the garlic in the hot pan for 7 minutes.

6. Sprinkle on the bacon drippings and cook for another 5 minutes, before adding the pepper and salt.

7. Combine grits and the shrimp and put in the half , cook for 5 minutes and then sprinkle on the sherry.

8. Cook for 3 more minutes and then season to taste.

9. Top the dish with green onions.

GRITS CASSEROLE

PREP: 15 M COOK:1 H READYIN: 1 H 15 M

INGREDIENTS:

- 8 Slices Bacon
- 1 Cup Quick-Cooking Hominy Grits
- 4 Cups Water
- 1 (8 Ounce) Package Processed Cheese, cubed
- 2/3 Cup Milk
- 3 Eggs, beaten
- Salt and Pepper to taste
- 2 Cups Shredded Cheddar Cheese

DIRECTIONS:

1. Pre-heat the oven to 350 F.
2. Fry bacon in a heavy skillet over medium heat. Keep it aside and save 3 tablespoons worth of the drippings.
3. Boil the water, and add in the grits.
4. Cook over medium heat for 5 minutes.
5. Crumble half of the bacon and put it in; pour in the drippings too.
6. Add milk, eggs and the cheese too and sprinkle on the salt and pepper.
7. Pour the whole mix in large baking dish and garnish with cheddar cheese.
8. Bake for 40 minutes.

LEMON-GARLIC SHRIMP AND GRITS

PREP: 15 M **COOK:** 30 M **READY**IN:45 M

INGREDIENTS:

- 4 Cups Water
- 1 Cup Stone-Ground Grits
- 1 Teaspoon Salt
- 1/2 Teaspoon Freshly Ground Black Pepper
- 1 Tablespoon Unsalted Butter
- 1 Pound Uncooked Medium Shrimp - peeled and deveined, (tails left intact)
- 2 Tablespoons Unsalted Butter
- 2 Large Cloves Garlic, minced
- 1 Pinch Cayenne Pepper (optional)
- 2 Tablespoons Water
- 1/2 Lemon, juiced
- 2 Tablespoons Coarsely chopped Fresh Parsley
- 1/2 Lemon, cut into wedges

DIRECTIONS:

1. Boil four cups of water in a pan and put in the grits, pepper and the salt. Lower the heat and cook for half an hour.
2. Add one tablespoon of salt free butter to the mix.
3. Salt and pepper to taste.

4. Remove from heat and cover.

5. Salt and pepper the shrimp to taste.

6. In a skillet, melt two tablespoon of salt free butter. Sauté garlic, shrimp and the cayenne pepper over medium heat for 4 minutes. The shrimp will become pink by then.

7. Pour 2 tablespoon of water over the shrimp and sprinkle on the lemon liquid and the parsley. Top with pepper and salt, as per taste.

8. Place the grits into bowls, top with sauce and the shrimp.

9. Eat with wedges of lemon.

SHRIMP AND GRITS ON THE BARBIE

PREP:15 M COOK:30 M READYIN: 45 M

INGREDIENTS:

- 8 Slices of Thick-Cut Bacon
- 1 1/4 Pounds Uncooked Medium Shrimp, peeled and deveined
- 3/4 Cup chopped Green Onion
- 3 Large Cloves Garlic, crushed
- 6 Cups Water
- 1/4 Cup Unsalted Butter
- 2 Cups Quick-Cooking Grits
- 1 1/2 Cups Shredded Sharp Cheddar Cheese
- 1 Tablespoon Barbeque Sauce, or to taste

DIRECTIONS:

1. Fry bacon in a big skillet over medium heat.
2. Drain the bacon and let it cool.
3. Save the drippings in the pan.
4. On a griddle over medium heat, heat the shrimp until it becomes pink. It should take about 10 minutes.
5. Put the shrimp, garlic, green onion and the bacon crumble into the bacon grease in the pan and heat on low.
6. In a big pan, boil water and add the butter and grits; cook for 5 minutes.

7. Lower the heat and put in the bacon drippings mix into the grits.

8. Add the cheddar now and mix well.

9. Serve with barbeque sauce.

RESTAURANT STYLE SAUSAGE GRAVY AND BISCUITS

PREP: 5 M COOK:30 M READYIN:35 M

INGREDIENTS:

- 1 (16 Ounce) Package Bulk Pork Breakfast Sausage (Such as Bob Evans®)
- 1 (26.5 Ounce) Can Condensed Cream of Mushroom Soup
- 2 Cups Water
- 1 (16.3 Ounce) Can Refrigerated Biscuit Dough (Such as Pillsbury Grands!®)

DIRECTIONS:

1. Begin by pre-heating the oven to 350 F.
2. Crumble and brown sausage in a skillet over medium heat.
3. Drain grease and set aside.
4. Combine the soup with the sausage and boil it. Then lower the heat and cook for 15 minutes. The gravy will become thick by then.
5. Now separate the dough of the biscuit and put them on baking sheet 2" apart.
6. Bake the biscuits according to the directions on the can.
7. Halve the biscuit and serve with the gravy.

FRESH SWEET CORN FRITTERS

PREP: 20 M COOK:30 M READYIN:50 M

INGREDIENTS:

- 1 Cup All-Purpose Flour
- 1 Teaspoon Baking Powder
- 3 Ears Fresh Corn, kernels cut from cob
- 2 Eggs, separated
- 1/2 Cup Heavy Whipping Cream
- Salt and Freshly Ground Pepper to taste
- 1 Quart Vegetable Oil for Frying, or as needed
- 2 Tablespoons Cane Syrup, or as desired (optional)

DIRECTIONS:

1. Combine flour, baking powder and corn kernels.
2. Mix eggs yolks and cream in a bowl before adding in the corn mix.
3. Sprinkle on the black pepper and the salt.
4. Whip the egg whites in a separate bowl, then fold the whites into the mix.
5. Now heat veggie oil to 375 Fin a deep pan.
6. Put the fritters over the oil (three tablespoons each) and fry for 3 minutes.
7. Serve with cane syrup.

TOMATO GRAVY

PREP: 15 M COOK:45 M READYIN:1 H

INGREDIENTS:

- 8 Slices Bacon, cut into 1/2 inch pieces
- 1 Large Onion, chopped
- 2 (28 Ounce) Cans Diced Tomatoes
- 1 (14 Ounce) Can Tomato Sauce
- 1 Teaspoon White Sugar, or more to taste
- 1/2 Teaspoon Ground Black Pepper, or to taste
- 1 Tablespoon Butter

DIRECTIONS:

1. Put the bacon inside the dutch oven and heat it over medium for 2 minutes.
2. Now put in the onion and cook again for 5 minutes
3. Now shift the tomatoes and the sauce to a pan.
4. Sprinkle on the black pepper and the sugar.
5. Cook until the sauce thickens.
6. Add butter and stir right before serving.

SAUSAGE BISCUITS AND GRAVY

PREP: 10 M **COOK:**20 M **READY**IN: 30 M

INGREDIENTS:

- 1 (19 Ounce) Can Southern-Style Flaky Refrigerated Biscuits (Such as Pillsbury Grands®)
- 1 (16 Ounce) Package Maple-Flavored Breakfast Sausage
- 3 Tablespoons All-Purpose Flour, or as needed
- 1 (12 Ounce) Can Evaporated Milk
- 1 1/2 Cups Milk
- 1/2 Teaspoon Salt
- 1/4 Teaspoon Ground Black Pepper
- 1 Teaspoon Butter

DIRECTIONS:

1. Begin by pre-heating the oven to350 F.
2. Now arrange the biscuits about one and half inches from each other over a baking sheet and cook according to package directions.
3. While they bake, brown and crumble sausage over medium heat. Drain and set aside.
4. To the drippings, add in the flour and cook until thickened (about one minute).
5. Lower the heat
6. Pour in the can of evaporated milk, then the milk and mix well.

7. Cook for 5 minutes before adding in the pepper and salt. (Add extra flour if you feel the gravy is not thick enough.)

8. Put the biscuits on a plate along with gravy.

DELICIOUS SOUTHERN CORNBREAD

PREP: 10 M **COOK:**20 M **READY**IN: 30 M

INGREDIENTS:

- 3 Tablespoons Vegetable Oil
- 1 Cup Self-Rising Cornmeal
- 3/4 Cup Buttermilk
- 1 Egg
- 1 Tablespoon Honey
- 1 Tablespoon Self-Rising Cornmeal

DIRECTIONS:

1. Begin by pre-heating the oven to 400 F.
2. In an iron skillet, heat the veggie oil over low heat.
3. In a bowl, and combine buttermilk, cornmeal, honey and the egg.
4. Add the oil and add one tablespoon of corn meal. Mix well.
5. Bake for 22 minutes in the oven.

HOW TO MAKE COUNTRY GRAVY

PREP: 15 M COOK: 35 M READYIN: 50 M

INGREDIENTS:

- 2 Tablespoons Butter
- 8 Ounces Breakfast Sausage Links (Casings remove and meat crumbled.)
- 4 Strips Bacon, sliced Crosswise
- 1/2 Cup chopped Green Onions (bulbs only)
- 1/3 Cup Packed All-Purpose Flour
- 1 Pinch Cayenne Pepper, or to taste
- Salt and Freshly Ground Black Pepper to taste
- 2 1/2 Cups Cold Milk
- 1 Tablespoon chopped Green Onion
- 1 Pinch Cayenne Pepper for Garnish

DIRECTIONS:

1. Begin by melting butter in a skillet over medium heat and cook the bacon and the sausage. Crumble sausage.
2. Add ½ cup of green onion and sauté for 3 minutes.
3. Add the flour 2 spoons at a time, stirring well, and cook for 3 minutes.
4. Pour milk into the meat, one cup each and mix well. The gravy should thicken within five minutes.
5. Raise the heat and sprinkle on the salt and both pepper types.

6. Reduce heat now.

7. Cook for ten to fifteen minutes and then garnish with green onion and cayenne pepper on top.

HOME FRIES

PREP: 10 M **COOK:**15 M **READY**IN: 25 M

INGREDIENTS:

- 2 Tablespoons Bacon Drippings
- 4 Large Potatoes, peeled and sliced
- 1/2 Vidalia Onion, chopped
- Salt and Pepper to taste

DIRECTIONS:

1. Cook onion and potatoes in bacon grease over medium heat.
2. Cook for 15 minutes and then dash the pepper and salt
3. Eat!

BREAKFAST GRITS

PREP: 10 M **COOK:**20 M **READY**IN: 30 M

INGREDIENTS:

- 3 Cups Water
- 1/2 Teaspoon Salt
- 1 Cup Hominy Grits
- Freshly Ground Black Pepper
- 1 Tablespoon Butter
- 1/2 Cup Shredded Sharp Cheddar Cheese

DIRECTIONS:

1. Boil water and salt in a pan
2. Put the grits in now and whisk for at least a minute.
3. Bring to a boil again.
4. Lower the heat and simmer for 15 minutes.
5. Add in the pepper, cheese and the butter.
6. Combine well and let the cheese melt.

BUTTERMILK BISCUITS III

PREP:5 M **COOK:** 15 M **READY**IN: 20 M

INGREDIENTS:

- 4 Cups Self-Rising Flour
- 1 Teaspoon White Sugar
- 1 Teaspoon Baking Powder
- 2/3 Cup Shortening
- 2 Cups Buttermilk
- 2 Tablespoons Buttermilk (for brushing)

DIRECTIONS:

1. Begin by pre-heating the oven to395 F.
2. Grease baking sheet.
3. In bowl, mix sugar, flour and baking powder.
4. Put the shortening in before pouring in the two cups of buttermilk. Mix well.
5. Roll dough to one-inch thick and cut with biscuit cutter (a clean juice glass can be used also).
6. Brush tops with two tablespoons worth of butter milk and then bake for 15 minutes.

SAUSAGE GRAVY WITH BISCUITS

PREP:45 M **COOK:** 10 M **READY**IN: 2 H 25 M

INGREDIENTS:

- 1 Pound Sage Flavored Ground Breakfast Sausage
- 2 Tablespoons Finely Chopped Onion
- 1 Tablespoon All-Purpose Flour
- 1 Cup Milk
- 1/2 Teaspoon Poultry Seasoning
- 1/2 Teaspoon Ground Nutmeg
- 1/4 Teaspoon Salt
- 1 Dash Worcestershire Sauce
- 1 Dash Hot Pepper Sauce
- 2 Packages Active Dry Yeast
- 1/4 Cup Warm Water (110 Degrees F)
- 2 Cups Warm Buttermilk (105 To 115 Degrees F)
- 5 Cups All-Purpose Flour
- 1/3 Cup White Sugar
- 1 Tablespoon Baking Powder
- 1 Teaspoon Baking Soda
- 1 Tablespoon Salt
- 1 Cup Shortening
- 2 Tablespoons Butter, melted

DIRECTIONS:

1. Begin by pre-heating the oven to 450 F.

2. For the gravy: crumble the sausage over the pan and heat it over medium-low heat. Add the onions and cook until translucent. Then drain.

3. Add the flour, stirring well, cook for six minutes and now pour in the milk, poultry seasoning, nutmeg, the worcestershire, salt, and pepper sauce.

4. Mix well.

5. For the biscuits: Begin by immersing the yeast in the warm water for five minutes.

6. Pour in the buttermilk and mix well.

7. In a large bowl, combine sugar, flour, baking soda, baking powder and the salt. Cut in the shortening with a blender on pulse setting.

8. Stir the buttermilk and yeast mix in.

9. Turn out over the floured counter top and knead it well.

10. Roll ½ inch thick and cut with biscuit cutter (a clean juice glass can also be used).

11. Place on greased baking sheet and cover with a clean kitchen towel.

12. Allow to rise for 1 ½ hours in a warm location.

13. Then bake for 10 minutes and brush the tops with melted butter.

<u>CONCLUSION</u>

Thank you again for downloading this book!

The next step is to try the different recipes and share them with the people you hold dear.

Finally, if you enjoyed this book, please take the time to share your thoughts and post a review. It would be greatly appreciated.

Thank you and good luck!

Nancy Kelsey

DISCLAIMER

This BREAKFAST RECIPES is written with an intention to serve as purely information and educational resource. It is not intended to be a medical advice or a medical guide.

Although proper care has been taken to ensure to validity and reliability of the information provided in this book. Readers are advice to exert caution before using any information, suggestion and methods described in this book.

The writer does not advocate the use of any of the suggestion, diet and health programs mention in this book. This book is not intended to take the place of a medical profession, a doctor and physician. The information in this book should not be used without the explicit advice from medically trained professions especially in cases where urgent diagnosis and medical treatment is needed.

The author or publisher cannot be held responsible for any personal or commercial damage in misinterpreting or misunderstanding any part of the book.

18784980R00297

Printed in Great Britain
by Amazon